JULIE ANN GODSON

Julie Ann Godson

The Water Gypsy

*How a Thames fishergirl
became a viscountess*

FeedARead.com

Published in 2014 by FeedARead.com
Copyright © Julie Ann Godson

First Edition

The author has asserted their moral right under the
Copyright, Designs and Patents Act, 1988, to be identified
as the author of this work.

A CIP catalogue record for this title is available from the British Library.

Front cover: Main illustration by Stephen Godson;
portrait of Elizabeth Viscountess Ashbrook based on an original
by Daniel Gardner, courtesy Viscount Ashbrook.
Portrait of William Flower, third Viscount Ashbrook,
courtesy Viscount Ashbrook. Engravings: thegraphicsfairy.com;
The Book of the Thames from its Rise to its Fall, Mr and Mrs S. C. Hall
(Virtue, London 1859).
Watercolour of Charlotte Augusta Flower by Harriet Cheney,
Northumberland Archives.

In memory of Mick and Jean Godson

On seeing a beautiful picture of the Right Honourable Lady Ashbrook

OFT as I view that pictured form, and trace
In that sweet smile, and in that lovely face,
Virtue's soft image, and affections kind;
The genuine goodness of a feeling mind;
Charms that thro' life could happiness impart,
And win an Ashbrook's, and a Jones's heart;
Pensive I turn aside, and sighing say,
"Oh! why were these permitted to decay?"
"Short-sighted mortal," Reason quick replies,
"Grieve not that beauty's fading flow'ret dies;
While that alone is to the tomb consign'd,
Waft the blest Spirit to the realms above
To reign in regions of eternal love."

Anon, The Gentleman's Magazine, *April 1813.*

Betty Ridge, Lady Ashbrook 1745–1808
Based on a portrait by Daniel Gardner

Contents

Introduction

HOW AN ORDINARY girl negotiates her transformation into a princess is a subject of continuing fascination even today. The Cinderella story never loses its appeal, and I feel this is a tale that should be available to everyone. I have therefore set aside much of the careful training I received in writing comprehensively-footnoted academic history, and I must apologise to my former tutor at Oxford for the minimal academic references. But everything in this account is sourced in the proper way, and anyone who wishes to see the documents for themselves can find the appropriate references in the *Bibliography* and *Documents* sections. In quotations I have retained enough of the archaic spelling and punctuation, I hope, to convey a flavour of the period.

The repetition of names within and over generations can create confusion, and the frequent intermarriage between cousins or closely-allied families renders the inter-relationships somewhat mind-bending. The family charts are offered in a spirit of sympathy for the reader, and not simply as another way of bringing on a headache.

I have learned many things during the course of this project, amongst which are: never reject oral history before you've checked it for yourself; always listen to local farmers; and *never* underestimate the women of Northmoor.

Julie Ann Godson
May 2014

Acknowledgements

S O MANY PEOPLE have helped with the writing of this book, but special thanks must go particularly to that patient and hardy band whose members have accompanied me every step of the way. They are Hilary Hicklin, David Lamb and Judy Webb.

I must also thank Lorian Edwards for her generous assistance in the National Archives and tactful modification of authorial assumptions, as well as Peter and Shelley Stokes and their staff at lovely Castle Durrow for their kind hospitality during the trip which convinced me that this story does indeed have a beginning, a middle, and an end.

Others who have given me the benefit of their time and expertise are: Colin Buddin, former lock-keeper at Northmoor; Peter Buckman; Yvonne Cornish, Director of Studies, St Benet's Hall, University of Oxford; Keith Crocker, Relief Lock and Weir-keeper at Northmoor; Judith Curthoys, archivist, Christ Church, University of Oxford; Robin Darwell-Smith, archivist, Magdalen College, University of Oxford; Ross Dean; Dr John Evans; James Ferguson; Charles Foster; Roibéard Ó Gallachóir, Representative Church Body Library in Dublin, for clarifying the position regarding qualification for a clerical situation; Stephen and Julie Greenslade (and my apologies for adopting the prevailing spelling of 'Eirke' and not their preferred 'Erke'); Mrs P. Hatfield, archivist, Eton College; Clare Hopkins, archivist, Trinity College, University of Oxford; Amanda Ingram, archivist, Pembroke College, University of Oxford; Christopher Jeens, archivist, Jesus College, University of Oxford; Máire Kennedy, Divisional Librarian, Special Collections, Dublin City Public Libraries; Pádraig Ó Macháin, Professor of Modern Irish, University College Cork; Jane Mulvagh; Michael Riordan, archivist, St John's College, University of Oxford; Juliet Robertson; Myles Shortall; Kay Sweetman, parish archivist, St John's, Hillingdon, Middlesex; Jolly Wade.

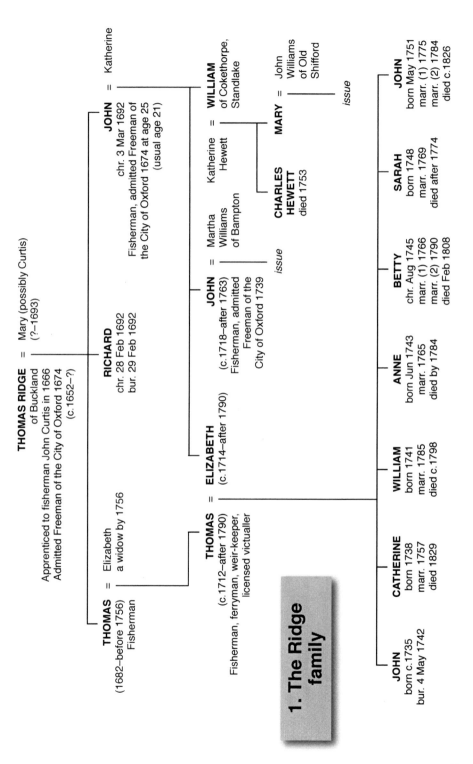

THOMAS RIDGE
of Buckland
Apprenticed to fisherman John Curtis in 1666
Admitted Freeman of the City of Oxford 1674
(c.1652–?)
= Mary (possibly Curtis)
(?–1693)

THOMAS = Elizabeth
(1682–before 1756) a widow by 1756
Fisherman

RICHARD
chr. 28 Feb 1692
bur. 29 Feb 1692

JOHN
chr. 3 Mar 1692
Fisherman, admitted Freeman of
the City of Oxford 1674 at age 25
(usual age 21)
= Katherine

WILLIAM
of Cokethorpe,
Standlake
= Katherine
Hewett

THOMAS = **ELIZABETH**
(c.1712–after 1790)   (c.1714–after 1790)
Fisherman, ferryman, weir-keeper,
licensed victualler

JOHN
(c.1718–after 1763)
Fisherman, admitted
Freeman of the
City of Oxford 1739
= Martha
Williams
of Bampton

issue

**CHARLES
HEWETT**
died 1753

MARY = John
Williams
of Cokethorpe,
Standlake

issue

JOHN
born c.1735
bur. 4 May 1742

CATHERINE
born 1738
marr. 1757
died 1829

WILLIAM
born 1741
marr. 1785
died c.1798

ANNE
born Jun 1743
marr. 1765
died by 1784

BETTY
chr. Aug 1745
marr. (1) 1766
marr. (2) 1790
died Feb 1808

SARAH
born 1748
marr. 1769
died after 1774

JOHN
born May 1751
marr. (1) 1775
marr. (2) 1784
died c.1826

1. The Ridge family

11

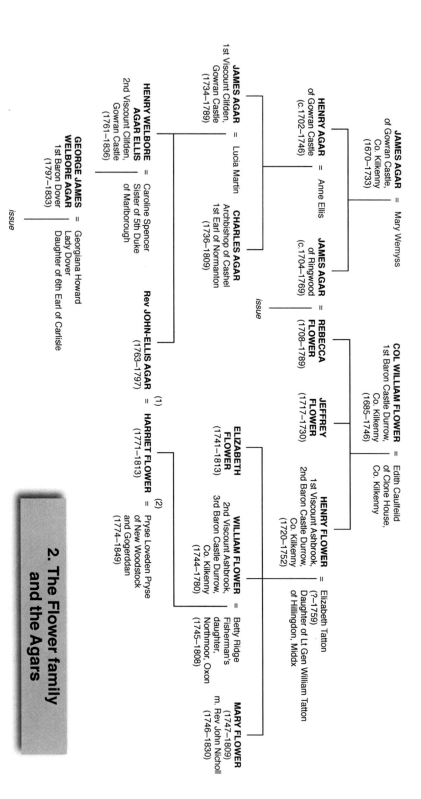

2. The Flower family and the Agars

JAMES AGAR
of Gowran Castle,
Co. Kilkenny
(1670–1733)
= Mary Wemyss

HENRY AGAR
of Gowran Castle
(c.1702–1746)
= Anne Ellis

JAMES AGAR
1st Viscount Clifden,
Gowran Castle
(1734–1789)
= Lucia Martin

JAMES AGAR
of Ringwood
(c.1704–1769)
= REBECCA FLOWER
(1708–1789)

CHARLES AGAR
Archbishop of Cashel
1st Earl of Normanton
(1736–1809)

HENRY WELBORE
AGAR ELLIS
2nd Viscount Clifden,
Gowran Castle
(1761–1836)
= Caroline Spencer
Sister of 5th Duke
of Marlborough

Rev JOHN-ELLIS AGAR
(1763–1797)

GEORGE JAMES
WELBORE AGAR
1st Baron Dover
(1797–1833)
= Georgiana Howard
Lady Dover
Daughter of 6th Earl of Carlisle

issue

issue

COL WILLIAM FLOWER
1st Baron Castle Durrow,
Co. Kilkenny
(1685–1746)
= Edith Caulfeild
of Clone House,
Co. Kilkenny

JEFFREY FLOWER
(1717–1730)

HENRY FLOWER
1st Viscount Ashbrook,
2nd Baron Castle Durrow,
Co. Kilkenny
(1720–1752)
= Elizabeth Tatton
(?–1759)
Daughter of Lt Gen William Tatton
of Hillingdon, Middx

ELIZABETH FLOWER
(1741–1813)

WILLIAM FLOWER
2nd Viscount Ashbrook,
3rd Baron Castle Durrow,
Co. Kilkenny
(1744–1780)
= Betty Ridge
Fisherman's
daughter,
Northmoor, Oxon
(1745–1808)

MARY FLOWER
(1747–1809)
m. Rev John Nicholl
(1746–1830)

(1)
HARRIET FLOWER
(1771–1813)

(2)
Pryse Loveden Pryse
of New Woodstock
and Gogerddan
(1774–1849)

12

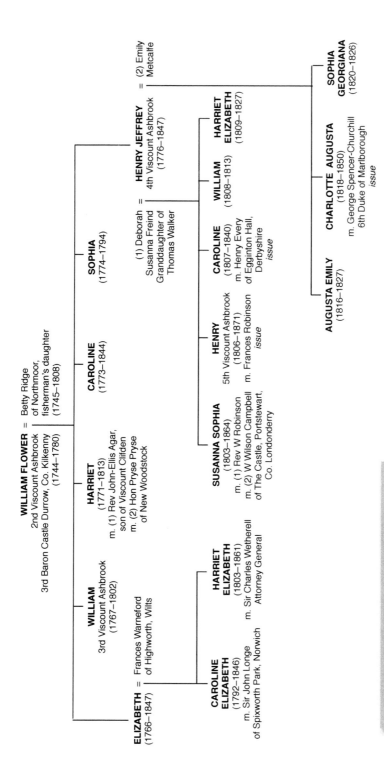

WILLIAM FLOWER = Betty Ridge
2nd Viscount Ashbrook   of Northmoor,
3rd Baron Castle Durrow, Co. Kilkenny   fisherman's daughter
(1744–1780)   (1745–1808)

ELIZABETH = Frances Warneford
(1766–1847)   of Highworth, Wilts

WILLIAM
3rd Viscount Ashbrook
(1767–1802)

CAROLINE
ELIZABETH
(1792–1846)
m. Sir John Longe
of Spixworth Park, Norwich

HARRIET
ELIZABETH
(1803–1861)
m. Sir Charles Wetherell
Attorney General

HARRIET
(1771–1813)
m. (1) Rev John-Ellis Agar,
son of Viscount Clifden
m. (2) Hon Pryse Pryse
of New Woodstock

SUSANNA SOPHIA
(1803–1864)
m. (1) Rev W Robinson
m. (2) W Wilson Campbell
of The Castle, Portstewart,
Co. Londonderry

CAROLINE
(1773–1844)

HENRY
5th Viscount Ashbrook
(1806–1871)
m. Frances Robinson
issue

SOPHIA
(1774–1794)

HENRY JEFFREY = (2) Emily
4th Viscount Ashbrook   Metcalfe
(1776–1847)

(1) Deborah =
Susanna Freind
Granddaughter of
Thomas Walker

CAROLINE
(1807–1840)
m. Henry Every
of Egginton Hall,
Derbyshire
issue

WILLIAM
(1808–1813)

HARRIET
ELIZABETH
(1809–1827)

AUGUSTA EMILY
(1816–1827)

CHARLOTTE AUGUSTA
(1818–1850)
m. George Spencer-Churchill
6th Duke of Marlborough
issue

SOPHIA
GEORGIANA
(1820–1826)

3. William Flower and Betty Ridge's family

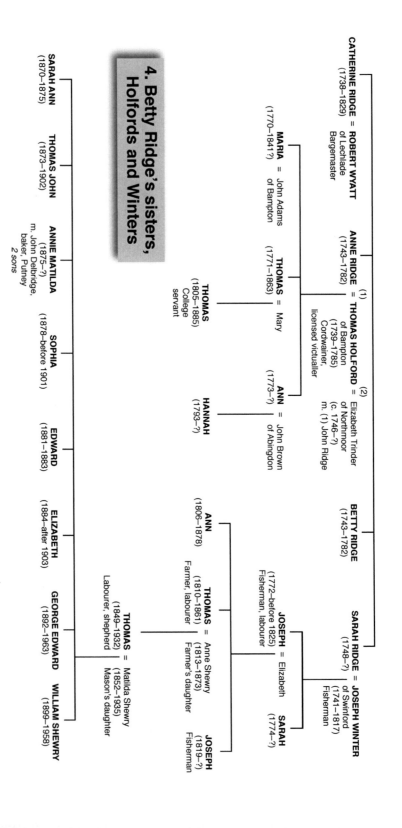

4. Betty Ridge's sisters, Holfords and Winters

CATHERINE RIDGE (1738–1829) = **ROBERT WYATT** of Lechlade, Bargemaster

- **ANNE RIDGE** (1743–1782) = (1) **THOMAS HOLFORD** of Bampton (1739–1785) Cordwainer, licensed victualler m. (1) John Ridge
  - **MARIA** (1770–1841?) = John Adams of Bampton
  - **THOMAS** (1771–1863) = Mary
    - **THOMAS** (1805–1885) College servant
  - **ANN** (1773–?) = John Brown of Abingdon
    - **HANNAH** (1793–?)

- (2) **THOMAS HOLFORD** = **Elizabeth Trinder** of Northmoor (c. 1746–?)

- **BETTY RIDGE** (1743–1782)

- **SARAH RIDGE** (1748–?) = **JOSEPH WINTER** of Swinford (1741–1817) Fisherman
  - **JOSEPH** (1772–before 1825) Fisherman, labourer
    - **ANN** (1806–1878)
    - **THOMAS** (1810–1861) Farmer, labourer = **Anne Shewry** (1813–1873) Farmer's daughter
      - **THOMAS** (1849–1932) Labourer, shepherd = **Matilda Shewry** (1852–1935) Mason's daughter
        - **SARAH ANN** (1870–1875)
        - **THOMAS JOHN** (1873–1902)
        - **ANNIE MATILDA** (1875–?) m. John Delbridge, baker, Putney 2 sons
        - **SOPHIA** (1878–before 1901)
        - **EDWARD** (1881–1883)
        - **ELIZABETH** (1884–after 1903)
        - **GEORGE EDWARD** (1892–1963)
        - **WILLIAM SHEWRY** (1899–1958)
  - **SARAH** (1774–?) = Elizabeth
    - **JOSEPH** (1819–?) Fisherman

Prologue
A tall story

I DIDN'T BELIEVE this story when I first heard it. During the eighteenth century a young viscount came up-river to our village on a fishing trip, fell madly in love with the local innkeeper's daughter, and insisted on marrying her. To me, this smacked of one of those village myths claiming that the beams in the local pub come from a wrecked Spanish man o' war, or that the old manor house is riddled with secret passages.

In the spring of 2010 I had moved to the Oxfordshire village of Northmoor, and found a close-knit and lively community enjoying the sort of neighbourly spirit most of us imagine disappeared at the end of the 1950s. By the time I arrived, an enchanting collection of photographs of life in the village over the years had been amassed with a view to staging a free exhibition in the village hall. Images in ragged-edged sepia, smudgy black and white, and perpetually-sunny Kodachrome—the most heartbreaking medium of all—allow us to gaze on the faces of our predecessors, just as future residents will one day look upon ours. Turn-of-the-century postmaster George Baston leans proudly on a garden fork amidst his splendid vegetable patch; tractor-driver Jack Lay holds a protective arm around his little boy Fred in the 1920s; Bill Bint squints into the low winter sunshine as he collects milk from Stonehenge Farm in 1966; children dance the ring o' roses in the playground at the now-defunct village school in the 1970s.

Churches and the village halls are in constant need of funds and so, keen to ingratiate myself with my new neighbours, I offered to write a small local history book to accompany the exhibition. Then, in answer to the visitor's inevitable enquiry, 'Can I get a copy of that photo of my cottage?' we might surely reply: 'Certainly. If you'd like to hand over £7.99 on your way out, you can have a souvenir book containing *every* picture in the exhibition.' The idea was agreed and I set about my research. A little booklet compiled by the village parson Reverend Stowell in the 1930s revealed the unlikely tale: there was talk of a secret hideaway on an island in the river Thames, and of a crash course for the bride in how to conduct herself as a lady.

Stowell was doubtful and so was I, so I could hardly complain when I encountered a degree of scepticism during the course of my research. One archivist remarked crushingly that, yes, 'such things happen all the time in *Downton Abbey*'. But if I discounted the story and it turned out to be true, I would look very foolish indeed. I sought out the original marriage register for the parish church of St Denys in the county archives, and there among the marriages of farmers and pig-dealers, sawyers and labourers, was the rather startling entry in the curate's looping handwriting: 'William Lord Viscount Ashbrook Bachelor and Betty Rudge a Maiden (a Minor) both of this Parish were married by Licence in this Church with the Consent of Thomas Rudge the Father of the said Minor this 20th Day of March one thousand seven Hundred and sixty six.' The marriage was witnessed by the bride's father and brother, and they signed themselves Thomas and William 'Ridge'.

Of course, while answering one question the entry simply raised many others. Once the characters in the story have names, they become real people rather than shadows. How did Lord Ashbrook, a member of the Anglo-Irish Flower family of County Kilkenny, come to be in Northmoor? Who were these Ridges, and why did Betty so captivate a viscount? And most intriguing of all: what happened next? Gradually over the next two years the answers fell into place. An unexpected encounter between a lonely aristocrat and a working family in Northmoor led to a fairytale romance with an element of tragedy. Eventually, thanks to the adaptability, dynamism, and ambition of the Ridges, the episode culminated in the rescue from oblivion and ultimate triumph of the Ashbrook family.

1

A remarkable young man

ACCORDING TO local legend, it was in 1763 that young William Ashbrook came up the river on a fishing expedition and landed a wife. The date seems reasonable bearing in mind that William matriculated at Christ Church in the winter of 1762; his earliest opportunity for a jaunt up the Thames fly-fishing would come in the spring or early summer of the following year. He probably walked or rode the four miles across country from Oxford to Cumnor, then crossed the river at the Bablockhythe ferry. An attractive target for footpads and highwaymen, he would have avoided travelling along quiet lanes alone, being accompanied for the sake of safety by an attendant or a friend.

The first decent fishing ground up-river from the ferry crossing was the weir pool at Noah's Ark island. There he could also obtain refreshment at the Ridge family's licensed premises. At 17 years old, the inn-keeper's daughter Betty Ridge was already playing her part in the family business. When William first encountered her, she would have been wearing a plain dress for working, fitted into the bodice and with three-quarter length sleeves and full, ankle-length skirts. A long apron was essential for the working woman, and on her feet she wore clogs. A poem written much later by someone who evidently knew Betty in life, and which may be found reproduced at the beginning of this book, describes her sweet smile and lovely face. One (admittedly romanticised) report describes her 'milk and roses' complexion, her 'blue eyes and wealth of rippling hair'.[1] A portrait at Castle Durrow reputed to depict Betty at this stage in her life is currently lost, but it seems more likely that the skin of a girl spending a good deal of her time out of doors would be bronzed by the sun, and her hands roughened by hard work. Unlike William's own two sisters, whose hands would never have been deployed for anything more rigorous than an afternoon's embroidery, Betty was involved in a family enterprise that required her to help with gutting fish, piloting a boat, brewing ale, preparing food and handling money.

---

1   See Appendix C.

A much later portrait of a more matronly Betty shows that her seductively-hooded eyes were indeed blue, her nose straight and her mouth a pretty pink bow (see page 75). In the portrait she wears a fashionable powdered wig, but, as an unmarried girl her hair, rippling or not, would have been confined modestly under a white bonnet with a stiffened brim. Maidens through the ages have, of course, been well aware that an escaping tendril arranged with artful carelessness has a particular allure. But the rough-and-ready bargemen who surely formed the greater part of Thomas's custom would have needed little encouragement to express their appreciation of a pretty serving-girl's charms, and any female in Betty's position quickly acquired the skills necessary to evade wandering hands. Saucy remarks would have been countered with a cheerful riposte delivered in the rolling local burr. Betty Ridge proved irresistible to William Ashbrook; he fell madly in love.

And what would Betty have seen as she beheld the young gentleman out for a day's angling? No portrait of William Flower is known to survive, so we must guess. At the more sober end of the menswear favoured among eighteenth-century sports-men was a long waistcoat and skirted coat with wide cuffs to the sleeves. Knee breeches were worn with hose (stockings) and buckled shoes, though buckskin boots may have been more appropriate for clambering in and out of boats. Hats might be round-brimmed, tricorn or cocked. A wig was rather formal for undergraduates enjoying a day out on the river, so William probably wore his fashionably-long hair in a pigtail tied with black ribbon. The proximity of the university meant that the presence at the Noah's Ark inn of privileged young men would have not have been so very rare. Doubtless at first Betty took William's protestations of love as nothing more than the typical banter of yet another gallant.

Betty was the fourth of the six surviving children of Thomas and Elizabeth Ridge. She had three sisters and two brothers. Eldest sister Catherine had presumably been carried off to Lechlade by her husband of five years, the bargemaster Robert Wyatt, and the next girl Anne's eventual marriage to a Bampton man indicates that she may already have been away in the town in domestic service. But Betty's 22-year-old brother William was there helping his father in the business and, at 15 and 12 respec-tively, Sarah and John no longer needed Betty to act as nursemaid. Even in the absence of the two eldest Ridge girls, the appeal to a lonely teenager of a cheerfully-rowdy family home is obvious. At 19, William Ashbrook slotted in perfectly. His college vacations would otherwise have been spent at the Tatton family home at Hillingdon in the company of his mourning sisters and grandmother. Perhaps the presence of both Ridge parents within a family environment awakened happy memories of William's childhood, and the two Ridge brothers on Noah's Ark must have lent a masculine rumbustiousness to proceedings unknown in the exclusively-feminine domain at Hil-lingdon. The whole package might have been tailored for William Ashbrook, and in time the family realised that he was absolutely serious in his intentions towards Betty.

But the orphaned viscount was too young to marry without the consent of his guardians. Until he reached the age of 21, William needed his two maternal uncles' agreement to any proposed marriage, and their consent was not forthcoming. Their position was perfectly reasonable, of course. Colonel and Reverend Tatton were simply safeguarding the interests of their sister's vulnerable young son, a lad who had lost both his parents before his fifteenth birthday and had no other close male relatives to guide him. William had no option but to obey. If he wanted his heirs to inherit the Ashbrook titles and estates any children must, in the contemporary legal phrase, be 'lawfully begotten'. And anyway, William was no rebel. The idea of defying his guardians and muddying the dynastic waters by marrying Betty before he came of age very likely enjoyed little consideration.

Today William Ashbrook's choice of such an 'ordinary' girl as his bride would be regarded as commendably egalitarian. Not so for William's contemporaries, however hardworking or respectable her family might be. But before condemning as snobs those who disapproved of marriage down the social scale, it is worth examining the matter from an eighteenth-century point of view. Upper-class marriage was an institution designed to join together representatives from two families for dynastic, political and financial purposes. A brief review of previous Ashbrook brides bears this out. William's great-grandmother Mary was the daughter of Sir John Temple, Irish Solicitor General and Attorney General, MP and Speaker of the Irish Commons, and sister to the first Viscount Palmerston, MP for three English boroughs. The Temples owned land in Dublin, Kilkenny, Meath and Westmeath courtesy of the Cromwellian settlement. William's grandmother was Edith Caulfeild, daughter of a high sheriff of County Kilkenny and granddaughter of the first Viscount Charlemont who served as a Privy Councillor in Ireland, whose family had been granted land in Ireland in return for service to King James I. His mother Elizabeth Tatton was the sister of Lady Abergavenny, wife of William Neville, fourteenth Lord Abergavenny.

At a time when political power was divided between a relatively small number of families, these women were accustomed to the system of patronage, and were well aware of the part they were expected to play in order to advance their husbands' interests. Lavish entertainment was provided as a form of obeisance to social superiors controlling the disposition of lucrative offices, with balls and suppers for the local gentry and yeomanry who would be expected in return to support their host in parliamentary elections. Such occasions required a hostess capable of making the necessary arrangements, of knowing what was appropriate to each event, a woman gracious towards social inferiors, at ease with her husband's equals and with his betters too. Offering hospitality was a method by which the elite hostess might contribute to the maintenance of her husband's social credit and political power—and from which she might herself derive a degree of influence by means of the inclusions or exclusions manifest on her guest list. Naturally an aristocratic wife's primary duty was to provide an heir, but this other role in furthering the family fortunes by means of hospitality was well understood. Furthermore, the ideal marriage candidate would bring with her money and property which would in themselves enhance her husband's status. The prospect of such a crucial role falling to a country girl from a family of river people will have caused William's guardians considerable unease. But William was clearly confident that Betty was capable of learning the ways of a lady. After all, he knew that the Ridges were no ordinary family.

EARLY ON A June morning in the year 1734 a remarkable young man and his intended bride slipped quietly away from the hamlet of Chimney in Oxfordshire. Thomas Ridge and his cousin Elizabeth had to get onto the river very early indeed if they were to avoid discovery. They came from a tight-knit family of fishermen, and Thomas's face in particular would have been well-known to other river users. Anyway, they needed to reach their destination before midday for a marriage ceremony to be performed.

An experienced boatman setting out for a new life with his intended bride and all their worldly possessions would travel by water rather than by road. From Chimney as far as Newbridge the Thames is winding and narrow. But at Newbridge its nature changes. The river Windrush delivers the run-off from the Cotswolds into the Thames at just this point, and this made the river deep enough in those days for gaily-painted barges laden with coal to offload at Newbridge wharf. But Thomas and Elizabeth had a particular destination beyond Newbridge in mind. Where the river turns north before sweeping back down through Oxford, there came a river crossing known as Hart's where the track from Northmoor on the Oxfordshire side passed through flat, marshy Moreton and spanned the river, rising gently towards Netherton and Fyfield on the Berkshire side. Having eschewed the impressive edifice of St Mary the Virgin in their own parish of Buckland and ignoring the nearby church of St Denys in Northmoor, Thomas and Elizabeth disembarked and made their way uphill, bypassing churches in Appleton and Fyfield, and slogging on in the summer heat to the tiny roadside church of St Lawrence at Besselsleigh. Why?

Something was going on at St Lawrence's, and a comparison of the marriage register with those of other villages in the area does raise awkward questions. During the 1720s, in Thomas and Elizabeth's much larger home village of Buckland there were 21 marriages, and in their future parish of Northmoor, a village closer in size to Besselsleigh, there were ten. In Besselsleigh during the same period, the number of marriages was 154. During the long incumbency of the Besselsleigh rector John Bromwich the astonishing frequency of marriages involving outsiders suggests that the little church of St Lawrence, so conveniently situated beside the main road into Oxford, was a known venue for clandestine unions.

Marrying in a parish where neither partner lived required a licence from the bishop or archdeacon. A few days before the wedding, the applicant—generally the groom—would swear an allegation that there was no impediment to the marriage and provide a bond for a sum of money to be paid if the allegation proved subsequently to be false. But this seemingly-watertight arrangement was much abused both by the clergy and their flocks. Abuses of the system included the abduction and rape of heiresses, multiple marriages, and same-sex ceremonies with one partner dressed in disguise. None of these melodramatic scenarios is alleged in the case of Besselsleigh, but while those of a generous disposition might assume that Bromwich was a kindly old gentleman who could not bear to see true love thwarted, the more cynical might suspect that he was operating a profitable scam. When Bromwich arrived in the parish in 1703 a licence could be had for 2s 6d, but by 1721 it had reached 10s—a three hundred per cent rise during eighteen years when inflation was in single figures and wages hardly rose at all. Then, for reasons at which one can only speculate, from 1722 Bromwich thought better of recording the fee at all. Finally, from 1732 he ceased even to record whether a licence was presented, having done so scrupulously for the previous thirty years or so. Was Bromwich entering into a private arrangement with couples from other parishes whereby he would, for a consideration, call the banns in Besselsleigh—far away from any possibility of discovery and interference by disapproving families back in the couple's home parish?

As Thomas appears to have been quite open about his and his wife's parish of origin, it looks as if his licence was one of those which went unrecorded. Blank licences might be obtained illegally from the Bishop's court and sold on at a discount. Indeed, even without a licence, a marriage was still valid in the eyes of the Church if the couple were of legal age, both gave their consent, and there were no impediments. The overlap of lingering medieval country practice with the efforts of the Church to oversee people's personal arrangements had rendered the institution of marriage much in need of reform. And so the church of St Lawrence marriage register shows that Thomas and Elizabeth Ridge, 'both of the parish of Buckland', were married on Thursday 25th July 1734 when the groom would have been about 22 years of age, his bride about 20. But why did Thomas and his intended bride Elizabeth, cousins from what appears to have been a typically close-knit fishing family, feel the need to run off and marry in secret?

Boatmen in general enjoyed a life less dependent on the bonds of employment by the local yeomanry, they retained a freedom of movement envied by those dependent on the local lord for their livelihoods, and so they were better placed to exploit whatever opportunities came their way. Their loyalties were to their own families and to the river community, and this detachment from parish-based life caused suspicion and resentment amongst their static neighbours. Compounding this 'otherness' was the fact that river people inter-married all along the Thames rather than into the settled communities of the nearby villages. A linear community of inter-related families looked to their own for support and succour rather than to the parish. Members of this mobile and self-sufficient community were branded 'water gypsies' by their more circumscribed contemporaries, particularly once the carrying trade took off and families might live full-time on the new canals.

Fishermen could aspire to become respectable businessmen by becoming freemen of the city of Oxford. In 1674, having completed an apprenticeship to John Curtis of Fisher Row in Oxford, Thomas Ridge's grandfather was admitted as a freeman. This meant that he could trade within the city; an ordinary fisherman would have to sell his catch to a freeman who would expect to make a profit and therefore offer a lower price for the catch. Once a man had been admitted to the guild of freemen, he was entitled for a fee to propose one son for membership; further sons were permitted, but would cost over twice as much. Elder sons would expect to be proposed first, but something went awry in the Ridge family because Thomas's father was overlooked and his uncle John, the second son, was proposed instead. Why Thomas's father was bypassed is unclear. Was he unsuitable in some way? Had he been incapacitated by ill health or accident? Had he gone off the rails or absconded? Even non-church-goers needed to buried, but there is no entry relating to Thomas's father in the register of burials at Buckland. It looks as if he left the parish altogether, abandoning both his wife and the infant Thomas, who was aged no more than five at the time of his uncle John's admission as a freeman in 1717.

As Thomas grew up, it must have dawned on him that he would be obliged to settle for a lifetime of playing second fiddle to his uncle John's son. He would be restricted to the task of labouring to provide the catch in order that a younger cousin might enjoy playing the businessman in town. Sure enough, cousin John was admitted as a freeman of the city of Oxford in 1739. Cousin John's marriage two years later illustrates perfectly how the social cachet of belonging to the guild of freemen could enhance a family's expectations, and why Elizabeth's alliance with her own cousin was deemed a wasted opportunity. John's wife was Martha Williams, a member of a highly-respectable and well-established farming family—decidedly *not* river people. Martha was a sixth-generation descendant of a sixteenth-century judge in the Court of the King's Bench, Sir David Williams of Ham Court (now known as Bampton Castle) and of Kingston House, Kingston Bagpuize.

It seems that, long before their collision with the aristocracy in the 1760s, the Buckland Ridges were already lifting their eyes from the river and contemplating a better future by means of the marriages of their children. Elizabeth's preference for her cousin Thomas, destined forever to labour as a humble fisherman, would have been received less than warmly by her parents. As the granddaughter, daughter and sister of freemen, Elizabeth embodied certain Ridge family hopes regarding her marriage prospects. An alliance with her own cousin Thomas would hardly advance her fortunes or social status—or so her family must have thought. But now it was a *fait accompli*.

IN THE MAGNIFICENT surroundings of St Paul's Cathedral, a rather different wedding took place six years later. On 9th March 1740 the Honourable Henry Flower, son and heir of William Flower, first Baron Castle Durrow of County Kilkenny, led to the stylish new altar Elizabeth Tatton, daughter of Lieutenant-General William Tatton of Hillingdon in Middlesex, former colonel-in-chief of the 3rd Regiment of Foot. Henry had not expected to succeed to the family title. But when his elder brother Jeffrey died aged 13, Henry became the heir.

The Flower family originated in Oakham in Rutlandshire, for which county they had frequently served as sheriffs since the reign of Richard II. They were rewarded for service to the Crown in Ireland with an estate centred on Durrow (at that time in County Kilkenny), and Henry's father began construction on the Ashbrook family seat around 1715. Castle Durrow was a tall, blue-limestone house of perfect pre-Palladian proportions. The house was flanked on both sides by L-shaped service wings, and the front and back elevations of the main house were each punctuated with four classic columns topped with stone urns the height of a man. Lawns sloped gently down to the river Erkina, deer roamed the estate and thousands of acres of dense oak woodland— of which Henry was extremely proud—enveloped the castle grounds.

Henry and Elizabeth had first a daughter, Elizabeth, and then a son, William, both born at Castle Durrow. Finally another daughter, Mary, was born in Dublin where the Flower family had property at Finglas. As second Baron Castle Durrow, Henry took his seat in the House of Lords in October 1747, and was further advanced in the peer-

Castle Durrow, formerly in County Kilkenny: family seat of the Ashbrooks

age of Ireland a few years later when he was created Viscount Ashbrook in 1751. He did not have long to enjoy his new title however. In the following June, Henry died in Dublin aged just 32, and his only son William inherited the new title along with the blue-limestone pile at Durrow. Within days of his ninth birthday, young William Flower became Lord Ashbrook.

After what must have been a bewildering summer for William, he was enrolled at nearby Kilkenny School, overlooking the river Nore in John Street, Kilkenny. The school was reckoned to be the Eton of Ireland at the time, and many of William's peers would have attended there before going on to Trinity College Dublin. But in the following year his widowed mother made a decision which led to a severing of ties between the Flower family and Ireland that lasted for almost eighty years. Amidst a whirl of rumour suggesting that, a mere six months after the death of her husband, she was about to marry Lord Bessborough's son, Elizabeth fled with her three children to her own mother's home in Hillingdon. William was transferred to nearby Eton College.

In fact, Lady Ashbrook never remarried. In 1759, during William's sixth year at Eton, news reached him that now his mother, too, had died. He was not yet 15, and the loss of both of his parents within such a short period appears to have created in him a longing for a return to family life.

Castle Durrow today: the south side, overlooking the magnificent gardens

THE PLACE CHOSEN by Thomas and Elizabeth Ridge for their life together was Northmoor. The parish occupies low-lying land between the rivers Windrush and Thames; the very inclusion in its name of the word 'moor', a Middle-English term for boggy marsh, hints at the frequent flooding local farmers have had to deal with over the years. Across the northern side of the parish lay the Oxford Way, and scattered along it were the church and several farms. A large, central strip of common land separated this part of the parish from the hamlet of Moreton, another straggle of farms running more-or-less parallel to the river. Households numbered about fifty.

The Ridge family home was a willow-fringed island just up-river from the ferry crossing at Bablockhythe. It lies adjacent to the Oxfordshire bank of the Thames and was once connected to the Berkshire bank by a weir. The property is described in Thomas's lease—signed the day after that faraway marriage in St Paul's Cathedral—as a 'Messuage or Tenement Called or known by the Name of Noahs Ark'.[2] A messuage was understood to comprise a dwelling-house plus its accompanying outbuildings (barns, piggery, dairy, malthouse, boathouse) along with any orchard, vegetable gardens and so on necessary to the life of the main house. An eighteenth-century traveller described the scene as a sort of cosy, bucolic paradise with the banks so thickly wooded on either side that the trees created an arch over the water. Here the river divided into one major and two minor streams, forming two islands. 'The weir stretches across from the meadow bank to these islands,' he wrote, 'and is a principal feature of one of those home scenes, which frequently afford a more complacent delight to the mind than the wide expansive variety of distant prospect.'[3] The parcel of land comprised in all one acre, two rods and twenty perches—something over 6,500 square metres. Three small islands around the main one provided opportunities for additional weirs and associated fish pools and for growing osiers for making and repairing fish traps. So many gushing weirs would have made Noah's Ark a noisy place both day and night—indeed the relief keeper at the present (Victorian) Northmoor lock points out that the most worrying sound for a weir-keeper at night is utter silence. Only in times of severe flood do the levels above and below the weir level off and fall silent.

A fisherman had no need for fields; what he needed was access to the river bank, known as the 'water staff'. In the case of the land at Noah's Ark, this was a strip nine feet wide along the Oxfordshire bank of the Thames extending north-east in the direction of Bablockhythe, and south-east to a fourth small island, now incorporated into Northmoor lock. For an annual consideration of £13, the lease on Noah's Ark gave

2   Magdalen College Archives, DY-33 'Lease from Mabell Wheeler and others to Thomas Ridge for 12 years', 10th March 1740. This may, of course, have been the renewal of a previous agreement. A survey drawn up at the time of the renewal of the lease in 1798 (Magdalen College, MP/2/Oxon./1, 'Map, with detailed reference key, of estates at Northmoor by John Gutteridge, dated 1768') shows conclusively that this 'Noah's Ark' should not be confused with the building of the same name shown on the Berkshire bank in the Rocque map of 1762.

3   William Combe, *An History of the River Thames* (London, 1794).

Thomas a means of supporting his family. The offspring of river people would grow up with a respect for the water, and all would have mastered the art of handling a boat from an early age, boys and girls, first on the green-scented streams and channels which criss-crossed the marsh, and then on the faster-moving river itself. Not only was the Noah's Ark complex a self-contained economic unit, it was a children's paradise too.

The difficulties of farming the flood-prone fields meant that the parish of Northmoor was not as prosperous as Buckland, but the registers show that from around 1700 baptisms usually outnumbered burials. Baptism was not a sacrament to which the Ridge family had hitherto shown itself especially devoted, so the unusual circumstances of the Ridges' next appearance in the record three years after their marriage suggest that, as ever where Thomas was concerned, a plan was afoot. In August 1737 the whole family was christened at the church of St Denys in Northmoor as a job-lot: Thomas, his wife Elizabeth, and their two-year-old son John. But this was no sudden religious revelation.

Thomas looked around at his adopted parish and concluded that here was an opportunity for a man of ambition to better himself. Anyone with the necessary ability and drive who was prepared to conform to the expected proprieties, for example by being fully received into a church upon whose parochial system local administration was largely based, might emerge as a leading light in village society. Of course, this was a considerable change in focus for a family of water gypsies. Integrating quite so fully into parish life ran counter to the instincts of the river people, but Thomas Ridge was sufficiently outward-looking to see possibilities for himself and his family if he carved out a place in the village. And he had a very particular goal in mind designed to reduce or eliminate his dependence on the diminishing fishing trade. Thomas wanted to run a riverside inn.

It was not unusual for the better-placed weir-keeper's accoutrements to include a victualler's licence. Traversing a weir caused an unavoidable delay in a boatman's journey, and this provided the canny weir-keeper with an opportunity. Ale would be brewed on site and dispensed by the women in the parlour of the weir-keeper's cottage—or quite possibly simply handed out through a window. Is it beyond the bounds of reason to imagine that the weir-keeper may even have taken rather longer than was strictly necessary to complete the boating manoeuvre in order that his pretty daughter might ply thirsty gentlemen anglers and hard-drinking bargemen with as much ale as possible, giving the income of a simple fisherman a considerable boost?

The body from which an ambitious young man needed to gain support in any application to the local magistrates for a licence was the vestry committee, members of which elected the parish officers. The vestry committee—named after the room in the church where the vestments, plate and parish chest were kept—was made up of parish notables, usually householders and therefore ratepayers, who gathered together in the vestry to form the collective decision-making body for the village. By the beginning

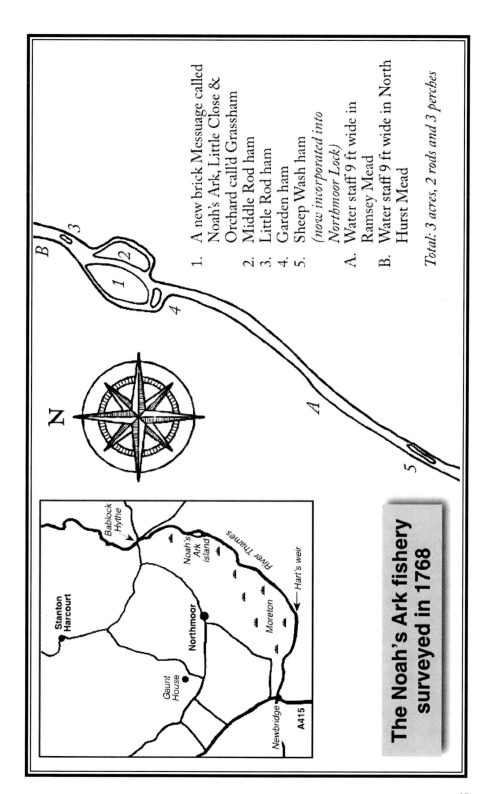

1. A new brick Messuage called Noah's Ark, Little Close & Orchard call'd Grassham
2. Middle Rod ham
3. Little Rod ham
4. Garden ham
5. Sheep Wash ham *(now incorporated into Northmoor Lock)*
A. Water staff 9 ft wide in Ramsey Mead
B. Water staff 9 ft wide in North Hurst Mead

Total: 3 acres, 2 rods and 3 perches

N

B
3
2
1
4
A
5

Bablock Hythe
Stanton Harcourt
Noah's Ark island
River Thames
Northmoor
Geunt House
Moreton
Hart's weir
Newbridge
A415

The Noah's Ark fishery surveyed in 1768

of 1745 Thomas is recorded in the vestry accounts serving time as parish constable, a role nobody relished. Like other parish offices, the job was unpaid apart from the reimbursement of expenses. Duties included maintaining law and order by apprehending offenders and taking them before the magistrates at the Quarter Sessions, establishing who was liable for tax and collecting the payments, acting as the coroner's officer in the event of a sudden or suspicious death, and keeping accounts of his own expenditure. All these functions required the office-holder to be both literate and numerate, as well as trustworthy and reliable. Organising watches and searches in times of peril, and also—more rarely—mustering the local militia, all came under the purview of the constable. And the year of 1745, when Elizabeth Ridge gave birth in late July to a daughter christened Betty, was indeed considered a time of peril in these parts.

During that unsettling summer of Betty's birth, England was on heightened alert because of the Jacobite rebellion. Taking advantage of the absence of most British soldiery fighting the French on the Continent, James II's grandson the 'Young Pretender' Charles Stuart landed with a force in Scotland with the intention of reclaiming the throne from the Hanoverian George II for his father James. The fact that during the Civil War Charles I had moved his court to Oxford when he fell out with Parliament has given rise to an impression ever since that the entire county was solidly Royalist. As ever in that bitter conflict, the situation on the ground was far more nuanced, with no less a Parliamentarian than House of Commons Speaker William Lenthall residing just over the river from Northmoor at Besselsleigh. Lenthall's nephew Sir Edmund Warcupp was lord of the manor of Northmoor from 1671 and served as a Parliamentary captain during the war. In 1745 parish constables in the area would have been aware that it was their job to keep a special lookout for papist sympathisers who, emboldened by Charles Stuart's initial successes, might conspire to assist the cause of the Catholic James. Thomas Ridge was in office throughout this worrying period, submitting his final signed account to the vestry in October 1746, a month after the Bonnie Prince's ignominious return to France. Thomas had paid his dues to his adopted community, and his plan came to fruition. In 1755, at the age of about 43, Thomas Ridge was listed as a Northmoor licence-holder in the register kept by the Clerk of the Peace at the Quarter Sessions.

By this time he and Elizabeth had six children: Catherine, 17, William, 14, Anne, 12, Betty, ten, Sarah, seven, and finally John, the baby of the family at just four years old. After at least three successive generations of Thomas Ridges, our Thomas had had four sons, but not one had been named Thomas. A baby called William had died in 1740, followed by the eldest son John in 1742. Both names were later re-used, making two Williams and two Johns, but no Thomases. Broadly, first sons were named after their father and second sons frequently after the mother's father. First daughters were named after their mother, second daughters after their paternal grandmother. The custom confirmed the specific context of an individual within the community, it provided

A paddle and rhymer weir like the one operated by Thomas Ridge at Noah's Ark, with a typically humble weir-keeper's cottage in the background

a way of acknowledging and commemorating one's forebears, and even offered a kind of immortality. Of course there were exceptions, but Thomas and Elizabeth's choices support the theory that Thomas's father had disgraced himself in some way and thus disappointed Thomas of his hopes of being proposed as the Buckland Ridge family's freeman of the city. By naming their boys after Elizabeth's father John and younger brother William and avoiding 'Thomas' altogether, the couple could hardly have chosen a more obvious way to make a point.

Thomas Ridge's determination to make the best of every opportunity is clear from the sequence of his actions. Each step appears to have been carefully thought through, and formed a necessary precursor to the next. Realising that he would be limited in his prospects if he stayed in Buckland, he sought a new opportunity elsewhere. Seemingly not good enough for his intended wife's parents, he absconded with her and married her clandestinely at Besselsleigh, a manoeuvre requiring considerable forward-planning. Recognising that anyone aspiring to become a pillar of his new community needed to be christened, Thomas presented himself before the minister along with his wife and child, even though the Ridges had shown themselves largely innocent of any church-going urge in the past. A twelve-year indenture on a property on the river indicated a firm intention to make Northmoor his family's future home. And having served his time in the unpopular role of parish constable, he was at last rewarded with vestry support for his application to become a licensed victualler.

Thomas Ridge must have regarded his progress with satisfaction. Having left his home village of Buckland as an ambitious young man with little to his name but a remarkable potential, he had at last arrived. He was the next-best thing to the respected man of business that he would have been had he gained the freedom of the city of Oxford.

SOME OF THE GRANDEST rooms in the grandest college in Oxford are in Peckwater Quadrangle at Christ Church. The height of fashion at the turn of the eighteenth century, the Classical style would, to many of the building's aristocratic undergraduate occupants, have been reminiscent of their own family seats in the country. One young man in particular would have felt perfectly at home moving into his spacious, oak-panelled rooms in 1763. When 18-year-old William Ashbrook, already nine years a viscount, had arrived at an overcrowded Christ Church as a freshman from Eton in November 1762, he had had to make do with a room on the second floor. But this year he was allocated high-ceilinged rooms on the first floor; this was some of the most desirable accommodation in Oxford, and thus more befitting of William's noble status as second Viscount Ashbrook and third Baron Castle Durrow, County Kilkenny. William's mother Elizabeth had appointed her brothers Colonel Neville Tatton and Reverend Dr William Tatton guardians and trustees of her children and their fortunes. In Michaelmas term 1763, therefore, William still had to defer to his uncles on matters concerning his inheritance and his future. However, apart from the need to keep those who settled their debts sweet, the young blades at Oxford during the eighteenth century would not otherwise have been much taxed with displays of deference.

Accounts of life in the university at this time concentrate chiefly on the various jolly diversions available to undergraduates rather than the actual curriculum presented to them, and it seems that this approach largely reflects the attitude of the students themselves. Of course, as so often in England, the trick was to be born an aristocrat. For a start, where other students wore sober black gowns of varying intricacy according to their status, young men of rank swished about in full silk gowns in a colour of their choosing, adorned with gold lace. A velvet cap with a gold tassel topped off this eye-catching ensemble, and served as a helpful identifier to every hawker, good-time girl, and shady dealer frequenting the streets hoping to part reckless young bucks from their allowances.

During this period the once-hallowed medieval seat of learning had become virtually a finishing school for the sons of noblemen. In 1759, a mere 182 freshmen were admitted and only Christ Church was thriving—to the point of overcrowding. This is why the social order was disrupted so violently as to oblige William Flower, already a viscount, to accept second floor lodgings in his first year; rooms became less grand the further away they were from the ground. Thankfully, propriety was restored in Wil-

Peckwater Quad at Christ Church, Oxford: William's windows are shown in the corner on the first floor

liam's second year when he moved down a floor and thus had fewer stairs to negotiate before neglecting to visit his tutor, produce any work, or sit any examinations. This is not to cast aspersion on William in particular, and a few brilliant minds were still toiling away in quiet corners. Such diligent souls doubtless awaited eagerly the completion of Peckwater Quadrangle at this time by means of a magnificent Palladian library, though whether the higher-ranking undergraduates were impatient to examine the library's treasures is debatable. Young nobles generally lived the life of Riley, mingling with the dons in the senior common room and dining at high table (when they were not breaking the rules by dining in one another's rooms), and filled their days with sports and entertainments of varying degrees of riotousness.

Indeed, rioting itself was a favourite pastime, preceded by its customary companion drinking and succeeded, with any luck, by a rampage through the streets pursued by irate university proctors. It is to be hoped that young William was discouraged from such racketing around by the presence in college of the erudite Charles Agar, a smooth operator who later became archbishop of Dublin. Agar was a relative of William's through the marriage in 1741 of his aunt Rebecca Flower to James Agar, sometime member of parliament in the Irish Commons for Gowran and Tulsk. The influence of both Charles Agar and his brother, another James, would prove to be critical to the course of events which will unfold in these pages.

Team sport of the sort practiced in the university today had not properly arrived in the eighteenth century, but many a young gentleman brought with him into town both his horse and the rural pastimes of his home life: fox-hunting, badger-baiting, horse-riding and shooting. Another popular diversion of the period was cockfighting, especially as it involved the irresistible coupling of violence with betting. In vain did the vice-chancellor issue an order announcing that: 'All Persons are hereby strictly Forbidden to keep or to Frequent an Cock-Pit, or to beat any drum, calling to such unlawful Game, within the University or City of Oxford.'[4] Bolder students simply defied the edict and risked rustication by attending the two cockpits in Holywell; more law-abiding souls had only to ride a few miles across country to the river Thames to find convenient spots in which to indulge in the quieter sport of angling.

THE STORY GOES that, once the marriage was agreed upon, Betty was sent away to the house of a suitable dowager a few miles off in order to be taught the ways of a lady. This would certainly seem to be a sensible use of the years of hiatus, but the identity of the dowager in question is unrecorded. A potential mentor might be Mary Marchant at Gaunt House on the edge of the village of Standlake, about three miles across country from Noah's Ark and easily accessible by boat via the nearby Thames tributary, the Windrush.

The Marchants were yeomen farmers who sometimes even described themselves as gentlemen, tenants—strikingly—of William's college Christ Church. Mary Marchant had lost three young daughters back in the 1730s, and now in 1763 she was newly-widowed, her husband having died the previous summer. Moated and fortified Gaunt House, where this eminently respectable gentlewoman lived on with her son, may have seemed to William Ashbrook a good place to which Betty might retire in order quietly to acquire the accomplishments necessary to a lady. And Mary Marchant's 22-year-old unmarried daughter Sarah was the perfect companion to introduce Betty to a more refined way of life.

So what were these skills which Betty needed to move more smoothly into the higher echelons of society? In the previous century it would have been perfectly normal to find the lady of any substantial country establishment directly involved in or at least supervising the day-to-day necessities—brewing beer, overseeing the dairymaids, distilling herbal preparations, monitoring and mending precious household linen. But as the eighteenth century progressed, ladies of quality became estranged from the nitty-gritty, handing the basic running of the household over to a housekeeper. Whilst an aristocratic wife might no longer have to deal personally with household accounts, the advent of a reliable postal system rendered literacy essential for those wishing to communicate with friends and family at a distance.

The long hours of the day not occupied in paying social calls and conducting correspondence had to be filled somehow, so tutors were appointed to instruct the daughters of the well-to-do in music, sketching, painting, dancing, embroidery, deportment, good manners and French. Much of this was designed to attract the attention of eligible bachelors; one is reminded of the number of otherwise rational men in the novels of Jane Austen who were struck dumb by the accomplished warbling of a blushing maiden who had then only to venture outdoors for a life-threatening walk in the rain to

---

4   G. Midgley, *University Life in Eighteenth-Century Oxford* (London, 1996), p. 117.

seal the deal. Let us hope that the already-affianced Betty, a girl accustomed to serving up vittles to rowdy bargemen and well capable of handling a rowing-boat unaided, was spared any such improvement.

But still, Betty was being expected to make a leap of Olympian proportions up the social scale. The friends she grew up with would shortly become her inferiors. Members of the community to whom she would hitherto have been expected to curtsey would now be her equals because they were her husband's equals. Even in an age where relationships across the classes within a household had not yet assumed the starchy stratification that they would do under the Victorians, a lady would expect a degree of deference from her subordinates—particularly in the presence of other elite ladies. There were many Rudge and Ridge families in the surrounding villages and the spectacular news of a betrothal between a humble Ridge girl and a lord must have been difficult to contain. If the couple chose to remain in the area, Betty faced the prospect in her new life of paying a social call upon a member of the local gentry and perhaps having the gates opened to admit her carriage by a grinning acquaintance or, as the tea tray was carried in, enduring the giggles of her hostess's parlourmaid who happened to be some sort of a cousin. Loss of dignity in public would have been a distinct danger.

Even if William decided they must return to the Ashbrook family seat at Castle Durrow in Ireland, Betty will have been well aware that her metaphorical skid into

Gaunt House, Standake: home of Mary Marchant, Betty's possible tutor

society's drawing-room would cause her to become an object of surprised curiosity which could so easily tip into derision amongst her new colleagues at the higher end of the social scale. Bored wives of stuffy men twice their age selected for them by their mothers might not automatically be well disposed towards a ravishingly pretty creature who had married for love and landed a titled youth with a fortune to boot. It seems reasonable to speculate that some members of the sisterhood might have enjoyed an opportunity to brighten dull days with gossip of how the poor dear girl had tripped up socially once more. When contemplating tackling the pitfalls of such a daunting change in status, one can see why the simpler option of life as a comfortable kept-woman might recommend itself. William and Betty must have been deeply committed to making a family life together to take the more difficult course with its attendant social hazards and potential slights. Or perhaps clever Thomas Ridge persuaded his daughter to hold out for marriage or nothing.

IF WILLIAM ASHBROOK'S guardians were hoping that, while Betty exploited the three-year delay in order to equip herself as a lady, William would make even better use of the time by transferring his affections to a more suitable girl, they were destined to be disappointed. William and Betty were at last married on 20th March 1766 in the little church of St Denys at Northmoor. The contrast with the wedding of William's parents in St Paul's Cathedral hardly needs emphasis. Doubtless Thomas made sure that his daughter was furnished with an up-to-the-minute dress in fashionable pale-blue or silver silk, corseted and with a full skirt. Sleeves were elbow-length with falling lace cuffs, and full-length pleats from shoulder-height adorned the back of the dress. Brides wore bonnets, not veils, which were kept on inside the church. Elegant grooms wore a silk suit with an embroidered waistcoat. Weddings were a much more low-key affair in the eighteenth century than they are today, but no mother in any period would need prompting to turn out to see her daughter married to a viscount. Perhaps Betty's other siblings were present too, including her unmarried sister Sarah who, at 17, was the perfect age to serve as bridesmaid.

The bride's father Thomas formally witnessed the marriage along with his elder son William, now 25. The signatures for all three Ridges are confident, but something about Betty's is not right. Betty's sister Catherine had signed her own name upon her marriage to Robert Wyatt, as would all the Ridge siblings save the youngest, so it seems unfair to quibble over Betty's signature in particular. But why would Betty sign herself 'Betty Rudge' on a document that her father and brother sign as 'Ridge'? When Thomas and Elizabeth Ridge had arrived in Northmoor, there was already a Rudge family in the village—possibly some sort of cousins. Where the Buckland Ridges had used Rudge and Ridge more or less interchangeably, Thomas seems to have wished to differentiate his family from his nearby cousins and by the time of Betty's marriage

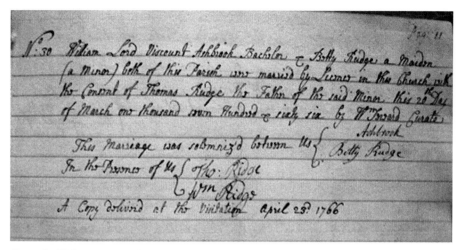

Entry for William and Betty's marriage in the Northmoor parish register: would Betty really call herself 'Rudge', or did somebody else sign the register on her behalf?

the family was calling itself exclusively 'Ridge'. A further problem is that Betty's signature in no way matches the second known example of her handwriting written some twenty-four years later (by which time, of course, she was signing herself 'Elizabeth Ashbrook'). The signature of 1766 is not just a wobbly, inexpert version of that of 1790; it is in a completely different hand. Any literacy training Betty underwent in the years prior to her marriage evidently produced limited results. At her wedding to Lord Ashbrook in 1766, someone else signed the register in Betty's name, arguably rendering the marriage technically invalid. Who was it?

It must be admitted that individuality does not appear to have been encouraged in the teaching of writing during the period; the four hands that do appear genuine—Lord Ashbrook's, Thomas Ridge's, William Ridge's, and the curate's—do not differ greatly. This is not surprising; well into the twentieth century pupils were presented with a copperplate guide which was to be reproduced diligently, with whoever came closest to the original even winning a prize. Everyone from the highest to the lowest learned the same style so, providing all were reasonably familiar with the practice, social class could not be divined from a person's handwriting. Thus it is with William and Betty's marriage entry. The difference between the writing styles of the two Oxford men, Lord Ashbrook and the curate, and that of the two fishermen, Thomas and William Ridge, is negligible. Credulity would be strained to breaking point by the suggestion that William Ashbrook had not, in the course of a long courtship, cottoned on to the preferred family name of his beloved and had signed for his wife as 'Rudge'.

Our attention therefore lights upon the officiating curate, William Seward. A formidable, multi-exhibition-winning scholar and Fellow of St John's College, the 36-year-old expert in civil law would seem no push-over when it came to introducing an irregularity into the register. On the other hand is it too outrageous to imagine that Seward might have been prevailed upon by a fellow Oxford man discreetly to insert Betty's name in order to avoid the embarrassment of an Ashbrook marriage entry being marred by the mark of an illiterate bride? Seward seems the most likely candidate to enter 'Rudge' instead of 'Ridge' into a parish register already bursting with Northmoor Rudges. In all the excitement, would he even have known the difference? Probably not.

Where or whether the party celebrated the marriage immediately after the ceremony is not known. We must hope that the young couple did not waste too much time in setting off for their marital home in the village of Shellingford, over the river in Berkshire. Two days after the wedding, thunder, lightning and hail buffeted the area so badly that a barn was destroyed at Hinksey. Snow began to fall that evening and continued relentlessly over following days. On Wednesday 26th March it snowed heavily for twelve hours. 'Along the Chilterns, and that Chain of Hills which runs through Oxfordshire, Bucks, &c. they have rarely known any Snow equal to this,' reported *Jackson's Oxford Journal*, adding that 'many of the Hollow-Ways filled to a Level, which could not be passed till the Drifts were cleared away.'[5] Even at a height of only three hundred feet, Shellingford must have experienced severe cold. But meteorological matters were unlikely to be much on the mind of the young Lady Ashbrook as she said goodbye to her childhood home on Noah's Ark island. She knew, as she set off with her husband for Shellingford some eleven miles off, that she was already pregnant with her first child.

It seems that William and Betty had followed the old country custom of ascertaining a potential bride's fertility before a formal marriage took place. An alliance with a bride who brought no dowry was in effect an expensive luxury for an aristocrat and, with no brothers to act as back-up heirs, William needed to know his marriage would secure the Ashbrook succession, and Thomas Ridge was realistic enough to appreciate his position. Within a week of a pregnancy becoming evident, William and Thomas had obtained the licence necessary for the marriage of a minor. Clearly Betty's father calculated that the risk of damage to Betty's reputation in the event of a marriage failing to materialise was worth taking when weighed up against the great benefit to his family if all went according to plan. For the father of an aristocratic bride, this gamble would have been unthinkable. For a humble fisherman, pragmatism prevailed. But at that time, a pregnancy did not by any means necessarily lead to a live birth. Clearly William was determined that, whenever the Ashbrook heir did arrive, the child's mother would be Betty Ridge.

---

5   *Jackson's Oxford Journal*, Saturday 29th March 1766.

2
A happy family

IN ORDER TO REACH the little village of Shellingford in the Vale of the White Horse, eighteenth-century travellers from Northmoor had somehow to traverse the river Thames from Oxfordshire into what was at that time Berkshire. The poetic heart yearns to imagine that the newly-weds took a ferry across the river and retraced the steps of Betty's parents up the slope to Besselsleigh, and past the little church where their clandestine marriage was performed thirty-two years before. More likely, however, a groom considerate enough to find a home close to his expectant bride's family would also have insisted that she should depart for her new life comfort, poetry notwithstanding. A carriage crossing the river at Newbridge and winding through the lanes of Longworth and Hinton Waldrist, then through Pusey and across the furze-covered downs of Hatford would take between two and three hours to reach Shellingford, and we know the weather was poor. At the entrance to the village, the horses had to pick their way across an icy ford through the Mill Brook before the carriage passed the smithy on the left. A sharp left-turn into the village itself took them past Home Farm, the Tudor rectory and Church Farm. Just beyond St Faith's church, lights burning in the windows of the old manor house must have been a welcome sight for the cold and tired young couple.

An old drawing of Shellingford Manor shows a substantial sixteenth-century stone house built in the old, half-timbered style. At the front a wide central gable sat between two narrower ones, and each gable was topped with a stone cross hinting at a pre-Reformation date of construction. Large, stone-mullioned windows on the ground and first floors afforded maximum enjoyment of the views across open fields towards the glorious sunsets for which the Vale is renowned. Projecting from the north-eastern corner of the front of the house in the drawing is a range of buildings, presumably domestic offices, and a map of 1878 suggests a second wing facing the first, perhaps stabling, creating an open quadrangle at the front of the main house for turning carriages. Beyond the site of the walled garden once adjoining the manor to the south-east, the remains of fishponds in the eponymous Fishpond Copse show that the gentle slope down towards Holywell Brook and the river Ock on the southern boundary of the parish assisted in the exploitation of the local stream in order to provide a supply of fresh fish for the manor's table—no commercial fishermen required. Such an arrangement was popular before the Reformation when the site belonged to the Abbey of Abingdon and may suggest an even older, medieval house pre-dating the Tudor one.

By the standards of the day, it was an outdated old pile. A nobleman of William Ashbrook's generation would expect to hold court in a Palladian mansion set in extensive, landscaped grounds—just like Castle Durrow, in fact. It is a sign of William's devotion that ostentation and status were dispensable providing he could be with Betty. And perhaps it is a further demonstration of his consideration towards her that he chose this rambling old house tucked away down a lane in an obscure village; it was surely less intimidating to a girl of humble origins than a super-modern Classical show-home isolated within its own grand park. The manor was acquired by Sarah, Duchess of Marlborough during the 1730s. She had developed a mania for accumulating property which she thought was a protection against currency devaluation. Shellingford passed to Sarah's grandson John, first Earl Spencer, who let it to Viscount Ashbrook and his new wife. Doubtless the arrival of new tenants at the big house caused a ripple of interest among the villagers, especially if rumours had leaked that the young viscountess came from a background no more elevated than their own.

The curate of the neighbouring village of Stanford-in-the-Vale made a conscious effort to record the disappearing way of life of the people of the Vale of the White Horse. In his charming memoir *A Berkshire Village* the Reverend Maine described the attire of the villagers at the time of William and Betty's arrival, recalling the clean white smocks of the men and the red cloaks of the women, once almost universal in the Vale. He attempted to capture a dialect that he claimed was once pronounced the closest thing then spoken to the original Anglo-Saxon language. In the Vale the plural of houses was *housen*, a gate was a *gaeat*, when folk were lonely they would declare themselves *unked*. Inanimate objects were referred to by personal pronouns; one day Reverend Maine heard one lad say to another who had presented him with an apple: 'Whoever gave you he to give to I?'[6]

One characteristic of the people of the Vale in Betty's time did persist into the nineteenth century, to the great satisfaction of Reverend Maine. They were industrious, early-risers: 'There is scarcely a farmhouse in this neighbourhood where the duties of the day do not commence at the very earliest possible hour. For cows must be milked, and dairy-work attended to.'[7] Consequently, right through to Maine's day, the universal lunch-hour across all classes remained half-past eleven, and the hour for supper half-

---

6   Lewin G. Maine, *A Berkshire Village, its History and Antiquities* (Oxford and London, 1866), p. 10.
7   *Ibid.*, p. 38.

Shellingford Manor near Faringdon: home to Betty Ridge and Lord Ashbrook

past three. Once upon a time, the mistress of Shellingford Manor would have been up and about just as early as the women in the more humble farmhouses and cottages. But the advent of the housekeeper meant that the lady of the house was freed (if that is the word) to concentrate on ladylike pastimes such as paying and receiving calls involving the wildly popular new craze of taking tea, displaying philanthropy towards the local poor, and tending to the intricacies of her increasingly impractical toilette. A lady's magazine of the period warned that a mistress who betrayed too great a talent for practical matters risked being landed with 'the reputation of a notable housewife, but not of a woman of fine taste'.[8]

Perhaps Betty would have assumed more comfortably the role of the chatelaine of a previous generation, the transition from a family home and business to a substantial country house being at that time one more of scale than nature. Indeed, the young viscountess might well have preferred to cultivate in her new walled garden something rather more useful than gracious manners. The plot at Noah's Ark island was a substantial one and a girl like Betty had to lend a hand in growing the family's food. But for the lady of the house in the higher echelons of society to carry out such work would have been unthinkable. Anyway, for all we know, Betty was perfectly happy to hand over such back-breaking labour. Her knowledge alone of pickling, preserving, brewing and laundry probably worked in her favour, increasing the respect in which she was held by her household staff. Her maids could hardly claim that the mistress had never done a day's work in her life. It seems reasonable to suppose that Betty's efforts concerning her domestic staff were directed towards retaining her authority while discouraging resentment of a mistress who gave the orders 'even though she's no better than we are'.

---

8   Roy Porter, *English Society in the 18th Century* (revised edition, London, 1991), p. 29.

The north range: all that remains of Shellingford Manor today

WILLIAM ASHBROOK'S sisters Elizabeth and Mary Flower left Ireland as children and came with their mother and brother to their Tatton grandmother's home in Middlesex in 1753. When their mother died they were aged 18 and 12 respectively; it would have been quite improper for Elizabeth, as a young woman, to return to Castle Durrow alone, and Mary was still a child. At the time of their brother's marriage in 1766, Elizabeth was 25 and Mary 19, and they could be forgiven for experiencing a twinge of concern about the effect on their own marriage prospects of an alliance between the Flower family and a tribe of Thames fishermen. Their Ashbrook grandfather had negotiated a match for their aunt Rebecca with a member of the Agar clan, a family prominent in Irish politics who owed their extensive landholdings to the victory of King William of Orange. Elizabeth and Mary doubtless hoped to do at least as well. But their brother's marriage and subsequent abandonment of the family seat at Castle Durrow threw their expectations into doubt.

Indeed at 25, the elder sister Elizabeth might have expected to have been married for some years already, and it is tempting to suspect that William's obsession with Betty after 1763 diverted him from performing the duty which devolved upon him following the deaths of his parents: arranging good matches for his sisters. It is hard to see how he could have attended to such an important project if the boisterous attractions of the Ridge household kept him in Northmoor during his university vacations instead of accepting invitations to the country homes of his peers. Plenty of eligible bachelors surrounded him in his days at Christ Church, but perhaps they had heard the rumours of a romance with a village girl which appeared to be getting out of hand, and were wary of connecting themselves with the Flower family. A chap might take his pleasure with a pretty girl to his heart's content, but insisting that the thing went as far as marriage was simply tiresome.

The fact that only members of the Ridge family acted as witnesses may hint at the sisters' absence from the little wedding ceremony in Northmoor. Generally the bride's signature would be witnessed by a relative or friend of the groom, and vice versa. Women frequently served as witnesses, so had William's sisters been present it would have been perfectly in order for one of them to have done the job. However, the practice was not invariable so perhaps we should not read too much into it. Certainly, upon the death of their grandmother late in 1767 they had little choice but to come to Shellingford. The presence of these women in the marital home presented another test of Betty's diplomatic skills, and it would be intriguing to find any evidence of the temperature of the sisters' relationship with their brother and his new wife whom they had very probably never met prior to the marriage.

Elizabeth and Mary's fates were now tied irrevocably to that of their brother, and any initiatives directed at carving out fulfilling lives for them must come from him. Buried away in Shellingford, all hope of meeting any of the Anglo-Irish beaux they would have encountered at Castle Durrow must have seemed lost, and all because of their supposed-protector's determination to follow his own heart's desire. To add insult to Elizabeth's injury, just at the point when her own dreams of presiding over an establishment of her own were fading, she must defer to a fisherman's daughter several years her junior. For the eldest child of a viscount, having to curtsy on a daily basis to a woman hailing so recently from a class which was not just humble but viewed even with mistrust must have been a novelty.

Betty at least had the advantage of almost two years on William's younger sister, Mary. However, immaturity may have rendered Mary immune to any claim to respect which seniority in rank gave Betty, especially if Elizabeth decided to pass on to her younger sister any grievances of her own. If Mary had not yet realised the degree to which her own prospects were compromised by a secluded existence far from the social circle where her family enjoyed maximum prestige, a resentful elder sister could surely be relied upon to clarify the situation for her. Of course, this is speculation; it may be that the disappointed spinster and the sulking teen were in fact souls of tact who stayed with their grandmother for the first year in order to give the newly-marrieds a little privacy, and then descended as angels of mercy, filled with compassion for the nervous fawn their brother had brought into the family. Their knowledge of the conduct and duties of a lady would certainly have been invaluable to an apprentice like Betty. Perhaps it depends upon your view of the likely nature of the atmosphere where two sisters are thrown together with a pretty girl they don't know, but who has the ear of the pivotal figure in their lives, their brother. Whatever were the individual attitudes of the three women, negotiating their relative places within the household was doubtless challenging where the social norms had been overturned.

AT LEAST if Betty wished to keep a low profile in these first few months for fear either of disgracing herself as a notable housewife in the eyes of her sisters-in-law or of being branded Lady Muck by her maids, her pregnancy allowed her the latitude to ease herself gently into her new position. In general, eighteenth-century women did not retire from public life just because they were pregnant—indeed, those who were obliged to work continued to do so up to the last minute. But an expectant mother is a universal figure of special consideration. Betty's condition may have prompted a mood of feminine solidarity within her household, and she may also have derived from it a degree of confidence; no aristocratic battle-axe was going to close her doors to a woman who may be carrying the heir to a viscountcy. As far as onlookers were concerned, the chances of Lord Ashbrook regretting his youthful impetuosity and putting aside his embarrassing spouse were now significantly reduced.

Whilst no doubt enjoying the legitimisation that pregnancy afforded, Betty will have been aware of the hazardous nature of child-bearing at the time. Death during or shortly after childbirth was appallingly common, and the incidence of child mortality among infants under one year was to modern eyes staggering. For women aged between 25 and 34, perinatal complication was probably the most common cause of death. In larger villages young women might see a contemporary die in childbirth every third year, and even being a member of the elite offered no refuge from these terrible statistics. Women like Betty's own mother managed with the assistance of a village midwife, but the gentry could summon the local physician whom they probably knew socially.

Alternatively, during this period the phenomenon of male midwives emerged. The use of newly-developed equipment like forceps transformed childbirth into a recognised medical condition. A hitherto exclusively feminine realm might now be viewed as a profession, and therefore worthy of male consideration. Aristocratic women often migrated to London to give birth in order to take advantage of the very best practitioners, but the fact that Betty's children were baptised in the village church at Shellingford suggests that she remained at home for the births, probably with the assistance of her own mother, her sisters-in-law, and a respectable local physician. One person we can confidently exclude from the birthing chamber was the father; William was probably downstairs talking and drinking with his father-in-law and Betty's elder brother when his first child Elizabeth arrived in mid-November, just eight months after her parents' marriage.

The inconvenience of the early arrival after their marriage of William and Betty's first child was later smudged out by the publishing of a false birthdate for Elizabeth of 24th December 1766.[9] In fact the family Bible records the birth as 27th November, and the parish register shows that the little girl had been carried up the short path

---

9   Edward Kimber, *The Peerage of Ireland: A Complete View Corrected to Jan. 20 1768* (London, 1768), p. 209.

from the manor and into St Faith's church to be baptised on the last day of November. The high death-rate among newborns meant that it was regarded as essential to have a baby accepted into the church as soon as possible. The sacrament of christening was usually carried out within a few days of the birth, sometimes on the actual day if the child appeared sickly.

It is unclear how closely Betty would have observed the tradition of lying-in, the ritual by which a new mother re-emerged gradually into the world. In the enlightened eighteenth century, the elite preferred to distance themselves from the age-old customs of their social inferiors. Paradoxically, though, a woman in Betty's position, with an army of servants to attend to the running of the house, would have been at liberty to take her time and enjoy a slower progression from childbed back to normal life than Betty's own mother would have done. It stretches credibility too far to suggest that Betty would forgo a month's rest simply in order to demonstrate her intellectual superiority to her husband's tenantry.

The first of the three stages of lying-in lasted anything between three days and a fortnight and involved complete confinement to bed in a darkened room for the new mother. Next came the 'upsitting' during which the mother was allowed out of bed—but not out of the room—and the bed-linen was changed. Finally, after a week or ten days of this, the mother would begin to move about within the house—but not outside—once again for a week to ten days. The few female visitors allowed into the birthing chamber in the days following the birth joined the new mother in consuming a nourishing hot drink known as 'caudle', a mixture variously including cream or milk, eggs, spices, honey and wine, something akin to today's eggnog. The whole process of lying-in took around a month.

Once the lying-in had been completed, 'churching' was the ecclesiastical rite by which a woman emerged into the world once more. The ceremony originated in the Jewish faith, where it was seen as a means whereby a supposedly-unclean new mother was purified. The post-Reformation Church of England was keen to shift the emphasis away from purification and on to the giving of thanks for the safe delivery of the mother from the hazards of childbirth. At the end of her lying-in the new mother was escorted, veiled, to the church by her womenfolk where she paid her dues to the minister and the parish clerk. Before the usual church service, she knelt before the altar and the vicar would say a short prayer of thankfulness after which the woman returned to her customary pew. This ritual marked the official end to the child-bearing process, and normal life could now be resumed.

Aristocratic women often employed a wet-nurse to undertake the tiresome business of breast-feeding. A young woman who had recently given birth would be selected for the job; she might live in her employer's home or take the baby away to her own cottage. Betty's first baby had arrived in late November, her lying-in ended in late December (perhaps on the 24th, and this was why the date was selected as the baby's 'official' birthday), and as soon as her husband was re-admitted to the marital bed in January, she promptly became pregnant again.

It is interesting to observe how easily Betty slips into the ways of her betters; there appears to have been no urge to introduce an element of working-class grit into the proceedings. Her mother, who had dealt with eight pregnancies of her own, was no doubt quick to embrace any practice that would give her daughter an easier time than she had herself endured. As a working woman, her only option had been to pick up a hungry baby and interrupt her daily chores when necessary. And as the family grew, a mother relied on older daughters to look after the smaller children once they were weaned. The rich could afford to pay nursery-maids, and were therefore unconcerned about 'bunching' their offspring, that is, producing babies in such quick succession that the early ones were not old enough to take charge of the later ones while the parents worked. Whereas Betty's mother gave birth to eight children spread over sixteen years, Betty gave birth to the same number in just ten because she could afford the luxury of a wet-nurse and nannies, and because there was no specific family enterprise to which her contribution of labour was essential.

So, after just ten months of marriage, Betty was plunged for a second time into the agonies and ecstasies of eighteenth-century pregnancy. Her son William was born in late October and then, after just four months, Betty was pregnant once more. On the last day of 1768 Henry was baptised, the 'spare' to back up the Ashbrook heir. As usual, Betty was pregnant again by the spring of 1769 and she and William no doubt counted their blessings daily. Their determination to make a life together seemed to have been rewarded with a fairytale outcome, but they were about to endure a dreadful fifteen months.

FIRST, THERE CAME shocking news from Ireland. William's uncle, James Agar, husband of his aunt Rebecca and his only remaining adult relative on his father's side, had been shot dead in a duel. Duelling had become increasingly fashionable in Ireland by the late 1760s. Families of the Anglo-Irish elite assumed that they were automatically entitled to political power, and their attempts to arrive at pacts dividing up seats and boroughs between themselves sometimes led to acrimonious disagreements. In the eighteenth century it became common for such disputes to be settled by means of a duel. One such borough was Callan which had for some fifty years been passed agreeably enough between representatives of the Agar, Flood and Weymss clans. But by 1769 this well-established working agreement had collapsed.

James Agar had already shown himself to be something of a hothead by falling out with his own brother, and he had called his latest adversary Henry Flood out once before as well. Flood was considered a great Irish patriot and orator, keen to establish the same rights for Protestant Irish gentlemen as were enjoyed by their English counterparts. The mens' first duel had ended with Agar being slightly wounded, but the bitter rivalry over the borough of Callan had become so personal that this was not the end of the matter. An absurd incident at Burnchurch contrived by Agar resulted in his man Keogh becoming involved in a fracas with Flood's men, whereupon Keogh fled the scene minus the pair of pistols with which his master had supplied him. Agar decided to force the issue by accusing Flood effectively of stealing his pistols. In view of this, Flood had no alternative but to agree to a meeting and the location settled on was Dunmore, north of Kilkenny.

At two o'clock on the afternoon of Friday 25th August 1769, the antagonists lined up at fourteen paces alongside a hedge in Dunmore Park. Agar barked a question at Flood about the pistols, as he had done several times during the ten months since the Burnchurch set-to.

Coolly, Flood replied: 'You know I will not answer you while you ask me in that manner.'[10] Flood's second, Gervase Bushe, invited Agar to save himself considerable trouble and ask again more politely. By way of reply, Agar simply laid one of his pistols down on the ground, straightened up and, being left-handed, rested the other pistol on his right arm to take aim. Shouts of protest from both seconds rang out. Using a rest was considered unsporting behaviour, and especially so in this case since Agar's own second had declared that there should be no levelling. Agar accordingly lowered his right arm, turned to assume a more respectable stance with his left side towards his opponent, raised his arm, and fired. He missed.

Throughout, Flood stood with the muzzle of his pistol turned upwards. He watched calmly as Agar bent to pick up his second pistol. Convention dictated that, since his antagonist had already fired a shot, it was now his turn to take aim. He waited until Agar stood upright once more, and then paused a moment longer, observing the irascible enemy who had harassed him for so long.

Unable to stand the tension, Agar shouted: 'Fire! Fire, you scoundrel!' Flood fired, and the shot passed straight through James Agar's heart.

One should not overplay the extent of any personal attachment between William and his uncle; they probably met only rarely after William's departure from Ireland as a child. The significance of the event was this: if, after the death of his father, William Ashbrook ever had anything approaching a male relative who understood the lie of the land in Kilkenny, his uncle James Agar was it. And now he was gone.

---

10   James Wills, *A History of Ireland in the Lives of Irishmen*, Volume 5 (London and Edinburgh, 1897), pp. 212–213.

BACK IN NORTHMOOR, wily Thomas Ridge made sure the family held on to Noah's Ark, to its fisheries and to control of its weirs. And after Betty's marriage a splendid new brick house and outbuildings were erected for the Ridge family courtesy of Lord Ashbrook. Although brick had come into use for buildings of the very highest status as long ago as the Tudor period, most houses built locally at this time were of limestone rubble to the ground and first floors, with either thatched or stone-slated roofs over attics punctuated by dormer windows. Building in brick would certainly have reinforced the newly-gentrified status of the Ridges, and Lord Ashbrook could easily afford to make such a statement.

Not long after Betty left home, her eldest sister Catherine returned. In 1757 Catherine Ridge had married Robert Wyatt, a member of an energetic family of bargemasters. The carrier business to and from London had benefitted from improved navigation of the Thames, and a forward-looking man like Thomas Ridge will have kept his eye on such developments. Marrying within an allied trade was an obvious way to reinforce and advance a business-minded family's interests. But fishing was in decline; the triumph of Protestantism meant fewer fast days, and Oxford itself was in the doldrums largely thanks to falling numbers at the university. In the decades before turnpiking began to finance the improvement of the highways, and a century before the advent of rail, waterways provided by far the fastest mode of transport. Boats from as high upriver as Lechlade transported produce from the west such as cheese, iron and metal goods, and brought back some of the delights available from the capital. The carrying trade required reliable agents all along the river, and the Wyatts had a family presence at the head of the navigation in Lechlade as well as at the barge terminus at Folly Bridge in Oxford. For Thomas Ridge, what better way could there be to help his wife's disapproving parents in Buckland understand the error of their ways than for him to show that, even if he was never to enjoy the freedom of the city like their son John, he could still organise advantageous alliances for their grandchildren?

The involvement of one Richard Brookings in the selection of a husband for Catherine suggests the classic Ridge approach of careful forethought and exploitation of a well-placed contact. Like grandfather Thomas Ridge's master John Curtis, Brookings came from the community of fishing families based in Fisher Row in Oxford. The Brookings were involved in organising the traffic of the barge trade, and such activity was often the business of the perfectly-placed riverside alehouse-keepers; in 1716 Richard Brookings was licensed as a victualler at Bablockhythe, a location of particular significance to the carrying trade. In this period, boats were dragged up-river not by picturesque horses, but by raw manpower in a rugged business known as 'bow-haling'. A team of men would haul a boat along one stage of the river, and then pass it on to a new team for the next stage. Because of a looping diversion of the Thames north around Wytham Hill, Bablockhythe was about ten miles by river from Oxford. But a reasonably straight track from the Bablockhythe river crossing, through Cumnor

Noah's Ark island in the late 1800s: the remnants of the house built for the Ridge family by Lord Ashbrook following his marriage to Betty

and along the Botley Road back to Oxford, provided a convenient four-mile route by which the halers could return home at the end of the day and be in position for the next haul in the morning.

Although Brookings had probably moved away from Bablockhythe before the arrival of the Ridges at Noah's Ark, clearly some sort of acquaintance existed between the two families. It seems very likely that Thomas consulted the well-connected Brookings who then brokered the marriage with the Wyatts. Many river families failed to prosper whereas the Wyatts adapted to the new canal trade; by the 1790s they would be running weekly stage boats to Manchester and the Potteries, and in 1830 a Wyatt became mayor of Oxford. Perhaps this flexible and energetic approach to business was already evident to Brookings in the 1750s, prompting him to recommend Robert Wyatt as a good prospect for Thomas's daughter. And, it should be remembered, Brookings must have spoken well of the Ridges to the go-ahead Wyatt family too. Thomas was clearly keen, for Catherine was only 19 years old and could not marry without his consent. Such a young bride might be expected to produce a large family, the cost of which normally deterred early marriage among working people. In September 1757 Richard Brookings signed his name next to Thomas Ridge's as a witness to the marriage of Catherine Ridge to Robert Wyatt of Lechlade. There was every reason to look forward to a successful future for Catherine and Robert, and to a beneficial relationship for both families.

However, it became apparent in September 1769 that Robert Wyatt had been taking advantage of the peripatetic nature of his work and had fathered an illegitimate daughter in Henley-on-Thames. The liaison with an unmarried girl named Ann Wickett does not appear to have been a serious one on Robert's part. The Henley overseers were forced to obtain a court order in the November obliging Robert to reimburse them the £2 they had paid out for Ann's lying-in plus maintenance of mother and baby for the four weeks after the birth. Another 7s 6d was due for the maintenance of the child for the following three weeks.

Catherine and Wyatt had been married and apparently childless for twelve years by the time of Robert's dalliance with Ann Wickett. Perhaps the couple had already separated, but it seems reasonable to suppose that, if Catherine wasn't back from Lechlade already, she was after 1769. Robert Wyatt makes no further appearance in the registers of Northmoor. Thomas Ridge's careful plan to ally his family to the up-and-coming Wyatts had crumbled to dust, but from a business point of view it no longer mattered.

WHEN NEWS of the death of William Ashbrook's uncle James Agar arrived at Shellingford, the timing could not have been worse. At just eight months old Henry Flower, William and Betty's youngest child, was mortally ill. A wide range of diseases might snuff out the life of an eighteenth-century infant according to the season: smallpox, spotted fever and typhoid enteric fever in the warmer months, diphtheria and typhus in winter. Conditions such as measles, influenza or chickenpox, no longer generally considered life-threatening in England today, could kill. Little Henry died three weeks after James Agar and was buried at St Faith's in September 1769.

Anybody who is tempted to imagine that parents in Georgian and Victorian England somehow suffered less from an infant death because they were 'used to it' should spend some time poring over parish burial registers. There they will find the ages of dead children recorded often with painful accuracy, particularly once numeracy became widespread. Two little girls, now long-forgotten but once cherished, were buried within eighteen months of one another back in Northmoor; Hannah Harris, we are informed, was aged one year and seven months at her death in January 1796; and Sarah Brownot's life is recorded as lasting eleven days (four days longer than her twin brother William). These are not round figures, though they could easily have been approximated to eighteen months and two weeks respectively. Where asked, parents sometimes gave their dead child's age with an agonised precision that included not just years and months, but weeks, days, and occasionally even hours. Maybe the fact that Betty was already five months pregnant with her next child offered a degree of comfort, but there is no reason to believe that a new baby could replace a dead one in the eighteenth century any more than it can today. Two days after what would have been Henry's first birthday, William and Betty's second daughter, Catherine, was baptised.

But the little girl proved to be another source of heartache: a mere eight weeks later she was buried near her brother.

We can safely assume that warmth and nutrition were not lacking for the tiny girl, but congenital problems which modern parents would expect to be addressed in an operating theatre or critical care unit today simply took their course until well into the twentieth century. Parents had little but their own faith in God's wisdom to sustain them during a weakly baby's decline. The five months from the end of August 1769 through to the beginning of March 1770 were a period of unremitting misery for William and Betty, and they could be forgiven for wondering whether the fairytale was over and they were being punished for transgressing society's boundaries. Even after baby Catherine was buried there was no respite from worry for, as usual, Betty was pregnant once more. Would a new baby ever again be a source of joy? Or were they now locked into a ghastly cycle of hope followed by anguish, terror, and ultimately desolation?

In the light of these trying events, it is hardly surprising that William became yet further estranged from his Irish interests. It had been a gradual process, with no single step making the breach irrevocable, but the cumulative effect of a sequence of decisions rendered William Flower a member of that breed especially reviled in Ireland, the absentee landlord. The breach had begun years before at the time of his father's death. After his mother's flight to England, William was understandably kept close by being sent to Eton from where the natural destination was an Oxbridge college. Had the family remained in Ireland, William may well have accompanied his fellow sons of the Anglo-Irish aristocracy to Trinity College Dublin. This was not an invariable rule, but it does seem likely that if, upon graduating from Oxford William had had parents still living in Ireland, his return to Castle Durrow would have been the natural course.

As it was, there was only aunt Rebecca remaining in Ireland and she had been established at her marital home of Ringwood, some forty miles from Durrow, since before William was born. Of course, living in a rented property in England did not actively preclude visiting family possessions in Ireland—many Anglo-Irish landowners had country homes in England, and took houses in London and Dublin for the season too. Following the birth at Christmas 1768 of the doomed Henry, supposed 'spare' to the fourteen-month-old Ashbrook heir, William might have felt at liberty to leave his once-more-pregnant wife safely at home for the month or so that it would take to travel to Castle Durrow, but a pamphlet published in Dublin at the time suggests that he did not.

A List of the Absentees of Ireland and an estimate of the yearly value of their Estates and Incomes spent Abroad provided 'A List of Lords, Gentlemen, and Others who having estates employments or pensions in Ireland, spend the same Abroad'.[11] William Ash-

---

11   Thomas Prior, *A List of the Absentees of Ireland and an estimate of the yearly value of their Estates and Incomes spent Abroad* (Dublin, 1769), p. 6.

brook appeared in the First Class list, that is 'those who live constantly abroad, and are seldom, or never, seen in Ireland'. Second Class was reserved for 'those who live generally Abroad, and visit Ireland occasionally, for a very short time', so being absent from Ireland on a scale that qualified as First Class clearly required considerable commitment. The pamphlet also describes the actual amount of money which each absentee landlord was taking out of the country, but which the author believed should rightfully be invested at home in Ireland. The estimated yearly rental value of William's Irish estates is given as £3,000 which equated in 2005 to an annual buying power of around £191,000.[12] While this sum was no doubt a considerable loss to the Irish economy, it probably left William little surplus once the costs were met of maintaining a large family and a full staff in the appropriate style in a rented English country house.

MOST ORDINARY FOLK in the eighteenth century would simply toil on to the point of physical exhaustion, working into extreme old age—if they survived that long.[13] But Betty's parents Thomas and Elizabeth Ridge, in their fifties and parents of a viscountess, could now retire from the grubby business of trade. The lease on Noah's Ark was transferred into their son William's name, and Thomas relinquished his victualler's licence in favour of his daughter Anne's husband, Thomas Holford. Holford gave up his trade as a cordwainer and he and a pregnant Anne left Bampton for Noah's Ark. The Holfords had already lost two infant boys, so their new start must have seemed blessed when a healthy daughter, Maria, arrived in the summer of 1770. Next came Thomas in 1771, and then Anne in 1773. Betty's younger sister Sarah had been allowed to marry a humble fisherman, Joseph Winter, in 1769—why not, since the Ridge family's future was now assured?—and had moved away to Eynsham. How very convenient, therefore, that poor, dear Catherine Wyatt should be available to look after her parents and keep an eye on the Holford little ones as well. The role thrust upon her was that of the spinster-aunt, selflessly helping out in the background while her younger sister Anne gloried in the role of First Lady in the family business. Times were tough for a wife with no husband, and it was an especially galling outcome for Catherine, who had probably believed that her marriage would be the making of her family.

Thomas Ridge now considered himself a man of leisure. When the baby of the family, 19-year-old John, went up to Pembroke College Oxford in December 1771 to read law he gave his father's occupation as 'gentleman'. Thomas must have pinched himself occasionally when he reflected on the memory of that hazy June morning

12   [http://www.nationalarchives.gov.uk/currency/default0.asp#mid]
13   In the Ridge home-parish of Buckland in 1791 John Coombe was described as a wheelwright upon his burial at the age of 83. Four years later, 93-year-old Richard Fear was listed as a carpenter at the time of his death.

thirty-seven years before, and of the ambitious young man rowing stealthily away down the river Thames, away from his home and family, determined to make something better of his life.

John Ridge was the youngest of Thomas and Elizabeth's children. As such, he occupied a position in the family which has been known on occasion to enjoy a degree of parental indulgence. He was a boy of 12 when Viscount Ashbrook became a frequent guest in the Ridge home. Having been exposed to aristocratic company at such a formative age, he had more chance than anyone in the family to develop the demeanour of a gentleman naturally, rather than cultivating a manner designed to conceal humble origins. John was presented with opportunities which his father would have relished at that age. For Thomas Ridge grew up in an area where village life was heavily influenced by the university in Oxford. The colleges owned a large proportion of the farms, and the churches were stuffed with Oxford men. Thomas may have noticed that these clerics were not necessarily any sharper than he was, they simply enjoyed the benefits of a fine education coupled with impeccable social contacts. Any young man of means sufficiently ambitious and diligent to seek out and value such an education could enjoy his pick of the professions, and Thomas was determined that his youngest son John would be one of those men. A degree from Oxford combined with Ashbrook influence would give John a pass into society. A pathway smoothed by the tread of generations of privileged young men lay open before this son of a family of water gypsies.

After Betty Ridge's marriage into the Flower family in 1766, her two brothers William and John, by then aged 25 and 15, became perhaps the most eligible bachelors ever beheld by the maidens of Northmoor. The boys' father Thomas doubtless counselled caution—the exercise of rigid self-control in the present might open up the prospect of mixing with young ladies of quality later on. Whilst steady William Ridge's history shows that he saw the wisdom of biding his time, it must have been a relief to Thomas when the rather wilder John reached an age when he could be packed off to Oxford university and away from his village friends. But it may already have been too late.

John left river life behind in December 1771 and embarked on a course of study at Oxford leading to the degree of Bachelor of Civil Law, one of the university's higher awards for which candidates had to be of at least seven years' standing. This was a considerable commitment, and any student whose heart was not in it, or who was undertaking the course to fulfil the vicarious wishes of a parent, might very well run into trouble. Someone like John posed the ideal target for those wishing to distract him with all the delights now available to him and, perhaps even more dangerously, those of his own background who might see abstention in the face of ready access as simply perverse. On the day of John's matriculation, the Pembroke College bursar wisely obliged him to deposit a sizeable eight pounds' caution money into the hands of the college authorities. The money would be repaid if and when John left college with a clean record. One of the rules to which John was thereby agreeing was that absolutely forbidding undergraduates to marry. It is something of a surprise, therefore, to discover an entry in the Northmoor parish register showing that in 1775 John married a local girl named Elizabeth Trinder.

The Trinder family was (and still is) widespread around the Northmoor area. Elizabeth was baptised in Northmoor in March 1746, making her five years John's senior. In the following century when the Northmoor baptismal records included the father's occupation, all the local Trinders were recorded as labourers, so it seems likely that they always had been. This was not the calibre of wife that Thomas Ridge had in mind for John. Was the marriage a deliberate attempt on John's part to disqualify himself from a course of study at Oxford which he had undertaken only at the behest of his father? Or had he been caught out by his own intemperate conduct? Elizabeth Trinder, five years more worldly than John, may have claimed that she was expecting his child. He was, after all, the catch of a simple Northmoor girl's dreams, and Elizabeth may have felt pressed to take action before her beau began to mix with ladies of quality. Why should she be prevented from making a spectacular leap across the social divide when her neighbour Betty Ridge had already done so? Maybe the young couple even conspired to bring about an outcome that suited them both in their own ways.

John's father Thomas, however, favoured social mobility of the upward variety only for his own family. If a child failed to appear within the appropriate time-frame, an annulment would be sought. While the Ridge family waited to be convinced of the veracity of Elizabeth Trinder's claim, it was imperative to separate her from the easily-led John. It was essential that Elizabeth should be removed from Northmoor immediately after the marriage ceremony and placed in the care of a member of the Ridge family. This would prevent her from making further attempts on motherhood either by means of John or of an obliging stand-in. Shellingford was the obvious outpost to which to despatch her. Elizabeth Trinder and Betty Ridge will have known one another from childhood but, even if the two girls had been close friends, any suspicion of a personal desire on Betty's part to have a childhood playmate as a sister-in-law would disqualify her in her father's eyes from performing her policing role reliably; Ridge family interests took priority.

Upon the non-appearance of a child by the summer of 1776, action was required in order to liberate John to make a more advantageous connection. Divorce was available only by Act of Parliament in the eighteenth century and therefore at great expense. Cost would provide no barrier where Lord Ashbrook was involved, but such a procedure was hardly low-profile and offered none of the discretion that he and the Ridge family would have deemed desirable for a quiet resolution to the situation. However, an annulment (a legal separation) would allow John to continue his studies at Pembroke College, which he could not have done as an openly-married man. An application would be made to the church courts for the case to be considered by the Bishop of

Oxford and, by happy coincidence, the bishop's seat was Christ Church, Lord Ashbrook's own alma mater.

Evidently, an annulment was successfully obtained because John Ridge gained his degree in 1780. It is difficult to ignore the possibility that the university authorities, sensible of maintaining good relations with the Ashbrooks, co-operated in the swift smoothing away of any difficulties. John reclaimed his eight pounds' caution money from the Pembroke bursar in June 1780 and left college with a clean disciplinary record. In other words, he got away with it. But the family's collective sigh of relief soon turned to a gasp of despair for, within weeks of John's lucky escape, Betty's young husband William Ashbrook was dead.

FOLLOWING THAT dreadful period ending with the burial of baby Catherine in 1770, William and Betty enjoyed ten peaceful years in the private world they created tucked away in Shellingford. Another daughter, Harriet, arrived in November 1771. Those first few months of the new little girl's life must have been tense ones for William and Betty. Their daughter Catherine had died at eight weeks, Henry at eight-and-a-half months; an eighteenth-century parent could never breathe easy and assume all trouble was past. However, Harriet was followed by Caroline in 1773 and then Sophia in 1774, and the nursery became a happy place once more.

No doubt these girls were all loved and valued just as much by their parents as they would be today, but one difficulty remained: the lack of a 'spare' to replace Henry, a male child to succeed to the title in the event of the unexpected early death of the heir. William was well aware of such a possibility: his own father had been a second son whose older brother died young. We can never know whether the survival of baby Henry in 1769 might have marked an end to child-bearing for Betty, but we do know that this is exactly what happened following the birth of another son, this time a robust one. The last of William and Betty's children was baptised Henry Jeffrey in November 1776.

Modern squeamishness about re-using the name of a dead child would have baffled eighteenth-century parents. As we have seen, the naming of children, especially those who arrived early on in the brood, followed a rough formula. Having named his first son after himself, William wanted to call his second after his father. When that son died and another finally arrived, the same principle applied, though it is notable that a slight differentiation was introduced by the addition of the name of William's uncle, Jeffrey. Perhaps even in 1776 recycling the name of an eight-month-old child was not quite so easy as recycling the name of a tiny scrap who survived for a few days or weeks only. Maybe it is relevant, too, that 'Jeffrey' was the name of the heir who should in due course have succeeded to the Ashbrook title rather than William's own father, Henry. Combining the two names seems to be an expression of William's awareness that he had both his father and his uncle to acknowledge for his position as Viscount Ashbrook.

A brief glimpse of William living up to his part as a patron of the arts is shown by his appearance in 1774, along with other local notables including the fourth Duke of Marlborough, in the list of subscribers to a book of poetry, *Poems on Several Occasions* by John Bennet, a shoemaker of Woodstock. Such sponsorship was standard practice for a cultured gentleman of the time, but did William and Betty mix socially with aristocratic neighbours like the Throckmortons in their shiny new Palladian mansion in Buckland? How intriguing to imagine Betty's thoughts as she rode in her carriage up to the spectacular new house, knowing not only that her husband owned one just like it in Ireland, but also that so many of her Ridge cousins lived in the humble cottages of the surrounding parish.

Another eminent neighbour with property in nearby Nuneham Courtenay as well as in Stanton Harcourt, neighbouring on Betty's own home village of Northmoor, was Earl Harcourt, Lord Lieutenant of Ireland between 1772 and 1777. It seems inconceivable that the Anglo-Irish Lord Ashbrook could avoid paying his respects to such a powerful man, however bizarre the situation might be for Betty. Perhaps her state of near-permanent pregnancy allowed her licence to avoid accompanying her husband on potentially awkward social occasions. Anyway, any embarrassment regarding Earl Harcourt was resolved a few months after the Earl finally retired to Nuneham Courtney in January 1777; the poor man fell head-first into a narrow well-shaft, probably whilst trying to rescue his dog. He became wedged fast, and suffocated. The dog, of course, was found in the pink of health and displaying considerable resourcefulness by balancing on his master's upturned feet.

Whatever the extent of his social calls in England, we have already seen that William never visited his Irish estates. A man his rank, enjoying the privileges of that position, was expected to devote at least a portion of his time to public service from a young age. William's grandfather and namesake had served first in the army, and then as MP for County Kilkenny from 1715 through to 1727. Thereafter he represented Portarlington until 1733, being elected high sheriff of County Kilkenny in the meantime in 1731. Finally he served as a Privy Councillor of Ireland in 1735. Even William's father dizzy Henry at least managed a stint in a cavalry troop in the militia before his early death in 1752. While James Agar and Henry Flood slogged it out for the honour of representing the borough of Callan, William was busy making babies with Betty. He appears never to have picked up a firearm in defence either of his country or of his grandfather's seat in the Irish parliament. Today this might seem by far the more admirable course but William's contemporaries would have disagreed. Though he may occasionally have been obliged to travel to London, he seems to have been utterly content to spend his days with his family, oblivious to the wider world. His sisters remained living within his household unmarried, he had no brothers, and all his grandparents were dead. Where else would he go? For his wife, therefore, the shock of his death in the late summer of 1780 must have been profound.

William died aged 36 in August 1780, leaving Betty with six children under 14. He was buried in Shellingford church twelve days later, the second Viscount Ashbrook to die in his thirties leaving a child as his heir. Was there some congenital problem affecting the men of the Flower family? His father Henry suffered fainting fits as a young man, and of course his uncle Jeffrey had died at just 13 years old.

The wording on William's cherub-encrusted monument insists that he was 'blessed with strong natural Parts'. However, the rest of the inscription suggests that the text should be read with a degree of circumspection. It describes a man who 'would have conferred Dignity on any Trust or Employment in public life; But preferring the Tranquillity of Retirement, to the Tumult of Business, He devoted himself to innocent Amusements, And the Exercise of Hospitality, Charity, Benevolence & all other amiable Virtues which ennoble private Life, And are the only sure Foundation of social & domestick Happiness...'[14] That somewhat defensive assertion that William *would have* conferred dignity on any public service but chose instead to devote himself to his private life seems designed to counter criticism (real or imagined) that the second Viscount Ashbrook failed to play the role expected of him. Perhaps the strident assertion of physical strength gives the game away. Maybe William was never sufficiently robust in health for anything other than a quiet life.

One of the many objections of the family of an aristocratic young man to his marrying a humble village girl was that the proposed bride could not possibly bring with her a useful dowry either in cash or property with which to enhance the power, prestige and wealth of her husband. In return it was customary before any marriage for the bride's family to negotiate a 'jointure', or guaranteed share for life of the husband's estate. The jointure was to be paid in the form of an annuity in the event of the bride outliving her husband. Betty brought no dowry to the marriage but in his will William allotted her a handsome annual income all the same. He left Betty lands in County Kilkenny yielding just under £500 a year for life. William further directed that his wife 'shall have the Use of all her and the Family jewels and of all my Household Furniture Carriages and Coach Horses during her natural life...'.[15] Betty is clearly left in a comfortable position. It is touching to note the use of the phrase 'all her *and* the family jewels'. Such differentiation between the wife's personal property and family heirlooms is, of course, entirely to be expected where an aristocratic woman brings with her jewels of her own, independent of her husband's family possessions. Since it seems unlikely that Betty had much use for diamonds during her days brewing ale and gutting fish on Noah's Ark island, the fact that she had jewels which could be described as her own

14   Monument to William Flower, second Viscount Ashbrook (1744–1780), St Faith's church, Shellingford, Berkshire.
15   National Archives PROB 11/1069, 'Will of The Right Honourable William Lord Viscount Ashbrook of Kingdom of Ireland', 21st October 1780.

indicates that they must have been love tokens from the only person she knew who could afford such things—her beloved William.

Ten thousand pounds was to be divided between William's younger children upon their reaching the age of 21—Elizabeth, Harriet and Caroline at the time the will was written, and then with the addition of Sophia and Henry by the time of William's death—or, in the case of the girls, at the time of their marriages if such came earlier. In this way, the daughters were provided with dowries should they need them or a capital sum that would yield an income if not. No mention is made of William's sisters Elizabeth and Mary, but they had already each been allotted £6,000 in their father's will just as William was now providing for his daughters. The figures are revealing. William's father had left £12,000 between his two youngest children; William left £10,000 between five. Whilst William could afford to live comfortably day-to-day and buy his wife the occasional bauble, the family fortune appears to have been dwindling. He had neglected two important aspects of his financial responsibilities: to enhance the family exchequer by bringing home a rich wife, and to play the political game in Ireland from which members of the elite derived power, influence and ultimately financial advantage. A good marriage and an active role for the next Viscount Ashbrook was becoming a matter of urgency.

The actuality of William's absence from Betty's life must have been shattering. When she took the huge leap across the class boundary and left behind the world of the water gypsies, she had her husband to guide her. She had spent her entire marriage either pregnant or nursing young children. William seems to have been uxorious in the extreme and if ever there was much inter-action between Betty and the local aristocracy, no doubt he was hovering protectively nearby. Now, with her protector gone and the new viscount a mere 12-year-old boy, could she maintain her position? Or would any authority she had accumulated crumble away? The very thing which had made William vulnerable to the attractions of a pretty girl from a large and vibrant family, his lack of dynamic and supportive Ashbrook relatives of his own, now left Betty exposed.

She had become the protector: she had six children aged between 13 and three, four of whom were daughters who needed to be found husbands. There was no alternative but to maintain and encourage any social connections made as William's consort, for this is where the eligible young men would be found. The local grand-dames must be persuaded that the daughters of a fishergirl were good enough for their sons, and that the fishergirl herself was sufficiently respectable to be considered their own social equal. Betty was also now the legal guardian of a boy who was the proprietor of substantial estates in Ireland, Wales and England. His interests had to be protected, and this would involve dealing with lawyers, agents and tenants, all male and all far more experienced than she was in matters of business. At 35, and after only fourteen years in this new and bewildering world of the aristocracy, Betty's responsibilities must have seemed overwhelming.

3
A chip off the old block

BETTY'S ELDER BROTHER William Ridge was 22 when Lord Ashbrook wafted into the family's life. During the three years of William Flower's courtship of Betty, the ever-alert Thomas Ridge must have realised that something better might lie ahead for his two sons than a life of physical labour in a declining fishing trade. Even before the match between his daughter and the young aristocrat was settled, a man like Thomas would see the advantages for his boys of learning what they could while they could. While ever the somewhat startling circumstance of a viscount appearing regularly as a guest at their table persisted, it seems reasonable to imagine Thomas urging his sons to observe the manners and behaviour of a gentleman. Once the connection with the Ashbrooks became permanent, opportunities might open up and Thomas would want his sons to be equipped to hold their own in more elevated company.

Whether or not Lord Ashbrook intended ever to visit Ireland after his marriage to Betty, a family member on the spot overseeing Ashbrook interests would be a valuable asset. William Ridge's confident signature as a witness to his sister's marriage shows that like his father he was literate. Being from a family of self-employed men, he was numerate too. With Lord Ashbrook and Betty enduring their darkest days between late 1769 and mid-1772, Lord Ashbrook's neglect of his Irish possessions was finally made permanent. And there was his intelligent, capable brother-in-law: just the chap to keep an eye on business across the water. William Ridge left life as a fisherman behind and travelled to Ireland, first featuring in the Kilkenny press acting on behalf of Lord Ashbrook in December 1772.

At first William Ridge appears to be performing the role of enforcer alongside the existing Ashbrook man-of-business, William Hanson. Following the theft of timber and bark (for the tanning industry) from the Ashbrook estates, and especially from the magnificent oak stands in the woods of Durrow, William placed a notice in *Finn's Leinster Journal* offering a reward of ten guineas to anyone who could bring the offenders to justice. He also ran errands. Whilst Hanson conducted the desk-based business of administering the Ashbrook estates, William was despatched to England on a mission to find a way to improve the agricultural yield from the Castle Durrow lands. In January 1775, the *Journal* reported with satisfaction that a great quantity of Surinam potatoes had been produced, 'the seed of which were brought from England by William Ridge, Esq; they take little boiling, are remarkably dry and well tasted, and weigh from three pounds to four and a half pounds each'.[16]

Two significant events led to a change in the nature of William's role after 1780. First came Hanson's retirement on half-pay in June 1779, and then the death of Lord Ashbrook in the following year, leaving Betty in sole charge of her son's inheritance. William Ridge's promotion into Hanson's old job provided the vulnerable Betty with a representative she could trust implicitly with overseeing her and her 13-year-old son's interests in Ireland. And along with William's elevated status came a higher profile in Kilkenny society, the members of which he joined in condemning the latest outrage. One morning in February 1783 postman Patrick Hyland became separated from his postbag which contained a bank note and bills amounting to £244. Some of the bills were negotiated in Dublin the following morning. Amongst the nobles and gentlemen of Queen's County who pledged contributions to the enormous £800 reward was William Ridge. Alongside him in the list were his friends George Bathorn, the town apothecary, and Edward Harte, the doctor. William had become sufficiently self-confident to place himself among the pillars of local society.

He was also by now taking a leading role in the local militia, the Castle Durrow Light Dragoons, a role previously fulfilled by his sister's father-in-law first Viscount Ashbrook. As British soldiers were withdrawn from Ireland in increasing numbers to fight in the American War of Independence, and France and Spain were drawn into the struggle on the side of the United States, establishment fears grew of a Catholic invasion of Ireland. The men of each area were urged to do their patriotic duty and come together to form local defence corps. However, the opportunities for discussion occasioned by regular meetings of men of all classes gave rise to an unintended consequence: a degree of sympathy amongst Irish patriots with the spirit of independence of the revolutionary American people and their struggle against British oppression. A government-approved initiative designed to defend the status quo had in fact brought about a new political awareness and an empathy with elements among the nation's supposed enemies.

Man-on-the-spot William Ridge was as aware as anyone of the mood of unity engendered by dialogue between men of all levels of Irish society. The minutes of one particular meeting chaired by 'Lieutenant Colonel Ridge' and recorded by Jonah Barrington make the strength of feeling clear. Having elected in place of William as their new major John Barrington (the aforementioned author's brother), members of the

---

16   *Finn's Leinster Journal*, 18th January 1775.

Castle Durrow Light Dragoons resolved that they were: 'ready, with our *lives and for-tunes*, to co-operate with every Volunteer Corps, to obtain the Constitutional rights and liberties of [the Irish people]'.[17] Even accounting for a degree of bluster amongst companies competing to display the depth of their patriotic commitment, this was a long way from local worthies appointing themselves simply to protect their part of British territory from opportunistic Spanish adventuring.

A press report of the summer review of the Kilkenny Volunteer corps in August 1782 reveals the level of society in which William Ridge was now moving. Among his eleven fellow Kilkenny colonels were two Butlers, members of one of the grand-est families in Ireland, as well as three lords (Tyrone, Wandesford and Clifden). Such hurdling over the social divide from fisherman to familiar of the Kilkenny elite was doubtless expedited by the fact that two of the above-mentioned colonels also hap-pened to be relatives of William's sister Betty by marriage. Colonel of the Kilkenny Independents was Lord Clifden, aunt Rebecca Agar's nephew. At the head of the corps of the Callan Union was Colonel Agar, aunt Rebecca's son.

Each corps would have consisted of perhaps eighty to one hundred men, depend-ing upon how many able-bodied volunteers a parish or town could supply. They cannot all have been drawn from the landowning elite; they were men from every level of society whose lives were lived on Irish soil. One aspect in particular of the discussions among these newly-galvanised patriots doubtless rang alarm bells with William Ridge. Resentment against absentee-landlords was still as strong as it had been when Lord Ashbrook was branded a First Class offender in 1769. Jonah Barrington described this body of men as an obstacle to the prosperity of Ireland.[18] They lived, he claimed, exclusively at the British Court and knew their Irish demesnes by name only, feeling no interest for them apart from the income they yielded. It seems unlikely that Wil-liam Ashbrook ever left his wife's side for long enough to strut about at Court, but his ignorance of the lives of his Irish tenants and neighbours was undeniable; the portals of Castle Durrow had been bereft of Ashbrooks for more than thirty years.

Lord Ashbrook's early death means that we will never know whether he planned one day to return in triumph to Castle Durrow, taking the Ashbrook heir with him. However, what is clear is that once Betty's brother William Ridge became sufficiently established in Kilkenny society, he made his sister aware of the dangers neglect posed to her son's interests—and by extension to Ridge interests too. In the autumn of 1783 the local newspaper trumpeted in ninety-eight lines of excruciating verse the arrival at Castle Durrow of Lady Ashbrook along with her son William and daughter Elizabeth. The new viscount was by now aged 16, and had just left Eton. His sister Elizabeth was 17, and her attendance on the trip suggests that she was already 'out'—that is, she too had finished her education and was now allowed to appear among adults socially.

17   Jonah Barrington, *Historic Memoirs of Ireland*, Volume 1 (London, 1833), p. 353.
18   *Ibid.*, p. 34.

The ode, which alternates spoken verse with song, begins innocently enough but the poet, one 'Mr Lynch', develops several pertinent themes once he really gets going. He kicks off with a pretty picture of the local maidens celebrating:

Durrovian Nymphs, in whose joy-streaming Eyes
Th' o'er flowing Tears of Gratitude arise,
Whose Words but faintly express th'extatic Heat,
Wherewith your all-enraptur'd Bosoms beat...[19]

After a bit more of this Lady Ashbrook arrives, and readers are enjoined to break into song to the tune of *Rule Britannia*. A discussion of Betty's virtues follows, particularly her charity towards those in need and the calibre of her parenting skills. So far, so formulaic. Another burst of song follows, but then the subject matter begins to betray the true intent of the poet—as well as the fact that he clearly knows more of the mother than he does of the son. A decidedly martial tone is adopted for the introduction of the new viscount who is portrayed as a true Irish patriot, ready by his own example to inspire his gallant volunteers with the heroic fire necessary to check British selfishness and pride.

Perhaps the Irish Volunteers featured constantly in the verse of the day, but in this case the poem was written by somebody who was keen to address all the issues of contention then being discussed in Irish society. The new viscount's Irish ancestry is emphasised as if to counter local grumbling about Ashbrook absenteeism and adherence to Britain. His supposed martial qualities are highlighted, though time will show that young William Ashbrook was hardly the chap to furnish inspiration to anyone's heroic fire. The final verse of the poem addresses Irish concerns over being left behind in the booming new fields of science, manufacturing and trade. Readers are confidently assured that the third Viscount Ashbrook is just the man to lead the march towards the sunlit uplands of a prosperous Irish future.

As the boy was still only 16 years old, nobody was in a position to argue with this portrayal, and herein lies the essence of the work. It was not, as it might at first seem, a stream of obsequiousness directed towards the Flower family. It was aimed at the readers themselves and was designed to present the Flowers to the local populace in an ideal light, to reassure them that their grievances were well-understood by their young patron, and that they may feel assured that the solutions lay in his eager hands. Their new viscount was on their side against the selfish interests of the distant British establishment. As to the identity of the mysterious Mr Lynch, it seems we have no alternative but to brace ourselves for the possibility that William Ridge by now considered himself a self-taught man of letters. As we will see, another poem emanating

---

19   *Finn's Leinster Journal*, 1st November 1783. The poem can be enjoyed in full in
      Appendix E.

The stone-flagged entrance hall at Castle Durrow, now in County Laois

from Castle Durrow a few years later was published anonymously, but its subject is very close indeed to William's heart.

What a moment it must have been for Betty Ridge, fishergirl from Noah's Ark island in Northmoor, when she bowled in her carriage through the gates of the Ashbrook family seat, past the little church of St Fintan's and up the sloping avenue of limes to the front of the castle. It was not quite such a grand palace as Betty would have seen at Buckland House near Shellingford, but it was in a way more pleasing in its simpler lines. She must have moved through the gracious interior of her husband's family home with a sense of wonder. Glass-paned double doors at the main entrance opened onto a large, stone-flagged hall. Pretty, square morning rooms led off either side and enjoyed views across wide lawns running down to the tree-lined river Erkina. At the back of the hall, opposite the front entrance and beyond the stone-flagged cross-passage leading to the sweep of stairs, more double doors opened onto a magnificent saloon running the entire length of the house. Five lofty windows and a glass door gave onto a south-facing terrace and gardens and, on the floor above, the principal bedrooms enjoyed the same sunny aspect.

But the fractures in Irish society intruded even upon this fairytale interlude. During Betty's trip another of the frequent demonstrations of rural defiance against Anglo-Irish authority took place. At midnight on Monday 1st December 1783 a mob assembled at the Urlingford turnpike. They first demolished the toll house, and then turned their attention to the toll-gate itself. It was dismantled and, along with its posts, loaded on to carts. The gatekeeper was loaded up too, and carried off to the inn at Beggar's Cross where the terrified man was kept prisoner.

A meeting of concerned worthies was called at the house of Danniel Brennan in

The morning room at Castle Durrow, off the entrance hall

Durrow, i.e. the pub. William Ridge took the young Lord Ashbrook along to to demonstrate the new viscount's interest in local affairs. At the meeting twenty-one gentlemen of note signed an undertaking to contribute to the reward for the prosecuting to conviction of the guilty parties. (Before the introduction of a properly-constituted police force, those hoping to claim reward money evidently had to do rather more than quietly provide information to the authorities.) Young Ashbrook topped the list with a contribution of £5 13s 9d and William Ridge promised £2 5s 6d.

The momentous visit was probably over before the end of 1783. Betty had four other children aged eleven and under, and was no doubt anxious to return to them before the bad weather set in. William Ridge had pulled out all the stops to rescue the Ashbrook reputation in Ireland: he persuaded Betty to make the voyage to the family seat in order to introduce the tenantry to their new landlord; he arranged a review of the Castle Durrow Volunteers (though who was reviewing whom is debatable); and he either wrote or at least sponsored a work of poetic propaganda designed to manipulate local feeling in favour of his sister and her son. Eleven years in the business of running an absentee landlord's estate had given William a keen appreciation of the tensions involved in managing a potentially resistant tenantry whilst retaining political and social influence amongst the neighbouring Protestant elite.

Precisely when the gentlemen of the Grand Jury of County Kilkenny invited William Ridge to join them is unclear, but his public appearances alongside the young Lord Ashbrook during late 1783 will not have done him any harm. An address pub-

The principal bedroom at Castle Durrow today

lished in *Freeman's Journal* in January 1785 assuring the Lord Lieutenant of the loyalty of the Kilkenny Grand Jury was signed by a membership which now included one William Ridge.[20] Grand Juries performed the function of local government at county level and were made up of ratepayers. They selected new members from among their own kind, that is, landowners, substantial farmers and leading merchant families. They levied local taxes and then appointed their cronies to collect them. They inflicted fines, administered the law at the petty sessions, and generally distanced themselves from any activity likely to displease the Lord Lieutenant of Ireland, the monarch's official representative in Dublin.

Further light is cast on William's social ascendancy by the other signatures attached to the address. Foreman of the Jury was Henry Wellbore Agar, aunt Rebecca's great nephew; a fellow signatory was William Hanson, retired Ashbrook man-of-business; even Gervase Bushe, Henry Flood's second at the duel that finished off Lord Ashbrook's volatile uncle James Agar, was there. Furthermore, the Lord Lieutenant was at that time Charles Manners, His Grace Fourth Duke of Rutland, a county with which the Flower family had longstanding links. Any one of these men, or perhaps a combination thereof, could have been influential in facilitating William's selection onto the Grand Jury.

William's personal and political connections were now impeccable. The last thing he needed during this phase of his career was the arrival of an embarrassing relative.

---

20 *Freeman's Journal*, 13th January 1785.

JOHN RIDGE'S CONCEPT of duty to family and self contrasts sharply with that of his brother William. Having in spite of himself been equipped at great expense with a qualification which would set him up for life, John appears never to have practised as a lawyer. Along with the half-hearted marital scrape which should have cost him his place at the university, this suggests that the choice of the law may have been imposed upon him by others. Some other occupation had to be found for him. The end of his studies coincided with the death of his brother-in-law Lord Ashbrook, so the decision was taken to pack him off to Ireland to support his brother William in overseeing Betty's interests. John was installed at Prospect House near Durrow, the home, perhaps tellingly, of William's attorney friend George Frederick Lodge. William and Lodge could keep an eye on him, he would escape the orbit of those who knew of his somewhat compromised marital status, and he would be safe from the influence of the Trinders.

William's feelings at having to take responsibility for a troublesome younger brother when he was busy nurturing the upward-trajectory of his own career may be imagined. But, being his father's son, he managed to derive some advantage from the unpromising situation. For John arrived just as the nature of William's role was changing, and consequently John was placed in that subsidiary role which William once occupied in relation to William Hanson. The very presence of a subordinate threw William's seniority into relief and perhaps gave him confidence in the legitimacy of his position, especially when he became the agency by which the Ashbrooks were brought back into the lives of the people of Durrow. Next, a proper position needed to be found for the highly-educated John, and in an age of patronage such a project would best be facilitated by means of family contacts.

For the Flowers, that meant turning to their old allies the Agars. Since John evidently had no inclination to practise law, aunt Rebecca's nephew James Agar, Lord Clifden, was prevailed upon to arrange for John a career in the Church of Ireland. Today it would be baffling to discover a Bachelor of Civil Law operating as a clergyman in an established church without his having studied divinity in any form. In the eighteenth century it was a matter of whom you knew, not what. Indeed, there was no official training at this time for such positions; powerful friends would indicate their wishes to an archbishop and, once an applicant was approved by that archbishop, he was in. By great good fortune the archbishop approached in this particular case was Clifden's own brother.

Charles Agar, Archbishop of Cashel, was an immensely powerful man. He indicated his willingness to assist the brother-in-law of his esteemed friend and Oxford contemporary Lord Ashbrook, and in January 1783 John arrived in Dublin to collect a letter of introduction from Clifden in order that he might pay his respects personally to the Archbishop. The letter read:

My Dear Arch Bishop,

Permit me to introduce to Your Grace my very good friend Mr Ridge. From the obliging manner in which you were pleased to express yourself in His favour to me, & the regard you mentioned having for his late Brother-in-law Lord Ashbrook (of which I informed him) he is anxious to pay his respects & thanks to Your Grace. I beg to recommend Him as a Gentleman to whose family I am highly obliged, & any favour you are pleased to shew him will be considered as a high obligation conferred on My Dear A.B.

Your sincere friend & affectionate Brother,

Clifden[21]

The fruits of John's visit were prompt. Reverend Ridge's licence to practise as a curate in the Church of Ireland was granted within weeks. With John thus transmogrified from reluctant lawyer into newly-minted clergyman, it became a priority safely to marry off a young man apparently unencumbered by any sense of self-discipline. But, of course, there were complications.

THE SOCIAL POSITION of John's first bride Elizabeth Trinder Ridge, previously spirited out of Northmoor by Lord and Lady Ashbrook and parked in Shellingford, was highly anomalous. She had been married in church but she had no husband. Indeed, she had been married to Lady Ashbrook's own brother, but she could not be treated as an equal or welcomed into social gatherings at Shellingford Manor because that would necessitate awkward explanations. Was she, or was she not Lady Ashbrook's sister-in-law? In return for being supported financially by the Ashbrooks, Elizabeth was doubtless discouraged from mixing too freely with her Shellingford neighbours— initially to avoid the possibility of a liaison entered into with the express purpose of producing a child, and thereafter in order to prevent a disappointed Elizabeth from delivering her own particular version of events to eager ears. What must have been an uncomfortable stand-off for all concerned had dragged on for seven years by the time a solution offered itself, and Elizabeth was doubtless ready to accept a route back to a normal life.

Back in 1764, while Betty had embarked on her education and William had set about completing his, Thomas Ridge had turned his attention to finding a husband for his second daughter Anne. At 22 Anne was two years older than Betty, and it was only proper that she should marry first, for a girl who was preceded to the altar by a

---

21   Hampshire Record Office, M57/B23/9 'Lord Clifden recommending Mr Ridge, January 1783', Ecclesiastical papers of Charles Agar, 1st Earl of Normanton (1736–1809).

younger sister risked the taint of the old maid. The fact that Anne gave Bampton as her home parish at the time of her marriage suggests that she was already living away from Noah's Ark, perhaps in domestic service. The town was home to a substantial clan of Ridges, and it may be that Anne had been sent to help out in a house full of young cousins. Her marriage a few convenient months in advance of Betty's would avoid the embarrassment of a viscount's bride having a sister in service.

In June 1765 at the church of St Mary the Virgin in Bampton Anne married 26-year-old Thomas Holford. Holford was a cordwainer—a maker of shoes and boots using exclusively new leather, as opposed to a cobbler who repaired old ones. The distinction was jealously guarded by cordwainers everywhere. Holford was very much the sort of independent tradesman that Thomas Ridge would have approved of even before his family's collision with the aristocracy; Thomas does not appear to have expected the dramatic change in one daughter's fortunes to affect the marriage prospects of the others. To this day, ambitious parents discover to their chagrin that the spectacular marriage of one pretty daughter does not guarantee automatic elevation into the aristocracy for any sisters.

But in August 1782, her sister-in-law Anne Holford had died following three final pregnancies, all of which had resulted in infant deaths. Even the undoubted grief occasioned by such sad circumstances would not have blinded Anne's father Thomas Ridge to the potential of the situation. Anne's widower Thomas Holford was attractive husband material; his victualler's licence meant that his future was relatively secure in the terms of the period. The eldest Ridge daughter Catherine was already acting as a sort of housekeeper, and the position of landlord's wife in a smart, modern establishment was not one to be sniffed at. A marriage with her first husband's brother-in-law would preserve Elizabeth's dignity in that her connection with the newly-elevated Ridges would be maintained, and she would gain a presiding role in an establishment of her own.

Parish registers of the eighteenth century reveal that widowers frequently remarried within months of a first wife's death. This suggests not a lack of feeling on the part of bereaved husbands, but a pragmatic acknowledgement that a man on his own could not look after children, run a home and work the long hours required to earn a living all at the same time. It was not unusual for an unattached woman to be brought into the home as housekeeper and nursemaid and then, once a few months had passed in reasonable harmony, for the lady's position to be regularised and the gentleman's domestic difficulties resolved by means of marriage between employer and employee. But Thomas Holford was obliged to wait a full two years before escorting Elizabeth Trinder Ridge on her second sally up the aisle at the church of St Denys.

Following the non-appearance of a child by the summer of 1776, John Ridge and Elizabeth Trinder had obtained an annulment (a legal separation) in order to allow John to continue his studies at Oxford. But in order for the parties to remarry, a further application would have to be made for a declaration of nullity, meaning that the marriage was considered invalid from the start. One qualifying criterion was a misrepresentation on the part of one of the parties which had induced the other party to enter into a marriage under false pretences. An example of such misrepresentation might be a spurious claim of pregnancy where none actually existed. Elizabeth had no reason to co-operate in converting the initial annulment into a full declaration of nullity until a reasonable offer was made by her estranged husband's family. Once a sufficiently attractive situation presented itself by means of Anne Holford's death, the necessary legal proceedings could be initiated. Unfortunately, any consistory court records of proceedings in this particular case do not survive, but the matter no doubt oozed along at the frustratingly slow pace familiar to litigants of every era.

At last in December 1784 Thomas Holford of Northmoor, widower, was married to 'Elizabeth Ridge of the Parish of Shillingford in the County of Berks a Spinster'. Elizabeth used her married name—after all, the bishop himself had acknowledged that a form of marriage to John Ridge had taken place—while at the same time being described in the marriage entry as a spinster (though not, we note, as 'a maiden'). From Thomas Ridge's point-of-view, the sad death of his daughter Anne had provided an opportunity to deploy what was essentially a Ridge family asset, the victualler's licence, along with its current holder Thomas Holford to tidy away the tricky problem of Elizabeth Trinder Ridge.

THROUGH NO EFFORT on John's part, the way was now clear for him to make an alliance with a lady properly suited to the role of clergyman's wife. His brother's friend George Bathorn, the town apothecary and William's fellow officer in the Castle Durrow Volunteers, had a sister who might fit the bill. The Bathorns were gentry—not nearly so exalted as the aristocratic Ashbrooks, but still a substantial cut above the sons of fishermen socially. George's parents were Hugh Bathorn and Judith de Courcy, daughter of a family of impeccable lineage tracing back to the Norman Conquest. The Ridge forebears may have lacked such claims to grandeur but, once John was abstracted from his native surroundings, his quick wits and the Oxford education with which he had (perhaps forcibly) been furnished equipped him to move among the polite classes with ease. Now that his profession was assured, what gentry family would fail to take this close relative of the Ashbrooks seriously as son-in-law material? Certainly not the Bathorns, for the Durrovian nymph fixed upon by John—or perhaps by William on John's behalf—was George's sister Judith. Her hand was quickly sought and bestowed.

Parents would insist that a marriage went ahead only after the groom had shown he enjoyed sufficient income with which to support a family. In May 1784 John was presented as rector and vicar of Eirke some eleven miles from Durrow in the barony of Galmoy, and later that summer he and Judith de Courcy Bathorn were married. The newly-weds moved into Castleview, a Bathorn property a quarter of a mile outside Durrow. The house, now demolished, enjoyed a delightful view across the river Erkina to Castle Durrow itself, as well as an agreeable forty-two acres. Along with all the appropriate out-buildings went an orchard and two walled gardens stocked with finest-quality fruit trees. In May 1785 a son, John Agar Warren Ridge, was born. Named for his father's patrons and for the Warrens, local gentry connected by marriage with the Bathorns, John Agar was the first of a family of nine children. Castleview would for the next twenty-five years be a home filled with the sort of bustle familiar to William and John from their childhood on Noah's Ark.

The smoothness with which John had been eased into a new identity in Ireland must have come as a great relief to his brother William. Lacking the advantages of John's expensive education, William Ridge had been obliged to make his way by means of sheer hard work, irreproachable conduct, and loyalty to his patrons. He attained a position from where he could transform his undisciplined younger brother John into a clergyman arguably more eligible than he was himself in order that John might secure a gentlewoman for a wife and live a quiet and blameless life. Having drawn upon the credit built up among powerful friends to deal successfully with a ticklish situation which can hardly have formed part of his personal plan, William could now turn his attention back to his own career. With every precautionary measure now in place to contain John's waywardness, William—remarkable son of a remarkable father—was poised to enjoy his greatest triumph.

THE ANNOUNCEMENT CAME from Dublin Castle on 28th February 1785. William Ridge, a former Oxfordshire fisherman with no formal education or blue blood, was appointed high sheriff of County Kilkenny.

William's achievement was considerable. The high sheriff was the king's personal representative at county level. He performed a judicial role in overseeing the execution of High Court writs, as well as functions of an administrative and ceremonial nature. The Lord Lieutenant would make it his business to select only the most loyal and reliable candidate for each county, a man with a vested interest in preserving the status quo. Predecessors in the role included representatives of the foremost Kilkenny families: Agar, Ponsonby, Flood, and Caulfeild—as well as William Flower, builder of Castle Durrow and the second Viscount Ashbrook's grandfather. William Ridge had to gather sufficient support in order to be nominated as one of the three candidates for high sheriff put before the Lord Lieutenant at the beginning of each year. The calibre of William's contacts on the Grand Jury has already been highlighted, and his timing was perfect in that, at this time, the Lord Lieutenant of Ireland was the fourth Duke of Rutland, the county of origin of the Flower family.

At the age of forty-four, he had done the sensible thing and avoided romantic entanglements until he was firmly established in society and his origins among the water gypsies became obscured by more recent success. He may already have fixed his hopes upon 22-year-old Juliana Lidwill before 1785, but the announcement from Dublin Castle was certainly sufficient to finalise the matter. The Lidwills of Clonmore were a junior branch of an established County Tipperary family. In the early 1760s a young man named John Lidwill attended a school in Durrow. At weekends he walked the three miles westwards with other pupils through Lord Ashbrook's woods to Ballybooden House, the home of Mrs Patrick Fitzpatrick. Family legend has it that Mrs Fitzpatrick's daughter Anne seduced young Lidwill, whereupon Mrs Fitzpatrick encouraged him in the idea of marriage by pointing out that, if he failed to accept her suggestion, she would arrange for him to be called out by her relations (note the plural). John's father Thomas Lidwill promptly made him a counter-offer of £1,000 plus the lands of Clonmore to pull out of the marriage, presumably by way of compensation not only for losing his bride but for risking his life in multiple duels as well. John indicated his preference for the status of live pauper rather than dead rich man by marrying Anne in 1762, and their first child was a daughter named Juliana.

William's marriage to Juliana Lidwill followed precisely one month after the announcement from Dublin Castle. It was a nicely balanced match. John Lidwill, a man with four daughters and little cash, could not avail himself of tempting dowries for his girls, and anyway he had left the family home by this time, having fallen out with Juliana's mother. For William's part, he could not boast of exalted origins, but his political and social star was undeniably in the ascendent. Who knew what glories lay ahead during the next twenty or thirty years of his career? So Anne Lidwill decided to by-pass her own sons and transfer the house at Ballybooden to William and Juliana and their sons after her own death. It was all she had to offer to secure such a promising husband for her eldest daughter. The deed was witnessed by William Hanson, and the trustees were Juliana's brother George Lidwill and William's brother John Ridge.

It seems appropriate at this point to pause and imagine the feelings of William Ridge's father Thomas when news reached him of his son's astonishing triumph. His eldest son and ally in all his enterprises had surely exceeded even Thomas's expectations. Thomas had been the first to raise his eyes from the river and look to the settled parish where advancement was available to the bright and the ambitious. The advent of a viscount in the family's life and the subsequent elevation of William's sister into the aristocracy might be described as something of a fluke but the point is that William, like his father, deployed his aptitude and dynamism to make the most of the opportunities unexpectedly laid before him. As a result he marched both himself and his wayward brother away from the realm of the water gypsies and into the ranks of the gentry.

4

A quartet of brides

BACHELORS OF an optimistic bent in the areas of Berkshire, Oxfordshire and Wiltshire within a carriage ride of Shellingford cannot fail to have noticed that the death of Viscount Ashbrook, left four eligible females of marriageable age at the manor. William's sisters Elizabeth and Mary Flower, his widow Betty, and his daughter Elizabeth must all have been in want of a husband, and then there were three more potential brides in the pipeline: the younger girls, Harriet, Caroline and Sophia. Of course, William's sisters Elizabeth and Mary Flower had been available for courting all along and we can only speculate as to why no offers were ever successfully made for them before William's death. But perhaps the added attraction of a young and beautiful widow on the premises concentrated the minds of the local swains. And perhaps the jitters spreading throughout the ruling classes as the threat of revolution came ever closer to British shores concentrated the minds of the women also. For once events began to move, they moved very fast indeed.

Access to potential suitors was a difficulty for unmarried aristocratic ladies of a certain age. If the new viscount had been a young man rather than a mere boy, it would have been perfectly straightforward for him to host gatherings at which prospective grooms suited to his aunts might attend. But he was only 13 when his father died in 1780 and still had three more years at Eton ahead of him. Then in July 1785 he went up to Trinity College Oxford, leaving his eight-year-old brother Henry Jeffrey as the only man of the family remaining at home, and even Henry was probably away at school. Only one class of gentleman had legitimate access to such unprotected ladies: clergymen.

John Nicholl, son of an extensive and complicated family in the ranks of the Welsh gentry, first appeared as a curate in the Shellingford parish register in 1771 when he was 25. He was the son of Whitlock Nicholl Esquire of The Ham at Cowbridge in Glamorganshire, and a Fellow of Jesus College Oxford. He was said to be a generous man whose cheerful nature and gentle manner particularly endeared him to the young. Quite why Nicholl waited until he was 42 and Mary Flower was 40 before making his proposal is unclear. Assuming that he first came to Shellingford in 1771, Mary would have been 24, seemingly the perfect age to marry and start a family. Perhaps the newly-ordained young clergyman felt nervous about asking a viscount for the hand of his wealthy sister so early in his career. He had just been appointed a Fellow in 1771 and, in order to marry, he would have had to sacrifice the prospect of any academic laurels which lay ahead. At last in January 1788, perhaps emboldened by the absence of a patriarchal figure at the manor and satiated by the acquisition of two more Oxford degrees, Nicholl became the first groom to escort a Flower bride from Shellingford Manor to the altar.

Evidently no country wedding was going satisfy Mary after being buried away in the sticks for twenty years. The ultra-fashionable church of St George's just off Hanover Square in Mayfair was chosen for the ceremony. Among the witnesses was Mary's second cousin Henry Neville, second Earl of Abergavenny, and the presiding clergyman was the Honourable and Reverend William Neville, rector of Burghclere in Hampshire. The Nevills were Mary's relatives through the marriage in 1725 of her aunt Catherine Tatton to William Neville, fourteenth Lord Abergavenny. The Earl of Abergavenny was aunt Catherine's grandson. Upon marriage John Nicholl was obliged to resign his Fellowship at Jesus College, and a living was found for him at Remenham near Henley-on-Thames. John's brother Iltyd Nicholl had died in 1787 leaving a widow with six small children, and it was decided that the childless John and Mary would take in three-year-old Whitlock. The life thereafter of Betty's sister-in-law Mary might have become completely obscure were it not for a little book compiled for private circulation amongst the Nicholl family. *A Slight Sketch of the Life of the Late Whitlock Nicholl MD* is a collection of poems, letters and essays by the titular Whitlock, accompanied by an account of his life.

Mary provided a loving home in which the little boy thrived. The *Sketch* reveals that young Whitlock adored his aunt and followed her everywhere, helping her in the garden and accompanying her on visits to the poor. Mary spoke to him in French, sparking off a lifelong love of the language in the boy, and whenever he was given any sweet treat, he would always save half for Mary. Such a relaxed relationship seems very familiar to the modern parent, and evidently produced an environment in which the boy felt so comfortable that he dared to test the boundaries by cheeking Mary just as a son would his own mother. But the lack of formality imposed by Mary seems to have offended the author's dour Welsh sensibilities. 'She spoiled instead of guiding him, and by making herself more his plaything than his companion, lowered her own dignity in his eyes and caused him to treat her often with less respect than was her due…'[22] Who could this sneering Nicholl relative be?

In 1797 John and Mary took in Whitlock's 12-year-old brother Iltyd, who was supposedly too delicate to survive the rigours of the climate in London (although he

22   Anonymous, *A Slight Sketch of the Life of the Late Whitlock Nicholl MD* (London, 1841), p. 5.

somehow contrived to struggle on to the age of 86). Most of the letters written by Whitlock in later life and quoted in the *Sketch* are addressed to this same brother, so Iltyd seems the most likely candidate as author of the book. Does the faintly-resentful attitude towards Mary suggest that Iltyd found it difficult to fit in to a home where such close bonds had already been formed before he arrived? A reference is even made to Mary being 'unused to children'. It's a cheap shot. Although childless herself, Mary had known nothing but a home filled with and centred upon children for the whole of her adult life. Perhaps Iltyd regarded the easy affection between his brother and Mary as somehow threatening their real mother's claim to supremacy in little Whitlock's heart.

The happy life at Remenham was over. John Nicholl resigned the living in the following year and retired to Glamorganshire taking both boys with him, and Mary is suddenly written out of the story. Of course, she went to Cowbridge too but, though she had brought Whitlock up almost as her own son for sixteen years, the *Sketch* leaves the death in 1809 of this quietly heroic figure unmentioned.

'SHE ARRIVED WITH her brother, the young and elegant Viscount Ashbrook, driving a high-wheeled phaeton behind a pair of prancing chestnut horses. She was the cynosure of all eyes in her bottle-green habit with a hat of black beaver ornamented with a fox's brush.'[23] Thus the advent in the winter of 1787 of William and Betty's 21-year-old daughter Elizabeth Flower into the lives of the warring Warneford family of Highworth in Wiltshire, according to a descendant writing in the 1960s.

How seriously Mary Gibson's immensely readable account can be taken overall is a matter for debate, sprinkled as it is with such colourful passages, but she frequently brings the sceptical reader up short by quoting verbatim from family letters and diaries. Furthermore, while the eighteenth century seems far distant to the modern reader, the lives Gibson describes are those merely of her own grandparents and their parents; it is perfectly reasonable to imagine stories told over the family dinner table making an impression on an imaginative young girl. Perhaps she asked the right questions at the right time instead of regretting not doing so once it was too late.

The timing of the visit to Warneford Place just about adds up: Gibson claims Elizabeth met her future husband at a meeting of the nearby hunt. Maybe so, but certainly when her brother William Ashbrook had joined the Berkshire militia that same summer he found one Francis Warneford already serving as a lieutenant. Francis affected the gold-laced coats, the brilliant waistcoats, the flashy turnouts and the highly-bred horses typical of the young bloods of his day. He bowled along the Wiltshire lanes with

---

23   Mary Gibson, *Warneford: Being the life and times of Harriet Elizabeth Wetherell Warneford* (Private publication, 1966) p. 12.

Warneford Place, Wiltshire: home of Betty's eldest daughter Elizabeth

a complete disregard for others and raced his high-slung curricle against those of his fellow young squires. Most of all, says Gibson, he loved the chase, whatever the quarry: 'It was all one with him as long as he had a good blood horse between his legs and a fast pack of hounds nose down on the scent'.[24]

The Warnefords of Warneford Place, Sevenhampton, near Highworth in Wiltshire were a quarrelsome lot. They had contrived to be divided amongst themselves during most of the major national crises such as the Reformation and the Civil War, but the more parochial matter of the matrimonial choice of the heir would do just as well. When in the winter of 1787 Francis Warneford introduced Elizabeth to his family as his intended bride, the subject was seized upon as yet another excuse for a bust-up. According to Gibson, Francis was bewitched by Elizabeth's wit, her beauty and her brilliant horsemanship, but his mother showed her disapproval openly. After Elizabeth had driven away, Francis flung out of the house shouting that he would not spend another night at Warneford until his mother and brother had 'taken themselves off, as on so many recent occasions they had threatened to do'.[25] Evidently the mood

24   *Ibid.*, p. 11.
25   *Ibid.*

within the Warneford household was often tempestuous, but Gibson hazards no suggestion as to precisely why the beautiful Elizabeth Flower, daughter of a viscount, was so unacceptable to Francis's mother. It is difficult to avoid the suspicion that the problem lay not in Elizabeth being the daughter of Lord Ashbrook, but in her being the daughter of *Lady* Ashbrook.

Francis Warneford's mother Catherine Calverley was an immensely wealthy and ambitious woman. Indeed, it was her fortune which had rescued Warneford Place from ruin, but only after she had staged sufficient tantrums to persuade her husband, a man perfectly content with his lot as a Yorkshire parson, to come south and take up residence there. The root of Catherine's snobbishness may be found in the fact that, unlike the Honourable Elizabeth Flower's, her own fortune derived originally from trade. Her father had been a successful drug merchant in Southwark and, although the profession did not qualify for the negative connotations such a description might convey today, the family's wealth was decidedly not based upon the traditionally acceptable source: land. Warneford Place was Catherine's chance to effect a public transfer for herself and her children from the merchant to the landowning class.

A marriage for her son which invited description as an alliance between the grandson of drug merchant and the granddaughter of a fisherman was perhaps too uncomfortable a prospect. She therefore declined to attend at St Faith's, Shellingford in November 1789 when Francis defied her wishes and married Elizabeth Flower. Francis's brother Samuel did attend, presumably along with his own wife of one year, Margaret Loveden of Buscot Park—a woman whose grip on reality was feared to be fragile. Conducting the ceremony was John Nicholl's friend and fellow curate John Jones and the witnesses were Elizabeth's brother third Viscount Ashbrook, now a graduate of Trinity College Oxford, and her sister 17-year-old Harriet Flower.

Francis and Elizabeth settled down to the business of providing an heir for the Warneford estate in order to prevent it from passing to Francis's (naturally) despised cousin John. In 1794 Caroline Elizabeth Warneford was born at Eastbourne, and after a gap of almost ten years, another daughter, Harriet Elizabeth, was baptised at Highworth in December 1803. At last, after sixteen years of marriage, the longed-for son arrived. His baptism is not recorded but his burial is—on 4th October 1805—suggesting that he may have lived for only a few hours. The little boy was named Francis William Warneford, and he was the last child Francis and Elizabeth would have.

Bitterly disappointed by his lack of a male heir, Francis applied himself to concocting a scheme by which to retain Warneford Place firmly in his own branch of the family. Thus the disunited clan was provided with a *casus belli* that would keep them all entertained throughout the lives of Betty's granddaughters Caroline and Harriet Warneford.

BY THE TIME of Viscount Ashbrook's death in 1780, Dr John Jones had been conducting services in the church at Shellingford for nine years. He may even have officiated at the baptism of one or more of William and Betty's children. He hailed from Eglwys Fach near Denbigh and was a year or so younger than Betty. A man of culture with a particular talent for music, he was ordained in 1771 and attained the qualification of Doctor of Divinity in 1778, traditionally the highest doctorate available at Oxford. Dr Jones was the epitome of the educated country parson of the eighteenth

Betty Ridge, probably at the time of her second marriage to John Jones, aged 45.
Based on a portrait by Daniel Gardner, courtesy Lord Ashbrook

century. As well as his musical instruments and quantities of accompanying sheet music, his collections included minerals, shells, fossils, books, greenhouse plants and even a camera-obscura as well as the latest must-have novelty, an electrical machine. Such an eclectic assemblage reflected the full range of interests that behove a gentleman before the days of specialisation by one particular subject.

A degree of regard had evidently formed between the parson and the lady of the manor, but Betty seems to have been content to live for ten years as a widow. Why such a long delay before she took the matrimonial plunge once more? It may be that, in a situation where children of the marriage were not earnestly desired either for inheritance purposes or to provide care in old age, the potential risk to the mother's health simply wasn't worth taking. Betty was 35 when she was first widowed, and 45 by the time she remarried. It looks very much as if she waited until she was sure she was no longer fertile before inviting another husband into her bed. (The same might be said for her sister-in-law, Mary Flower, for whom marriage to John Nicholl was entirely optional; Mary was sufficiently secure financially to live independently for the rest of her life if she chose—as indeed her elder sister Elizabeth did.)

Only six weeks separated the marriages of Betty's daughter Elizabeth to Francis Warneford and that of Betty herself to John Jones. Betty's second marriage was this time presided over, not by a simple curate as in Northmoor twenty-four years before, but by Joseph Hoare, principal of Jesus College Oxford.[26] Naturally, no marks sully the register entry; signatures fill all the relevant sections, but that of 'Elizabeth Ashbrook' is in an entirely different hand from that of her first marriage entry twenty-four years before, so it seems likely that the 1766 signature was written for her by somebody else. However, the 1790 signature is still not necessarily her own, and it has to be said that it does bear an uncanny resemblance to that of her son given as witness to the Warneford marriage on the previous page of the register. When the register was signed in the relative privacy of the vestry with just the participants and witnesses present, who was going to object to a harmless cosmetic exercise that saved the viscountess's blushes?

Another revelation occasioned by Betty's second marriage concerns her parents Thomas and Elizabeth Ridge, then aged about 78 and 76 respectively. Apart from an entry in the Northmoor parish register showing Thomas witnessing a marriage in 1768, nothing further is heard of Betty's parents after her first marriage in 1766—at least, not until Betty made a new will consequent upon her second.[27] Betty's children

---

26 By coincidence, like Earl Harcourt, Joseph Hoare died following an animal-related injury—in his case, a cat scratch. Before rushing to judgement upon the cat, however, it must be recognised that when Hoare was at tea one day, 'somebody moved the table upon his favourite cat, and gave the animal such pain that it flew directly at the Doctor and the wound occasioned by its claws occasioned a mortification which put a period to the life of a very worth and learned man'. (*European Magazine and London Review*, Volume 41, January–June 1802, p. 502.)

27 National Archives PROB 11/1478, 'Will of the Right Honourable Elizabeth Dowager Viscountess Ashbrook', 5th May 1808.

and her new husband were the only other beneficiaries of the will which was made in the summer following her marriage and witnessed by her sister-in-law Elizabeth Flower. Trustees Francis Warneford and attorney Philip Deare were ordered to pay to her 'honoured Father and Mother' Thomas and Elizabeth Ridge an annuity of £25. No indication is given of Thomas and Elizabeth's whereabouts; presumably they disappeared into gentrified retirement and led a life which involved no further need for the sort of licences, leases and permits which might otherwise have left a trace in the written record. If they lived out their days in their splendid brick house on Noah's Ark, no record survives of their burial in Northmoor. If they decamped to live with Betty in Shellingford or with their sons William and John in Durrow, there is no record of their burial there either.

CASTLE DURROW ITSELF was the backdrop to the next Ashbrook wedding. In March 1792, in what looks very much like an attempt to reinforce an important alliance in Ireland, Betty's 20-year-old daughter Harriet was married to Reverend John-Ellis Agar, son of her uncle John Ridge's patron, Viscount Clifden. Not for fifty-odd years had an Ashbrook bride been married from the family seat, and the previous occasion cemented the alliance with the Agars too, when aunt Rebecca married John-Ellis's great-uncle James in 1741.

Betty's daughter Harriet was the first Ashbrook bride to be married at Castle Durrow for some fifty years

But it was not just towards the Agars that the Ashbrook family moved closer in 1792. In the same month, John-Ellis's elder brother, by now second Viscount Clifden following the death of John Ridge's patron in 1789, married Caroline Spencer, daughter of the fourth Duke of Marlborough (see Family Chart 2). This marriage between Harriet's brother-in-law and the sister of the future fifth Duke of Marlborough renewed the link, if it had ever been broken, between the latter and Harriet's own brother, William, third Viscount Ashbrook; the two had been exact Eton contemporaries. But, more importantly for the Ashbrooks, in becoming Viscountess Clifden of Gowran not only did Lady Caroline Spencer acquire a family home in Kilkenny, but she also became a member of that family already so closely involved with the Ashbrooks, the Agars.

Harriet's new husband commissioned the design and construction of a home fit for his future family. In 1794 Glebe House at Galbally in County Limerick was built under the auspices of the ubiquitous Charles Agar, Archbishop of Cashel. The house was generously-sized and set in fourteen acres. The ground and first floors were eight bays wide, and each window was glazed with twelve-pane, up-to-the-minute sash windows. Glebe House can still be seen from the lane today, enclosed among its gardens by a high stone wall. Harriet and John-Ellis settled down to enjoy the modern comforts of this handsome edifice together.

Galbally Glebe, County Limerick: the house built for Betty's daughter Harriet

WE WILL NEVER KNOW what plans there were for the marriage of Betty's youngest daughter Sophia. She died at Shellingford Manor a few months after her nineteenth birthday in February 1794. Fatal accident or death as a result of some other unusual incident was normally reported in the press, so it seems likely that she simply fell mortally ill, a misfortune that could befall anyone at any time in the eighteenth century.

In just a few years, Betty's life in Shellingford changed completely. Her elder son William, third Viscount Ashbrook, set up his own establishment at nearby Wadley Manor, and an ensign's commission was purchased for younger son Henry Jeffrey in the 60th Foot, a regiment associated with the Flower family's county of origin, Rutlandshire. So the once-bustling manor was now quiet, a home to just four people: Betty and her parson husband, her sister-in-law Elizabeth, an old maid of fifty-five, and the third of her four daughters, 22-year-old Caroline, who would remain Betty's companion for the rest of her life.

By marrying, Dr Jones had become obliged to resign his place as a Fellow of Jesus College, just as John Nicholl had done two years before. Alongside a new minister Robert Wetherell, whose brother will appear later in this history, Dr Jones continued in the function of curate at Shellingford. However, again like John Nicholl, he decided that a living of his own would give him the dignity of financial independence from his rich wife, and in May 1795 his appointment to the living of Shipston on Stour was confirmed.

Shipston had become rich from its involvement in the medieval wool trade, and among the many handsome houses and cottages along the south side of Sheep Street is the elegant old rectory. Central to the two-storey front elevation of honey-coloured limestone ashlar is a large porch supported by Doric columns. Flanking the porch on both the ground and first floors are bow windows. An extensive garden with duck and chicken pens stretched south at the back of the house, and at the far end of the plot was a lodge with a coach entrance giving on to West Street.

Dr Jones's acquisition of the living in Shipston on Stour signalled the end of the Ashbrook presence at Shellingford Manor. After reigning there as Lady Ashbrook for nearly thirty years, Betty chose to follow her husband once more and live as a clergyman's wife in a relatively modest but agreeable rectory in the pretty town of Shipston.

STRICLY SPEAKING, a fifth bride completed this decade of marriages in the Ashbrook family. Harriet and John-Ellis Agar enjoyed their handsome home together for only three years before Reverend Agar died in February 1797. Harriet married for a second time in the following year, once again at Castle Durrow. Her new husband was a member of that social nexus back in England which involved the Ashbrooks, Warnefords, and Lovedens.

Harriet was still only 26 so children remained a possibility; her groom was 24 and very rich. He was born Pryse Loveden at Buscot Park some seven miles from Shellingford, but in the year of his marriage he adopted the surname Pryse following the death of his maternal grandmother. From her he inherited 30,000 acres in Wales which yielded an annual income of some £6,000, as well as property abutting the estate of the Duke of Marlborough in Woodstock. Pryse was the brother of poor Margaret Loveden who had married Samuel Warneford, and whose mental health was considered somewhat unstable.

As a country squire of broadly-Whiggish views, Pryse was happiest riding to hounds over his Welsh estates centred on Gogerddan in Cardiganshire, though he would go on to represent the borough as MP later in life. There was always a coolness between Pryse Loveden Pryse and his father Edward Loveden, partly because of Pryse's refusal to sell his beloved Welsh lands and consolidate the family holdings in Oxfordshire. But the Lovedens will have been gratified by the match with the Ashbrooks nonetheless; wealthy though the Lovedens were, neither they nor the Warnefords could boast a title. Having the daughters of a viscount as mothers to the next generation meant that any children would be 'Honourables'.

ONE ASHBROOK BRIDE notable by her absence was that of the heir, Betty's son William, third Viscount Ashbrook. The press ensured that his eligibility as a husband did not go unnoticed by the damsels of the day. In May 1785, the year that he left his mother's hearth for Trinity College, William featured alongside other aristocratic bachelors in the *Gentleman's Magazine* beneath the inviting headline: 'Fair Game For the Ladies, or a List of the unmarried Peers of Ireland, for 1785'.[28] Doubtless William was as delighted as any modern 17-year-old would be by this helpful intervention.

During his years at Oxford brief glimpses began to appear of William Ashbrook finding his feet in the traditional role of the gentleman. In 1787 in his capacity as a cultured man of letters he subscribed to a volume of Persian poetry;[29] in the same year he fulfilled his martial duty by joining the Berkshire militia (though tellingly he was obliged to decamp within weeks to take the cure at a fashionable spa); and in 1788, the year of his graduation, William displayed the nobleman's natural aptitude for local government by becoming a trustee of the St John's Bridge-to-Fyfield turnpike. After this, though, William made few further moves towards fulfilling the public role expected of a scion of the aristocracy.

A small clue as to the reason for the quiet life lived by a titled bachelor with the world at his feet concerns that excursion to a spa made within weeks of his joining the militia. Buried in a list of notables arriving in Southampton in the summer of 1787 is

---

28   *Gentleman's and London Magazine 1785*, Volume 55 (Dublin, 1785), p. 280.
29   John Nott, trans., *Selected Odes from the Persian Poet Hafez* (London, 1787).

William Flower, third Viscount Ashbrook:
Betty's frail elder son at the University of Oxford

the name of Lord Ashbrook.[30] Today one might expect an arrival at the great port to signify either the commencement or the conclusion of a long sea voyage. Not so in the later eighteenth century. In 1750 the ailing Prince Frederick of Wales, son of George II, took a dip in the sea at Southampton. He declared the waters extremely efficacious and came back for a second visit later that year. Breezily ignoring the Prince's death in the following spring, Southampton proceeded to market itself as a spa town equipped with all the usual amenities such as hotels, ballrooms and assembly rooms. William's visit at the age of 19 suggests that his health had begun to fail very early in adulthood. In so far as he is remembered at all by the townspeople of Durrow today, third Viscount Ashbrook still has the reputation of having been delicate.

William was dealing with money problems too. His father's marriage to a penniless water gypsy had deprived the family firm of the financial shot in the arm that a dowry customarily provided, and his absence from the political scene in Kilkenny denied the family lucrative political influence for a generation. This could be why, shortly after Betty's son reached his majority at 21, he made the first of several moves to retrench the family interests in Durrow. His uncle William Ridge was instructed to offer for sale one hundred acres of Durrow's famous oak woodland—considered one of the estate's chief glories. His grandfather, first Viscount Ashbrook, had protected these woods for twenty-one years in his will, and Betty's husband had adhered to the provision. But that provision was made forty-seven years before, and William Ashbrook was even further estranged from his Irish possessions than was his father. Anyway, needs must.

The sale of the near-legendary Durrow oaks appears to have coincided with William's decision to move out of Shellingford Manor and into a home of his own. He chose as his residence Wadley Manor two or three miles off on the Oxford-to-Faringdon road. The precise timing is unclear, but it may have been as early as 1790. The estate was by then in the hands of the ubiquitous Lovedens of Buscot, and the lease was advertised in *The Times* in that year. Wadley was a very old stone house belonging to Oriel College Oxford with a very new Palladian front added in 1768. Distinguished visitors through the ages included Queen Elizabeth in 1574 and then James I and Queen Anne in 1603. Now it was to become home to the son of a fishergirl. The house boasted a dining room twenty-two feet by thirty, and a drawing room to match. Also on the ground floor was the library (twenty feet by thirty-one), two more reception rooms, and a handsome hall. Upstairs were five bedrooms and two dressing rooms.

Outside, in addition to the attractive grounds, there was an excellent kitchen garden, and the whole estate comprised a satisfactory 1,270 acres. Surely the acquisition of such a substantial home suggests that, still only in his early twenties, William yet retained hopes of marriage. The chronically-ill ward off despair only by nurturing the fantasy that this time next year they will be back at their best.

---

30   *The Times*, issue 798, 19th July 1787.

Wadley Manor near Faringdon: elegant home of the third Viscount Ashbrook

William made one final trip to Ireland. With the French Revolutionary Wars now underway and the French Revolution itself reaching fever pitch with the execution of Louis XVI at the beginning of 1793, the landed classes throughout Britain and Ireland became nervous at the prospect of a tide of sedition overwhelming the status quo. Of course, in Ireland there were the additional grievances of the Catholic majority as well as ongoing resentment of tithes. Peter Gale, high sheriff of Queen's County (which now embraced Durrow), became alarmed by the manner in which supposedly-treasonous elements had induced their followers to forsake their oaths of allegiance to the Crown. Eighty-six concerned subjects of the king vowed at a meeting in Maryborough in June 1793 to contribute to a fund designed to reward informers; Lord Ashbrook promised a substantial £50.

It is from around this time that evidence emerges of William dabbling in horse-racing, a pastime for which Wadley was well-suited. Stabling for eighteen horses, a treble coach-house, and a seventy-acre paddock made the property decidedly equine in today's terms—indeed, a stud still operates on the estate to this day. In 1795 the *Racing Calendar* informed its readers that William's four-year-old, Freedom, would run on the fourth day of the meeting at Bath, and in the following year that Lord Ashbrook's colt 'by Boxer, out of Psyché' would run on the Monday of the first spring meeting at Newmarket.[31] Assuming that the young viscount by now had an inkling that he would not make old bones, he can perhaps be forgiven for indulging himself during his last years with such an expensive hobby. But the money had to come from somewhere.

---

31 *Racing Calendar*, Volume 22 (London, 1794), p. 268; *Sporting Magazine*, Volume 9 (London, 1797), p. 382.

After William's visit to Ireland, his known actions are mostly negative ones. Having been promoted captain in the Berkshire militia in February 1792 before his journey to Kilkenny, he resigned in November 1794. He had enjoyed his captaincy for just twenty months. The need to curtail unnecessary expenditure, coupled with Dr Jones's acquisition in 1795 of a splendid rectory in Shipston on Stour, precipitated the end of Ashbrook involvement in Shellingford, and perhaps the beginning of the end of creaky Shellingford Manor too. Having as its swan-song served as a backdrop to genuine romance and as the birthplace of two viscounts, the venerable old house was eventually demolished, probably in the 1860s when a new manor house called Kitemore was built nearby.

Also in 1796 came notice of William's recognition that he would not be not be visiting his sumptuous Irish home again for a long time, if ever. A seven-year lease on the 'beautiful House and Demesne of Castle Durrow'—or 'such other Term as may be agreed on'—was advertised in *Finn's Leinster Journal* in November.[32] Use of the furniture at Castle Durrow was included in the lease. Also available at valuation were a 'quantity of excellent Port, Claret and Sherry in the Cellars' and 'upwards of eighty brace of free Deer in the Park'. Not included was the family plate. A total of 171 individual items of silver including cutlery for eighteen diners, candlesticks, dishes, ladles and 'a foxes head' (probably a stirrup cup) were packed into a chest under the supervision of William Ridge and despatched to England, doubtless to adorn Wadley Manor. Along with the silver, and perhaps to the relief of the eighty brace of deer and other fauna on the Kilkenny estate, came a collection of top-of-the-range sporting equipment appropriate to the well-heeled country gent. Three fowling pieces by Joseph Manton, the finest gunsmith of the day (and some say the finest ever) were accompanied in the chest by two rifles, a brace of pistols, a powder horn, shot belts, and a new saddle.[33]

In 1798 the ailing young viscount journeyed twice with the family solicitor Charles Deare (brother to Philip) to Ashbrook property in Cowley, Middlesex with a view to selling. The manors of Cowley, Hillingdon and Uxbridge had intermingled over the generations to the point where landholding patterns were 'complex and obscure'.[34] It is unclear, therefore, whether the property to be disposed of included the Hillingdon home where William's father and aunts grew up with their Tatton mother and grandmother. But there appears to have been little room in William's heart for sentimentality when it came to his property dealings. If he had no need for the family seat at Castle Durrow, then the state of the Ashbrook finances demanded that it must begin to pay its own way. If the property in Cowley would cost more to repair than it was

32 *Finn's Leinster Journal*, 5th November 1796.
33 ORO F/122/20/F10 'Inventory of Lord Ashbrook's plate, received by Philip Deare on 24th September 1796'.
34 'Hillingdon, including Uxbridge: Manors and other estates', *A History of the County of Middlesex, Volume 4* (1971), pp. 69–75.

Betty's son sent to his uncle William Ridge in Ireland for the family silver with which to adorn his lovely house a few miles from Shellingford Manor

worth, it must go. William cannot be blamed for the fact that his father made a marriage with a girl who brought no dowry to bolster the family exchequer, nor for the fact that he was too ill to attract a rich heiress himself. Two opportunities in succession had now been missed whereby the aristocracy would normally take steps to keep money and land circulating between themselves. If cash was needed, the disposal of assets was the obvious way to get it.

William Ashbrook made his will at the end of 1799. As ever, particular care was taken to make provision for unmarried female relatives; as well as taking steps to ensure that his aunt Elizabeth Flower received her due under the terms of the first Viscount's will, William allotted a generous £1,000 a year to his steadfast sister Caroline—twice the sum his mother had been left to live on by his father. The legacy was supposed to be funded by the sale of yet another property: the Abercynrig estate in Wales. Situated on the south side of the Usk valley in Brecknockshire and surrounded by formal walled gardens, Abercynrig is a late seventeenth-century house which came into the Flower family through the marriage of William's great-great-grandfather with a daughter of the Jeffreys family. (This also explains why the name 'Jeffrey' came into use in the Flower family.) Altogether, the sale would eventually raise over £24,000, a figure which demonstrates the importance of bridal dowries to a family's exchequer. In the same year that Abercynrig was put up for sale, William was obliged to make a codicil

Abercynrig Manor, Brecon: in the Flower family for two centuries before William was obliged to sell

to his will. His heir and executor Henry had recently been posted overseas to Malta from where his regiment, now designated the 58th (Rutlandshire) Regiment of Foot, would be deployed to fight the French in Egypt. Caroline was appointed executrix of William's will in Henry's stead.

By the end of 1801 it was obvious that William was dying. Henry Jeffrey was summoned home from Egypt, arriving on 5th January, and William died at Wadley Manor the next morning. He was the fourth Ashbrook heir in a row to die young; his great uncle Jeffrey had died as a boy, his grandfather died in his early thirties, his father at 36, and now William himself at 34. Two weeks later he was buried in Shellingford church, and a fashionable sculptor was commissioned to create a monument to be sited across the aisle from the rather grander one Betty had commissioned for her husband William. But the note of defiance in the description of Betty's husband as a man who *would have* conferred dignity on any public role is replaced in her son's case by a hint of the gentle saintliness traditionally—and indiscriminately—attributed to the invalid: 'A man of most unsullied purity of heart, in his nature noble, and unassuming, gentle and unaffected in his manners, in disposition humane, and benevolent to all.'[35] Naysayers might have been forgiven for declaring that, after all, the idea that an injection of peasant blood would do the inbred aristocracy a power of good had proved no more than a myth in the case of the Ashbrooks. The water gypsy had presented her husband with a weakling for an heir. But now Betty's younger son Henry Jeffrey was back, and his career would prove him to be a Ridge by nature through and through.

35   Monument to William, third Viscount Ashbrook (1767–1802), St Faith's church, Shellingford, Berkshire.

5
A poet, a parson, and a pragmatist

AMONG THOSE TO WHOM pensions were granted by the Lord Lieutenant of Ireland during William Ridge's tenure as high sheriff of County Kilkenny were listed the names of three Oxfordshire ladies who rarely appeared
in such a rarefied context: Catherine Ridge, Sarah Ridge, and Anne Ridge.

It was announced that from October 1785 onwards, and during the pleasure of the
Lord Lieutenant (rather than for life only), each was to receive an annual sum of £33 6s
8d. Payment of pensions to those who had done nothing to earn them, and especially
where they would be spent outside Ireland, had long been a bone of contention in the
Irish parliament. The Ridge sisters were a prime example. Anne Holford was unlikely
to contribute much to the Irish economy having, as we have seen, died in 1782. Sarah
disappeared from the record following the birth of her daughter in 1774, and may well
be the Sarah Winter recorded as being buried in Berkshire in 1786.

At some point, maybe on account of these deaths, the entire £100 was paid to
Catherine, but when the updated list was published in 1788 the arrangement was
amended, and the £100 was split between the three ladies once more.[36] Perhaps Catherine had been tardy in passing on the share due to Anne and Sarah's families and they
had protested to William. One way or another, the full payment for all three continued
to be made until 1830 when, presumably in a nod of acknowledgement towards the
demise of the last-remaining sister in 1829, the amount each lady's estate received was
reduced to £29 2s 8d.

The Ridge sisters' appearance on the civil list reveals not only the routinely corrupt nature of the patronage system, but also that taking care of family interests was
still William's priority. If his sisters were to be supported with funds derived ultimately
from the sweat off the backs of the labouring poor, so be it. In spite of an ever-widen-
ing airing of revolutionary egalitarian ideas, any nascent class consciousness had been
superseded for William by a traditional loyalty towards kin. As soon as he was in a

---

36 'Domestic Intelligence', *Gentleman's and London Magazine 1741–1794*, p. 165.

position to do so, William used his influence to provide his sisters with guaranteed financial security at the expense of the Irish government. We may contrast this with William Ashbrook's failure to secure the futures of his sisters by making good matches for them during his eighteen years at the head of the Flower family. The two Williams were very different characters indeed.

POOR JULIANA LIDWILL, married at 22 to Betty Ridge's brother William, was dead by the time she was 26. The announcement of William's loss of a wife 'whose sweetness of disposition could only be equalled by her delicate sensibility' appeared in *Finn's Leinster Journal* on 14th February 1789. Two years later, a poem appeared in the same newspaper, revealing that the sadness of Juliana's death ran deep within the soul of the writer. *Epitaph for the late Mrs Ridge, wife of William Ridge, Esq of Castle-Durrow* is no masterpiece, but anyone who has ever lost a companion will recognise the sentiment: 'They knew not how they loved her till she died.'[37] That William composed these lines personally is, as with the unforgettable nymphs of Durrow, speculation, but it is difficult to imagine a candidate more suitable as the originator or at least the commissioning agent behind the two poems. William had worked so hard for so long for the benefit of his family and waited until he was in his forties and at the zenith of his career to choose a companion, only to lose her soon after. It is touching to picture him agonising over fourteen lines of verse for almost two years, refining them to the point where at last he felt they approached some approximation of his grief.

By now William Ridge was living the life of a country gentleman, with interests and pastimes closely matching those of his nephew third Viscount Ashbrook back in England. Courtesy of his involvement in the local militia he occasionally indulged himself with the title 'Colonel Ridge'. And he adopted a hobby not generally embraced by the families of eighteenth-century fishermen: horse-racing. Alongside the likes of the Lidwills and the Bathorns, he entered a horse in the Durrow races of 1791 which took place north-east of the town in an area known to this day as 'The Course'. His bay gelding Gragara achieved second place behind Captain Bathorn's black colt Eclipse in the dash for the ten-guinea cup, one of several donated by Lord Ashbrook. Indeed, it may have been during Lord Ashbrook's visit to Durrow in 1793 that the uncle passed on to the nephew an enthusiasm for racing, though the horse-flesh at Wadley Manor would be a cut above the motley collection of mounts raced at Durrow where the stewards enforced a strict no-thoroughbreds rule. In October 1794 William stewarded the Castle Durrow races along with the town doctor Edward Harte. During race week, assemblies were held on the Wednesday and Friday nights in the town's smart new public house by the bridge, the Ashbrook Arms.

Betty's elder brother also demonstrated his erudition in the traditional manner—

37 See Appendix E for the full poem.

by subscribing to *Payne's Universal Geography*, an ambitious work promising to examine subjects encompassing detailed accounts of Asia, Africa, Europe and America, 'the history of man', 'the fossil and vegetable productions of the Earth', 'a short view of astronomy' and of the 'planetary system to which the Earth belongs; and of the Universe in general'. Perhaps in order to avoid fraternal squabbling over access to such a handy resource, William's younger brother Reverend John Ridge at Castleview subscribed for a copy of his own.

Meanwhile, William carried on overseeing the interests of his young nephew Lord Ashbrook. He was now in sole charge of the disposition of leases and rentals of Ashbrook land—applications concerning Castle Durrow business should be addressed to 'William Ridge, Esq; Seneschal of said Manor', said *Finn's Leinster Journal* in 1791. Consequently he became involved, if indirectly, in certain of the practices that contributed to the unrest among the agrarian lower classes. The land-holding system of the time meant that there could be multiple layers of tenants and sub-tenants between the landowner's middleman, or head tenant, and those who actually tilled the soil—sometimes up to five levels of increasing insecurity. The chain might fail at any stage and the tenants further down sometimes found themselves subject to 'land-jobbing' by a rapacious speculator. Land-jobbing was a practice where a landlord obtained a relatively cheap writ to serve on a middleman who had fallen into arrears. The middleman had six months during which to redeem the lease, or he and all his under-tenants would be ejected. However, unscrupulous land-jobbers might take over an unredeemed lease and then evict all the under-tenants anyway. Eviction was a serious business for those on the receiving end. Whilst the former homes of evicted tenants, which they had very likely been obliged to build for themselves, might have been only a cabin with an earthen floor and a leaking thatched roof, the alternative could be nothing more than a temporary shelter constructed over a ditch.

The Ashbrooks were regarded as liberal and well-meaning landlords. However, newspaper announcements show that William was involved in both reversionary leases and the recovery of debts. In March 1789, he invited offers for no less than twenty parcels of land belonging to Lord Ashbrook, all with named tenants. Perhaps all of these tenants, Catholic and Protestant, high and low, were willing participants in the process, perhaps not. The expense of legal counsel was beyond most, and among the so-called 'outrages' perpetrated at this time were the various robberies committed in order to fund a defence against eviction. Where rents remained outstanding, a defaulting tenant might find his goods seized and sold off, and it was in William's capacity as a member of the Grand Jury and former high sheriff of the county that he found himself on occasion overseeing the sale of the belongings of such tenants in order to recover monies owed. Feeling themselves otherwise powerless, the dispossessed and their allies set about creating an atmosphere of terror. They issued threats to those co-operating with landlords who initiated evictions; they maimed or slaughtered their livestock;

they even murdered tithe-proctors who assessed payments in what they considered an arbitrary and corrupt fashion. Whether or not William felt any sympathy towards these sons of toil who reacted rashly towards a shoddy and corrupt system we do not know. But he was certainly prepared to do his duty in order to counter outrages that were becoming all to common. In November 1797 he was among those setting up 'an Association for the Preservation of the long undisturbed Peace of this District, and for our mutual Support and Protection'. He contributed generously to a fund set up to reward informers and bring offenders to court.

A SPECTACULARLY obsequious letter to the archbishop of Cashel tells us a great deal about the life of Betty Ridge's younger brother John by 1790. A man who could apparently sign the Northmoor parish marriage register with only a mark fifteen years earlier churned out four hasty pages of guff in order to make a simple request for instruction on how to vote in the general election: 'It will ever be my particular Study to the utmost of my Abilities to Oblige your Lordship on all occasions,' John assured the archbishop, 'and as my greatest dependance for the support of Six small Children and a large family is chiefly trusting to your Lordship's Patronage, and the good will and Friendship of the Agar family, I shou'd think myself in the highest degree Ungrateful if I did not consult your Lordship on this or any other Occasion…'[38]

John had learned how to play the eighteenth-century game. He acknowledged his debt to his patrons the Agars, and very probably did so in every communication he made with them. This was a very different John from the young man who had thought his sister's marriage would be his ticket to a life of ease and entitlement. The resentful boy who had so undervalued the opportunity of an Oxford education that he had attempted to disqualify himself by marrying now understood what was required of him. Having a family no doubt helped to concentrate his mind too; after only five years of marriage John already had six children.

In all, Judith Ridge appears to have presented her husband with at least six sons and three daughters during their marriage. The eldest boys, John Agar Warren and William Thomas registered at Kilkenny School, aged 13 and 12, on the same day as their cousin William Ridge. William Thomas would later go on to Rugby school at the age of 15, then to Trinity College Oxford, and on into the army. Somewhere amongst these boys two daughters arrived, Elizabeth and Harriet Caroline. Third and fourth sons were Hugh De Courcy and Henry Jeffrey, both of whom were educated at Donnybrook near Dublin and then admitted to the Honourable Society of the King's Inns to train as lawyers in 1806 and 1805 respectively. A third daughter, Sophia, was fol-

---

38   Hampshire Record Office 21M57/C24/1, 'Letter from Rev J Ridge to Agar, 10th April 1790', Ecclesiastical papers of Charles Agar, 1st Earl of Normanton (1736–1809).

lowed by two more sons: George Henry Warneford, who became a soldier, and James Jones, who would follow his father into the church.

Once again, the choice of names is illuminating, this time highlighting family and social ties as well as reflecting patronage links. Having himself adopted the mysterious middle name of 'Bagshot' around the time of his ordination, John Ridge, younger son of a Thames fisherman, showed himself eager to display the exalted nature of his connections. John Agar Warren was a clear tribute to John senior's patrons the Agars and to the prominent Kilkenny family of Warren, connections by marriage of Judith's family. Whilst the fact that the name of John and Judith's second son William coincided with that of the third Viscount Ashbrook doubtless caused John no loss of sleep, it would be gratifying to imagine that the boy's full name, William Thomas, was a tribute to John's brother and father who had between them done so much to frogmarch him back onto the path of respectability and good sense. Hugh De Courcy was named for Judith's father, and the fact that the boy was always known as 'De Courcy' suggests a desire to flag up his maternal connection with that ancient family.

It was important to John to maintain a nominal link with the family of his aristocratic brother-in-law too, though. His next son Henry Jeffrey was baptised at a point where the demise of the third viscount, William, and the accession of the fourth, Henry Jeffrey, looked increasingly likely. As for George, his middle name 'Warneford' clearly reflects a link with his Warneford cousins. Evidently John was still in touch with family matters in England eight years after his own departure for Ireland. Finally, a 'James' and a 'Jones' appear occasionally in the record, and the various overlapping contexts suggest that the two names refer to the same person. John's chief patron, first Viscount Clifden, was a James. James Jones was born in the year of Betty's second marriage, and he may have spent a part of his childhood living in her household and being educated by Dr Jones. He gained his BA at Trinity College Dublin and would eventually attain the status of Doctor of Divinity, so perhaps it was thanks to Dr Jones's generosity that James followed in his uncle's clerical footsteps, and was thereafter known usually as Jones. The names of John and Judith's daughters, Elizabeth, Harriet Caroline and Sophia, echo those of Betty's daughters—no Catherines, Sarahs, or Annes here. John's choice of names does at least betray an acknowledgment of the part played in his good fortune by others.

Judith was fulfilling her expected role as a clergyman's wife by doing her bit to better the lives of others. The Treaty of Paris had formally ended the American Revolutionary War in 1783, but now ten years on, Britain was at war again. Having executed King Louis XVI in January 1793, the French revolutionary government declared war on Great Britain in the following month. Just before Christmas that year, *Finn's Leinster Journal* highlighted the need to raise funds 'for supplying our gallant soldiers abroad with *additional cloathing*, and for the humane and benevolent purpose of sending the wives and children of the soldiers *comfortably* to their respective homes'.[39] We learn from the subsequent list of Honourables, Ladies and assorted matrons that 'Mrs Ridge, Castleview' found time amidst tending her brood to donate six flannel waistcoats. Many more waistcoats would be needed. Once the French Revolutionary Wars became the Napoleonic Wars, hostilities between Britain and France would drag on for twenty-two years.

Cultivating the patronage of the Agar family continued to pay off. In October 1795 second Viscount Clifden found himself in control of the disposition of the parish of Gowran and presented John to the living. John Ridge had found his niche. The leisurely life of a comfortable country parson evidently suited his ideas better than the nine-to-five grind of the lawyer. And to be fair, he appears genuinely to have devoted a proportion of his time towards attempting to improve the lot of the rural dweller. 'Improvement' was a fashionable concept among an Anglo-Irish elite which believed itself intellectually and morally equipped to usher those over whom it presided towards a better future. In the context of the Irish Midlands this impulse manifested itself as an encouragement to modernise agricultural practices. To this end the Midland Farming Society was formed in 1801 with 'Dr' Rev Ridge amongst its number. Its mission was to 'excite a spirit of emulation in breeding neat cattle, sheep, and pigs, and to produce an attention to neatness and regularity in the management of their farms, in the husbandmen of the district'.[40] A competitive agricultural show held at Durrow was deemed to be the best way to achieve these aims. A list of thirty-five classes covering all aspects of farming practice was drawn up, from fashioning the best plough and breeding the finest pig through to producing the greatest yield of turnips per acre. Agricultural enterprises of all sizes were accounted for: winners in the classes suited to the better-off were rewarded with medals, winners in the classes aimed at the smaller concern walked away with a cash prize.

Another 'improving' initiative—a study commissioned by the Dublin Society of the geography, and economy of County Kilkenny—brought John Ridge into contact with a member of the prominent Tighe family. In his *Statistical Observations Relative to the County of Kilkenny* published in 1802, author and future Wicklow MP William Tighe acknowledged John's help in compiling population statistics. Whilst doubtless keen to assist in the betterment of the lives of his parishioners, John would have been happy also to cultivate a connection with the family of the report's distinguished author.

---

39 *Finn's Leinster Journal*, 21st December 1793.
40 Sir Charles Coote, *General View of the Agriculture and Manufactures of the Queen's County* (Dublin, 1801), p. 213.

Durrow's Georgian town square: the handsome north side

VISITORS TO the little country town of Durrow today will find a pleasing Georgian square at its centre. Received local wisdom attributes its creation to 'the Ashbrooks' on the very good grounds that William Flower, first Baron Castle Durrow, initiated the design of a planned town and granted leases for house-building with strict specifications as to the size and cost of each property. The policy continued under his successor Henry until the latter's death in 1752. However, since members of the family themselves were largely absent during the second half of the eighteenth century, the oversight of some of this elegance must be attributed to the family's man-on-the-spot from around 1770 onwards, William Ridge. For example, the stone bridge across the river Erkina was built in 1788, and near the bridge the plot on which the dwelling now

The stone bridge across the river Erkina in Durrow, built in 1788

known as Ormsby House stands was leased for building in April 1798 to William's friend the town doctor, Edward Harte. Over the road from Harte's house was the Ashbrook Arms, advertised in 1793 as: 'A large commodious new-built inn, with very convenient Offices of every Description, together with twenty-two Acres of Arable and Pasture Land adjoining the Concerns.' Proposals were to be made to William Ridge Esquire at Castle Durrow.

A major project facilitated by William Ridge was the building of a new Protestant church of St Fintan on the west side of the town square beside the castle entrance. The surviving Durrow vestry books, which begin in 1778, show that William Ridge was appointed churchwarden in April 1781. Minutes of a meeting held in April 1790 reveal that the old church was in 'a most ruinous condition', and tenders were invited for the building of a new church 'ninety-one Feet in the clear in length, and of a proportionable breadth and height, together with a Steeple'. William paid 5s 5d per yard for flagstones from the quarry at Rosenallis a few miles north of Durrow to be laid along the new aisle (being reimbursed 'part of the money' in March 1796). The church was completed in 1795 at a cost of £646 3s 0d. Perhaps out of a sense of entitlement following a levy on the parish eventually totalling several hundred pounds, the new church was promptly burgled during the night after the Sunday service of 7th June 1795. That appearance by William Ridge in the newspaper as a contributor to the peacekeeping fund in November 1797 was his last. He had not worked since the previous summer when the attorney James Kearney took over the administration of Ashbrook business. By the time William and Juliana's eleven-year-old son registered at Kilkenny School in the following September, William Ridge was dead.

The Ashbrook Arms in Durrow: completed under the supervision of William Ridge

The church of St Fintan in Durrow town square, completed in 1795

No poems appear to have been written in honour of this somewhat lonely figure. Born to a family of water gypsies on an island in the river Thames, he rose to high political office and died a gentleman on his nephew's estate in Ireland. In maintaining a political presence on behalf of the Flower family, he did what he could to influence the balance of power between the ruling families in the area. For at least twenty-six years he worked far away from his loved ones for the advantage of family interests, a proud river man submitting to the indignities and humiliations of the patronage system, and even expending hard-won social credit in order to rehabilitate his black-sheep of a younger brother. Having after thirteen solitary years embarked upon matrimony at last, William was rewarded with the companionship of his wife Juliana for just four years. After her death, he endured for another nine, promoting the Ashbrook cause and compensating for an indifferent third viscount.

Since William Ridge's death, this loyal and diligent man has disappeared from local memory. So seamlessly did he fill in during the period when the supposedly-presiding local family was absent in England that his accomplishments are today attributed vaguely to 'Lord Ashbrook' whereas in fact the involvement of the two contemporaneous Lord Ashbrooks was neutral at best. But there William's church still stands, as well as the stone bridge, the Ashbrook Arms, and the elegant houses added to the town square during his time. The welcome in Durrow accorded to the fourth Viscount Ashbrook must be credited largely to the stand-in part played for the second and third by a fisherman from Oxfordshire.

Fletcher's House in Woodstock: first home of Betty's dashing younger son Henry Jeffrey, fourth Viscount Ashbrook, and his wife Deborah Susannah Freind

BETTY'S YOUNGER SON Henry Jeffrey Flower rushed back to England and arrived at his brother third Viscount Ashbrook's bedside at Wadley Manor on Tuesday 5th January 1802. Whether or not William Ashbrook was aware of his globe-trotting brother's presence in his sick-room we do not know, but it is touching that Henry made such an effort to see his brother one last time. It must have been a great comfort to Betty, too, to have her only other son with her at such a dreadful time. William died the next day.

Henry was a man of action. Blessed with robust health, he was a very different figure from the somewhat passive figures of his brother and father. When he was summoned home with news of William's imminent demise, he was serving in Egypt as a captain with the 58th Regiment of Foot. Their colonel was Lord Charles Manners, son of that Lord Lieutenant of Ireland who had in 1785 acquiesced to William Ridge's request for pensions for Henry's three Ridge aunts in Oxfordshire. The 58th had taken part in the Battle of Alexandria the year before, helping to bring to a close the Egyptian campaign. Having succeeded to the title of fourth Viscount Ashbrook in January, Henry was married by May. His choice of bride was Deborah Susanna Freind[41], 22-year-old granddaughter of Thomas Walker of Woodstock, a close associate of the fourth Duke of Marlborough. She had a whopping £30,000 and a grandfather desperate for a title for one of his grandchildren. The wedding ceremony took place at St George's, Hanover Square. Henry gave his address as 'Ireland', Deborah gave hers as

41 The family's preferred spelling of their name at this time.

'Woodstock'. To mark the occasion, Betty presented the couple with the Ashbrook family Bible, and in time Deborah would solemnly inscribe in it the names of all seven babies she would bear, though not all these children would live.

Deborah's grandfather Thomas Walker was a wealthy lawyer who served as town clerk for Oxford from 1756. He established the University and City Bank in Oxford in 1790—which doubtless endeared him to the credit-hungry dukes of Marlborough—and following his resignation as town clerk in 1795 he turned his attention to one of his properties in Woodstock. The smart new classical front added by Walker to Fletcher's House in Park Street belies its Elizabethan interior. The rear elevation, however, gives the game away and in fact echoes Shellingford Manor with its triple gables. Facing the church of St Mary Magdalene and now housing the Oxfordshire Museum, this was where Walker's granddaughter Deborah settled down to start a family with her new husband Henry, fourth Viscount Ashbrook. One cannot help wondering at what point, if at all, Henry disclosed to Deborah that she was not the first young lady with whom he had started a family.

ON THE DAYS when death, mutilation or capture by the enemy were not on the cards, life in the British military could be very agreeable for the officer class, particularly if the posting was a pleasant one. Nelson's defeat of the French fleet at Aboukir in 1798 confirmed for the British government the importance of maintaining the Royal Navy's domination of the Mediterranean, and William Pitt the Younger ordered that secret plans be drawn up for an invasion of Minorca with its strategically valuable deep-water port at Mahon. The island was taken in a few days, and without loss to British forces. Highland troops of the invasion force were delighted to find a little patch of Scotland in the Mediterranean, with purple heather scrambling over rocky hillsides. The population, disillusioned with the Madrid government and recalling better times under a previous British occupation, were equable.

Twenty-two-year-old Captain Flower found himself enjoying all the usual enter-

tainments to which elite young men of the military were accustomed at the time, but with the addition of warm sunshine. In the evenings the regimental band played beneath the walls of the barracks on the shore of the bay at Mahon. On moonlit nights numberless small craft could be seen zig-zagging across the glassy water, while the masts of merchant ships bobbed above the crags of the many small coves that lined the bay's edge. At the numerous balls and concerts the contrast between the dress of the British and Minorcan ladies was striking. The head-dresses worn by the native women particularly betrayed a residual Moorish influence. A handkerchief drawn tight across the forehead was joined at each side by a piece of muslin or black crape draped under the chin. The whole lot was topped off with a kind of cape covering the head and extending down to the waist. Legs clad in white stockings and visible below the knee must have been a distracting sight for the British men. The Minorcan ladies very much longed to adopt the London fashions they saw in the ballrooms, but that their menfolk would not have it.

Even in such modest garb, the charms of one local beauty did not escape the notice of Captain Flower. Camp-followers like Josepha Fernandez knew the rules, and she must have been aware that her relationship with an aristocratic British officer would at some point be curtailed. However, the circumstances when Henry had suddenly to depart for England from Egypt were particularly poignant, for he was obliged to leave in Minorca not just his mistress but his baby daughter too. Betty Ridge's second grandchild was a little Minorcan girl born far away on a rocky island off the coast of Spain. Henry supported Josepha and her child financially throughout his life and under the terms of his will he directed that this should continue for the whole of their lives too, and even made provision for any children the little girl may have. His heir was persuaded to abide by this arrangement with the threat otherwise of having the family plate and pictures sold off to fund the bequest. Henry was a man who took responsibility to family seriously.

Eirke House, County Kilkenny: built by Betty's brother Reverend John Ridge

HAVING BROUGHT SONG into the hearts of Eirke youth and neatness into the byres of Midlands livestock, John Ridge obviously felt entitled to a little self-indulgence, and in March 1802 he took out a certificate to kill game. It is tempting to imagine that perhaps the fisherman's son cast a knowing eye over the salmon and trout waters of the river Erkina which separated his home from the property of his nephew Henry Jeffrey, the new Viscount Ashbrook. While work continued on John and Judith's new house at Eirke, the merry-go-round of patronage jangled on. In April 1806 John wrote to Baron Ponsonby of Imokilly, assuring him of his support for Ponsonby's son in the forthcoming election for the seat of Kilkenny, now incorporated into the new parliament of the United Kingdom. Having congratulated Ponsonby on his elevation to the peerage, he continued: 'If your Son shou'd require my attendance or assistance on this or any other occasion, I entreat that he or any other of your family may command me—as I was the principal person who formerly attended your dear and much lamented Father when he canvassed this part of the County in your behalf [in 1783].'[42] The Ponsonbys were one of the foremost political families in Ireland, and this letter reveals just how quickly after his arrival from England John had been put to work reinforcing the Ashbrook-Agar-Ponsonby nexus.

The early 1800s were the years when John and Judith's sons struck out into the

---

42   Durham University Archive, Ponsonby Papers GRE/E516 Castleview, 'Brother of Elizabeth wife of second Viscount Ashbrook, 13th April 1806'.

world to make careers for themselves. In 1805 Henry Jeffrey was admitted to study law at the King's Inns in Dublin, and De Courcy followed him there in 1806. Their father—an Oxford-trained lawyer himself, of course—signed an affidavit for both boys to certify that each was 'a fit and proper person to be admitted a Student in this honourable Society', a deed which, in the case of one son, he would later have cause to regret.[43] In March 1809 George Warneford was appointed ensign without purchase in the 8th Regiment of Foot, and in December of the same year William Thomas, whom the record suggests never actually graduated from Oxford University, became a lieutenant in the 56th Regiment of Foot. Of the six sons, only the mysteriously-aimless John Agar Warren was still at Castleview. With four of their boys now settled in to careers and Jones soon to depart for Trinity College Dublin, it was time for John and Judith to move to their new glebe house at Eirke. The advertisement appeared in *Finn's Leinster Journal* in February 1810: 'To let, house of Castleview and 30a, commands a prospect of Lord Ashbrooks mansion at Castle Durrow. Situated in Queens Co. Apply John A. Ridge, Castleview or Rev J. B. Ridge at his Glebe, Eirke, near Johnstown.'

Back in 1790 John had received a £900 loan from the church authorities topped up with a grant of £100 to build a new glebe house at Eirke. This substantial house stood beside the church atop the rise to the west of the Rathdowney-to-Kilkenny road, and face east towards Galmoy. The plan was that, like most elite houses of the period, its style would express a deliberate distancing from the single-storey, rubble-built, thatched dwellings of the native Irish. Georgian symmetry prevailed, with steps up to a central door beneath a generous fanlight. The entrance was flanked by windows set into arch-shaped niches reflecting the outline of the main entrance, the stone walls were rendered and the roof slated. The ground floor comprised a hall and three reception rooms, on the first floor were seven bedrooms, and the domestic offices were hidden in the basement. It was a pleasingly pretty version of classical elegance, and has been rescued from imminent demolition and tactfully restored in recent years. The old stone barn (to which we shall return) still stands alongside, but there seems also to have been quite a complex of buildings on the site when it was first developed. Local tradition suggesting a school is confirmed by an advertisement placed by John Ridge in September 1792 for a clerk 'fully qualified as to singing and keeping of School'.

Doubtless John and Judith looked forward to a quieter life with their daughters Elizabeth, Harriet Caroline and Sophia in their beautiful new house on the hill. But these were tumultuous times. Today the pastoral tranquility of the area belies Galmoy's early-nineteenth-century past as a hotbed of 'murders, beatings, intimidation, raids for arms, and ultimately execution', at the centre of which would be Eirke House.[44] John's life as a country parson would prove to be less than quiet after all.

---

43 E. Keane, P. Beryl Phair and T. U. Sadleir, *King's Inns Admission Papers 1607–1867* (Dublin, 1982). See facsimile affidavit of 1795 opposite title page.
44 Pádraig Ó Macháin, *Six Years In Galmoy: Rural Unrest in County Kilkenny 1819–1824* (Dublin, 1992), p. 1.

Woodstock House, adjacent to the Blenheim estate: built by Harriet's husband Pryse Loveden Pryse

A FEW STEPS from Fletcher's House, just around the corner in Rectory Lane, lay a plot of land belonging to Pryse Loveden Pryse, husband of Henry Jeffrey Ashbrook's sister Harriet. Pryse set about building Woodstock House, adjacent to the park wall at Blenheim. Also within a few yards at the closed end of Park Street was the Corinthian triumphal arch which served as the entrance to the Blenheim estate, home of the dukes of Marlborough. The Duke's heir George Spencer-Churchill, Marquis of Blandford, was an Eton and Oxford contemporary of Henry's brother William, and now the new Lord Ashbrook's marriage to the granddaughter of the Duke's friend Thomas Walker reinforced the connection. It would seem to have been the perfect, cosy set-up in which childless Aunt Harriet could enjoy the company of her brother's new family. For the new Lady Ashbrook, as for most women at the time, marriage heralded the commencement of almost annual child-bearing, and the first of five children, Susanna Sophia, arrived in 1803. But Henry Jeffrey was ambitious. Fletcher's House was simply a useful stop-gap to help tide him over his sudden change of circumstances. He was aiming even higher, and now he had lots of Walker money with which to fund his campaign.

In 1804 Henry Jeffrey sold his army commission and set about becoming an establishment figure. He moved his family from the gates of Blenheim Palace to the

Beaumont Lodge, Old Windsor: home of Betty's younger son, Henry Jeffrey

bounds of Windsor Great Park, purchasing Beaumont Lodge in Old Windsor for £14,000. Formerly the home of disgraced Governor-General of India Warren Hastings, the house was considered somewhat flashy at the time having being rebuilt in 1790 as a nine-bay mansion with an enormous portico supported by four Corinthian columns. The credentials of the gardens, however, were impeccable. A hundred acres rose gently from the banks of the Thames to an ornamented woodland walk of nearly two miles. A winding terrace provided a panorama of the towers of Windsor Castle, across the valley through which the great river flows and, in the distance, of the loftier edifices of London itself. The parish church of Old Windsor, approached by an avenue of majestic elms, was considered romantic, but the couple's first Christmas in their new home was not a happy occasion. Their first son, born on 23rd December, was dead within an hour and the romance of the approach to the church must have been lost on those accompanying the sad little casket to its resting place on Boxing Day.

In the spring Henry Jeffery returned to his mission. On a Wednesday in May 1805, he attended a levée at St James's Palace in the company of, among others, John Manners, fifth Duke of Rutland, brother to the colonel of Henry's former regiment and member of a family of long-time Ashbrook allies. Even on such exalted royal occasions Henry was not among strangers, but within a few years he would become as close to the royal family as any outsider could claim to be. From 1806 Henry Jeffrey took a lease on 19b Grosvenor Street, a more convenient base from which to make his presence felt at the Court of St James. Perhaps Deborah took advantage of the proximity the house offered to the best doctors when she was having her children too. For happier news emerged from the Beaumont Lodge nursery during these years. Up the avenue of elms to the church were carried for baptism Henry, the heir, in 1806, Caroline in 1807, William, the spare, in 1808, and finally Harriet Elizabeth in 1809.

Sadly, the family life that Henry and his wife had so rapidly created together came to a shatteringly premature end. Deborah died in March 1810, perhaps as a result of difficulties arising from the birth of her last child in the previous December. In modern terms, theirs might be described as nothing more than a marriage of convenience— and a rushed one at that. But the warmth of the tribute on Deborah's monument in the parish church at Hurley on the river Thames in Berkshire is notable. It concludes: 'Her much loved lord has caused this monument to be erected as a small tribute of affection to the sacred memory of a wife so justly endeared to him.'[45]

Perhaps most telling of all is the detail related to the family by one of Henry's granddaughters. For the rest of his long life Henry kept all Deborah's letters immediately by him in a white satin bag. They lay on his library table by day, and on his bedside table at night. Never again would Henry find the domestic happiness he enjoyed with Deborah Susannah Freind.

---

45   Monument to Deborah Susanna Viscountess Ashbrook (1790–1810), church of St Mary the Virgin, Hurley, Berkshire.

The former rectory in Sheep Street at Shipston on Stour: Betty Ridge's final home

NOW IN HER SIXTIES, Betty Ridge lived out her final days in genteel comfort in her second husband's rectory at Shipston on Stour. A picture of her life at home with Dr Jones can be pieced together by means of a catalogue of the contents of the house.[46] In the library books were ranged along the shelves of a large, glass-fronted mahogany bookcase with drawers below. Mahogany library steps gave access to the upper shelves, and three padded and comfortably-upholstered mahogany-framed easy-chairs around a hearth rug offered a cosy place to read before the fire with its gleaming brass fender and fire irons. In the private 'Museum' were mineralogy, shell and fossil collections, as well as various curios ('brain petrifaction', 'jaw bones of shark and tiger'), all kept in a glass-fronted mahogany cabinet incorporating divided drawers and cupboards. A large oak library table offered the perfect surface upon which to display maps of Oxford, Berkshire, Ireland and Europe. Doubtless a prized possession was a fine pair of globes made by the Adams brothers, mathematical instrument makers to King George III. The twelve-inch globes were mounted in mahogany frames with compasses incorporated into their tripod stands; one globe represented the Earth, the other the constella-

---

46   Warwickshire Record Office, EAC560, 'Catalogue of musical instruments, music, books, household effects of Rev Dr John Jones', 2nd–3rd January 1828.

tions of the night sky. A selection of embroidery frames dotted about the house remind us that not one but two ladies resided there: Lady Ashbrook herself and her unmarried daughter Caroline. Elsewhere in the house, and perhaps not quite so familiar to the rector and his wife, were the apparatus of the day-to-day business of running such an establishment; from the kitchen or scullery came a deal cupboard and a large deal table, presumably unscrubbed by Lady Ashbrook's fair hands, an ironing-board with trestles, various pewter dishes, a copper tea-kettle, and a mop and bucket.

Dr Jones's parishioners were well aware that their rector's wife was a lady of quality, though whether they also knew she was originally a simple fishergirl is unclear. In June 1804, a field day in honour of the King's birthday, she presented a new set of colours to the Shipston Loyal Volunteers. In a gracious speech she complimented the members upon the esteem which their conduct had excited, and revealed the anxiety she felt for their welfare. In his reply the Commander expressed the gratitude of the whole corps for the honour which she had conferred upon it from its inception.

Betty suffered from the usual discomforts of old age and she began to appear in Bath and Cheltenham to take the waters. She returned to Bath for one last visit in September 1807 and then, in February 1808, she died at home in Shipston on Stour. A few days later, *Jackson's Oxford Journal* noted solemnly that: 'The remains of Dowager Lady Ashbrook passed through this city on Thursday last, for interment at Shillingford near Faringdon.'[47] In line with customary practice Betty was buried alongside her first husband William Ashbrook at Shellingford, even though her second marriage had been four years longer than her first. Also in the family vault were William and Betty's two children, Henry and Catherine, who died as infants, Sophia who died at 19, and of course their son William, third viscount, who had died six years previously.

One line only was added to the second Viscount Ashbrook's extravagant monument after Betty's funeral on 4th March: 'Also in this Vault are deposited the Remains of Elizabeth Dowager Viscountess Ashbrook, Relict of the above mentioned William Lord Viscount Ashbrook, who died 23rd February 1808, universally lamented in the 63d Year of her Age.'[48] But it would be unfair to read too much into the brevity of this tribute, presumably commissioned by Henry Jeffrey, the man who would wax so lyrical about his wife upon her death two years later. In the terms of the times, Betty had not died young like Deborah; whilst doubtless mourning her absence, her children would have regarded her death as something in the natural course of things rather than a tragic loss. And anyway, what with all the Ashbrook children that predeceased their parents, the room left available on the second viscount's monument was by this time limited.

Betty Ridge's beauty inspired men to poetry, and it would be easy to dismiss her

47 *Jackson's Oxford Journal*, 5th March 1808, issue 2862.
48 Monument to William Flower, second Viscount Ashbrook (1744–1780), St Faith's church, Shellingford, Berkshire.

simply as a pretty face. But why should she not also have enjoyed the same sharp intelligence and determined application as her father Thomas and her brother William? Her personality was sufficiently arresting to detain for three years an aristocratic bachelor with a world of choices available to him. William Ashbrook might easily have tired of her and moved on to a softer target before he attained his majority. He did not.

It is a sad fact that the source of the scant knowledge we have with which to sketch Betty's character is also the source of her great grief, the early death of her husband. Had William Ashbrook lived out a normal span, his sons would have been grown men when he died, ready to step in and take charge, and his daughters would already be in marriages of their father's making. As a venerable dowager, Betty would have been able to melt into the background in dignified and passive retirement. As it was, she found herself exposed to an interregnum which demanded the mobilisation of all her strengths. Her ability to grasp her role prevented her background from compromising her children's marriage prospects. Even in the absence of her husband, the wealthy Lovedens and Warnefords (mostly) dealt with her children as equals, and the powerful Agars were happy to continue a time-honoured alliance between the two families.

Betty's courage cannot be in doubt. After a closeted life in Shellingford she ventured as a young widow over to Ireland to introduce her son to his staff, tenants and neighbours. She possessed enough political savvy to appreciate that such a visit was essential to help guard against the growing hostility shown elsewhere in Ireland towards the Protestant ascendancy—particularly the absentees. Perhaps her brother William had already tried to persuade Betty's husband towards the same course and failed; we do not know. But once Betty gained autonomy over her own actions, she did what was needed for the benefit of her family. She also brought with her to her first husband the loyal and trustworthy relatives he lacked, and William Ridge, particularly, did the Ashbrooks proud. For eighteen years between the deaths of the two Williams, Ashbrook then Ridge, Flower family interests were entirely in the hands of the children of an Oxfordshire fisherman. Their father Thomas Ridge had gifted them enough of his own inherent ability, self-confidence and ambition to render them capable of taking on such an alien project. Even John did his duty when his brother died, and filled in until a new man was appointed.

Whilst her two able brothers were the ones who actually moved to Kilkenny to take care of business, it was Betty who was pivotal to this remarkable Ridge team-effort. She lived long enough to see her beloved husband's legacy pass into safe hands in the form of their son Henry Jeffrey, and to know that the future was secured by the birth of Henry's own son. In her final years, while her son busied himself about the royal Court, she could enjoy the comforting knowledge that her husband's family would not, after all, be mortally wounded by his unshakeable passion for a simple water gypsy.

6
A house on the hill

WITH A HANDSOME INCOME from two parishes, Betty's younger brother John Bagshot Ridge needed never fear that his family might go hungry or lose their home. The tithes of Eirke yielded £750 a year, those of Gowran £507 13s 10¹/₄d. This annual income of some £1,257 contrasted starkly with the average wage for a labouring man in the Galmoy area of tenpence a day. As well as paying rent to the landlord, those working on the land were obliged by law to pay tithes to a Protestant minister, the services of whom the largely Catholic poor did not avail themselves.

The poorest were frequently deprived even of milk, living on a scanty diet of potatoes, clothed in rags and shivering in their comfortless hovels. John cannot have been unaware of the disparity in incomes between the 'haves' and the 'have-nots' of Irish agrarian society. As we have seen, his brother William had been involved in dealing with some of the consequences of rural dissatisfaction, both as the Ashbrook agent and as a member of the Grand Jury. In the year of William Ridge's death, rebellion broke out in counties Kildare, Wicklow, Wexford and elsewhere, leading to gruesome reprisals by the British. Several thousand died.

Trouble was by no means confined, therefore, to Kilkenny. Outbreaks of attack and reprisal flared throughout Ireland, and contributed to a general fear among the Protestant landowning class of their imminent downfall. The barony of Galmoy itself had a recent history of violence. Back in the 1770s, coinciding with William's arrival in Durrow, there had been violent protest among members of the 'Whiteboy' movement against the payment and collection of tithes. Tactics included murder, burying victims alive or cropping the ears of those whom they considered to be responsible for oppression or corruption. The Whiteboys were succeeded in the following decade, after John's arrival in Kilkenny, by the 'Rightboys' who adopted the same appalling methods. Houses and farms were set alight, livestock hobbled. Robberies designed to raise money to fund a legal defence for those arrested for these outrages were widespread, as was the theft of firearms by 'Ribbonmen' with which to carry out such raids. And, just as John and Judith made Eirke their home, another series of vicious incidents broke out locally.

The first bore many of the typical hallmarks. On his way to Cullahill fair one autumn morning in 1812, landholder John Little was ambushed by two armed men hiding in a ditch. Little was wounded in the shoulder, his horse in the thigh. A notice warned that Little was guilty of oppressing widows and poor families; his sheep were slaughtered. His herdsman suffered a serious beating, and was forcibly ejected with his family from his home. In the following month, an elderly toll-collector who had outbid the previous incumbent at the hated turnpike between Johnstown and Urlingford was attacked and beaten. The proprietor of a Johnstown inn was warned in a public notice to fire one of his drivers by New Year's Day, or face the consequences.

In January 1813, fire engulfed the barn, stables and coach-house of a local magistrate well-known to the Ridges. Garrett Neville had signed the £100 reward-notice issued in response to the attack on John Little. Three weeks later, a gang intent on ambushing the mail coach in the Longford Pass south-west of Urlingford was engaged by the militia; two of the raiders were killed and two soldiers wounded. On Palm Sunday, a Johnstown worshipper coming out of Mass was shot twice in the back in an attack probably related to the Little outrage. Then in late summer another local farmer, Robert St George at Balief, was obliged to ask the army to save his harvest when local labourers too intimidated by threats of reprisal refused to carry out the work for him.

The terror and indignation caused by these awful events was the talk of the district all that year. However, in the autumn dramas somewhat closer to home must have resulted in many an anguished discussion in the privacy of Eirke House. First, John and Judith's eldest son John Agar Warren was obliged to confess to his Protestant-clergyman father that the unmarried Catholic girl with whom he had been conducting a liaison was pregnant. Secondly, John Agar's brother De Courcy, whom we last saw in 1806 entering upon a coveted King's Inns place in Dublin to train as an attorney, had been sent to gaol.

PRISONER NUMBER 4168, first cousin to Lord Ashbrook, was committed to Kilmainham gaol in Dublin in September 1813 convicted of exchequer extortion. The term 'extortion' is usually applied to the unlawful taking by an official of a payment where none is legally due, perhaps, for example, to expedite the progress of a certain case. Bribery is where an inducement is offered, extortion is where an inducement is demanded. De Courcy Ridge was still in the very early stages of his legal career when he ran into trouble. He was caught augmenting his salary in one of the senior common law courts in Ireland, the Court of Exchequer in Dublin, by extorting unofficial fees. De Courcy's case recalls that of his father John as a young man; he was handed every conceivable advantage in life, and yet still resolved upon a course towards catastrophe. Why would he take such a foolish risk? Clearly, he was short of money, but what newly-qualified professional is not? Had he paid his dues by working his way up through the profession, he could have looked forward to life as a prosperous Dublin attorney with all the perks that such a position entailed: a comfortable income, membership of an agreeable gentlemen's club, access to Dublin society, and the means to provide his own sons with similar opportunities. There was a difficulty, however, and it involved De Courcy's heart.

The name of this apparently irresistible difficulty was Maria Praval. Maria's father Charles Praval, a Frenchman, claimed the distinction of being draftsman to the botanist Joseph Banks during his expedition round the world on board Captain Cook's bark HMS *Endeavour*. Praval is credited with working with Cook to produce maps and charts, and with copying the sketches of two of Banks's own artists who had died on the voyage, suggesting that, rather than actually travelling on board ship, perhaps he collaborated with Banks and Cook upon their return in 1771. He came to Dublin in 1773 and taught drawing and French. Modest success led to the acquisition of 'Platanus', a Donnybrook villa where Charles and his wife kept a school for young ladies. The Pravals, therefore, hovered somewhere at the lower end of the middle class, and it seems unlikely that there was much money with which to provide dowries for three daughters.

Charles Praval died in June 1789, and in 1796 his eldest daughter Frances married a promising young lawyer named Joseph Franklin Chambers. Chambers worked as an examiner in the Court of Exchequer, and this may be where he met De Courcy Ridge. The two became friends, and an introduction was effected between De Courcy and Chambers' sister-in-law Maria. De Courcy's father John Ridge was a modestly prosperous clergyman who had set his six sons on the road to careers by which they would be able to support themselves in the fullness of time. At the age of 27, De Courcy was still at the beginning of that journey, but once he met Maria Praval he appears to have wished to delay married life no longer. It seems likely that it was the lack of means to marry which prompted De Courcy rashly to extort money in order to boost his personal coffers.

In spite of Kilmainham being one of the most modern prisons in Ireland, conditions were harsh. Such luxuries as glass in the windows and lighting in the cells were unknown. The cold air whistled in, and prisoners were permitted one small candle every two weeks. A diet of bread, milk and oatmeal soup must have come as something of a shock to the privileged young man-about-town. De Courcy was obliged to endure this regime for five months before being discharged by the court in February 1814 as an insolvent, suggesting that he had been detained in the first place because of his inability to pay a fine (and an unwillingness, we note, on the part of any relatives to cough up). In June 1814, just sixteen weeks after De Courcy's release from

Kilmainham gaol, he and Maria were married in St Peter's church in Aungier Street with Joseph Chambers as a witness. One wonders whether the marriage would have gone ahead had the bride's father been alive. A high-flying legal career in Dublin was now out of the question.

Whether John and Judith attended their son's marriage in Dublin is unknown. At the time they were coming to terms with the fact that they were grandparents to a two-week old Catholic girl, the result of a relationship between their eldest son John Agar and a Durrow girl named Mary Delany. Having accompanied his nearest brother William Thomas to Kilkenny College in 1798, John Agar failed to move on with him to Rugby school or Oxford university. Perhaps recalling his own reluctance to knuckle down to the study of law at Oxford, John Bagshot does not appear to have forced the issue, and consequently John Agar was left kicking his heels in Durrow while his parents busied themselves with their move to the new rectory in Eirke.

Delanys from all stations in life were to be found in Durrow at the beginning of the nineteenth century. The most prosperous considered themselves 'esquires'. But however respectable Mary Delany's relatives may have been, the fact remained that they were Catholic and this ruled them out as potential marriage partners for the children of a Church of Ireland clergyman. Baby Mary was baptised in Durrow on 27th May 1814, and little family was soon spirited out of the town where their connections with the Anglo-Irish Ashbrooks and the Protestant clergyman John Bagshot Ridge were so well known.

Two years still remained on the lease at Castleview, so De Courcy and Maria moved in as John Agar departed. John Agar took up farming at Bawnmore, Ash-

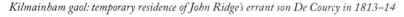

Kilmainham gaol: temporary residence of John Ridge's errant son De Courcy in 1813–14

brook property a few miles south-east of his father's parish at Eirke. He never married and the fact that he had two more children presumably with Mary Delany suggests that, like his brother De Courcy's, his partnership was a love-match. But the wilfulness of both men would also have lasting consequences for their children. John Agar's descendants would be obliged to abandon farming in Ireland for the cotton mills of Derbyshire. De Courcy's sons would become police officers in Liverpool—a respectable enough fate, but still a long way from the inns of court and gentlemen's clubs of Georgian Dublin that might have formed the milieu of a different De Courcy's sons.

A DEGREE OF DISQUIET had arisen within the Flower family. For Betty's daughter Caroline, the years since the third Viscount Ashbrook's death had been filled with legal business concerning the late lord's will. The Royal Hotel on Pall Mall was a favourite of Caroline's at this time, and served as the venue for a meeting with the family solicitor Charles Deare in October 1803 where he informed her that there was insufficient money to meet William's obligations 'without the aid of the personal estate'.[49] William had clearly foreseen this when he initiated the sales of the Cowley and Abercynrig estates, but the negotiations for the disposal of these properties dragged on for some years necessitating copious correspondence and consultations.

Discussion on the matter may have arisen when the Flower family gathered at Shellingford for Betty's funeral in March 1808. Caroline reported to Deare in March that the new Lord Ashbrook had complained to her of delays in resolving the family finances. For some six years now Henry Jeffrey's focus had been on reviving Ashbrook prestige from the extravagant backdrop of Beaumont Lodge in Old Windsor. His impatience betrays an anxiety over money that would cause further friction in years to come.

After Betty's death Caroline was somewhat cut adrift. Her sister Sophia, Betty's other unmarried daughter, had died fourteen years earlier at the age of 19 and her cousin James Jones Ridge, who probably spent some of his boyhood in Betty and John Jones's family, was now 16 and presumably moving on in preparation for his matriculation at Trinity College Dublin a few years later. At the age of 35, Caroline cuts a lonely figure. Evidently it was deemed inappropriate for a single lady to remain under the same roof as a widower who was not a blood relative. In spite of a demonstrable affection between Caroline and Dr Jones, she appears to have left the rectory at Shipston. This part of her story is hazy; spinsters of the Regency period who were past marriageable age troubled the written record very little. Perhaps she spent the next couple of years shuffling back and forth between her sister Elizabeth Warneford and her brother

---

49   ORO, F/122/20/F/6, 'The honourable Miss Flower Executrix of the late Lord Ashbrook, Bill from Philip Deare, 1803–1806.'

Henry Jeffrey. She was certainly with her brother in 1811 when the widowed viscount squired his sister to a ball at the Assembly Rooms in Staines one Friday night in April. The Ashbrooks were among the party of the Duke of Clarence, son of George III, an early indication of the growing friendship between Henry Jeffrey and the Prince. Henry Jeffrey had clearly positioned himself at the very epicentre of fashion, but upon Caroline the appeal of kicking up one's heels at the heart of the *haut ton* was apparently lost. Many would have relished the prospect of life in such a glittering milieu, but Betty Ridge's youngest-surviving daughter turned her back on the opportunity. Towards the end of the summer she departed for Crowfield Hall near Stoneham in Suffolk, where she appears to have been invited into the home of the Middleton family.[50]

Formerly MP for Ipswich, by 1811 Suffolk landowner Sir William Middleton was primarily 'a country gentleman devoted to agricultural pursuits… the improvements of his estates and the employment of the poor.'[51] He could well afford to improve his estates and employ the poor, having in that year inherited the £20,000 his younger brother John had won in a lottery as well as the £50,000 John held in the three per cents. Sir William had married Harriet Acton of Bramfield Hall, Suffolk in 1774. He held considerable estates in Carolina, a circumstance rendered particularly intriguing by his abolitionist sympathies. How Caroline made the connection with the Middletons is unclear. The Middletons' two daughters were both married by 1811 so if these marriages had left their mother in need of a companion, Caroline was excellently qualified having fulfilled a similar role for her own mother all her life.

In the New Year of 1813 there came terrible news, and Caroline was obliged to make haste for Wales. The life of her sister Harriet Pryse hung in the balance following a dreadful fire at her husband's favourite property Gogerddan in Cardiganshire. There had clearly been jollifications to welcome in the New Year because, we are told, Harriet did not retire to bed until the early hours of the following morning. The *Hull Packet* offered the official line: 'As Mrs Pryse was preparing to go to bed between two and three o'clock on the morning of New Year's day, her night dress came in contact with a rush-light that was burning in the room, and was instantly in a blaze.'[52] As a lady of breeding, Harriet did not allow such a circumstance to lead to undignified panic: 'Notwithstanding this alarming situation, Mrs Pryse had sufficient presence of mind to ring the bell; but, unfortunately, though almost immediate assistance was afforded, it had only the effect of preventing instant death.'

Betty Ridge's second surviving daughter lingered in what must have been great agony for almost two weeks, dying eventually on 13th January. Then rumours of a

---

50 A reference in a letter of 17th March 1810 from Charles Deare to Caroline in which he describes her as being on her 'way to Suffolk' suggests that she may have been established at Crowfield Hall before the ball at Staines (ORO, F/122/20/C/1a, 'Extract of letter from C. Deare to the honourable Miss Flower,' 17th March 1810).

51 'William Middleton (1748–1829) of Crowfield and Shrubland Park, Suffolk,' R. G. Thorne, ed., *The History of Parliament: the House of Commons 1790–1820* (London, 1986).

52 *Hull Packet*, 23rd February 1813.

Plas Gogerddan, Cardiganshire: scene of the strange death of Betty's daughter Harriet Pryse

quite different sequence of events began to emerge Had Betty's daughter been murdered? For those under the impression that Harriet had been bed-ridden for some years with a rheumatic complaint, the official account did not add up. How could she attend festivities downstairs into the small hours, and then take herself off up the stairs and change into a nightgown with nobody in attendance? Throughout the holiday period the guests at Gogerddan had included the family of Pryse's friend Peter Cavallier of Guisborough in Yorkshire. The alternative version of events suggested that under cover of the festivities downstairs, one of the Cavalliers sneaked upstairs and tossed a lighted lamp on to Harriet's bed. Anyone who has ever been felled by a serious rheu-

A distraught Pryse Pryse depicted on Harriet's monument in the church of St Padarn at Llanbadarn Fawr

matic complaint throughout the body will recognise that even reaching out to ring the bell may have been more than Harriet could manage. And her apparent lack of initiative in taking any other measures to save herself would also seem to be explained by an incapacity to move. But why would the Cavalliers want to dispose of the wife of the staggeringly-rich Pryse Loveden Pryse?

The shock of Pryse's loss caused him to live for a while as a recluse, during which period his father—always ready to leap to Pryse's vilification—feared that his son's behaviour was a manifestation of that same mental instability generally attributed to Pryse's sister Margaret Warneford. At Pryse's side to comfort him during this difficult time were his ever-reliable sister-in-law Caroline Flower as well as Jane, the unmarried daughter of his friend Peter Cavallier. Indeed, Jane Cavallier, who at 30 was running out of time to find a husband, so comprehensively comforted Pryse Pryse that by September 1814 she was expecting his child. Pryse married the heavily-pregnant Jane in April 1815 and she gave birth to a son four weeks later.

One way or another, Jane Cavallier had got her man.

A PERIOD OF relative calm descended on the barony of Galmoy in Kilkenny after two notorious gangs were eliminated by means of the rope: the last members of the Grant gang in 1817 and the Ryans in 1819. But no sooner had the judge at the 1819 Kilkenny assizes congratulated the magistrates on the tranquility of their county than trouble broke out again.[53] In December livestock grazing on the south-westward slope of the hill of Eirke and belonging to the universally unpopular land-jobber John Marum were attacked. This rapacious farmer had recently expanded his landholding in Rathpatrick at the expense of defaulting landholders. Having assured the tenants under him of their tenure, he promptly went back on his word, evicted them and sold off their household effects in order to recover the rent. Eight men were arrested for the attack on Marum's animals, but things would get much, much worse in the countryside around the home of John and Judith Ridge, and Eirke House itself would be central to the coming conflict.

Unlike De Courcy Ridge, John and Judith's other sons managed to stay on the right side of the law, and most of those who had been away were gradually making their way back to the fold. George Warneford was probably back in Kilkenny when he was placed on half-pay in 1816 having served in North America as a captain in the New Brunswick Fencibles. While posted abroad he had married Montreal merchant's daughter Anne Gerrard who gave birth to a son, Samuel, in 1818. A daughter, Anne Amelia, followed in 1819. Farmer John Agar had his two sons, John and William,

---

53 *Six Years In Galmoy: Rural Unrest in County Kilkenny 1819–1824* (Dublin, 1992), Pádraig Ó Macháin's thrilling account of events around John and Judith Ridge's home during this period, is highly recommended and extensively plundered here.

during this period, and De Courcy and Maria Praval had two daughters, Catherine Ann and Judith, followed by two boys William and John, possibly twins (though only John seems to have survived). Late in 1817 Jones was appointed curate to his father at Eirke having gained his BA at Trinity College Dublin the year before. Six weeks later, duly equipped with a professional qualification and a post, Jones married Alicia Alexandrina Moore at St Paul's church in Dublin. De Courcy's fellow law-trainee Henry Jeffrey disappeared from the record after entering the King's Inns at Easter 1805 so the chances are that he had died as a very young man. Only the soldier William Thomas, who was serving as a lieutenant with the 56th Regiment of Foot on garrison duty in Mauritius, was absent. Once again at an uneasy point in the parish of Eirke, events within the Ridge household took precedence. The transfer of William Thomas to half-pay in February 1820 might seem a reasonably mundane development were it not for the announcement in *Finn's Leinster Journal* of the death of Judith three days later, apparently after a long and painful illness. Perhaps news of his mother's failing health prompted William Thomas to rush home from his army posting. Whether Judith's malady extended over weeks, months, or years is unclear, but at least she was granted the comfort of having her five remaining sons around her in her last days. If any further demonstration of Ridge family solidarity were needed, that year the newly-widowed John appointed Jones his curate at Gowran.

The world outside, meanwhile, moved on in that indifferent way that it has. One night in October, the quiet within the mourning household at Eirke was shattered when the nearby cottage of the Phelans was set on fire, and Mrs Phelan was shot and wounded as she fled from the blaze. Her husband, John Marum's herdsman, returned fire. His two dogs, vital tools of their master's trade and financially valuable to boot, were shot dead. Did John Ridge pause amidst the chaos of that night to remember Noah's Ark island in the darkness, where the only sound after dusk was the rushing waters of the weirs? Next in the firing line among John's neighbours was George Brophy. For over twenty years Brophy had acted as a tithe proctor, that is, assessing the value of crops in order to calculate the amount due to the established church. However, Brophy had recently become a tithe-farmer as opposed to a proctor. The distinction was that a tithe-farmer rented the tithes from the rector and added on a profit margin for himself. Brophy immediately doubled the amount John Ridge had been charging. He was murdered in his home by a gang of intruders on a Sunday night in December 1820. Matters had now gone too far and the gentry decided to act. A meeting was convened in the house of Reverend Ridge on 28th December, and the host might have been forgiven for wondering whether life as a Dublin lawyer might have been easier after all. Fifty-five subscribers signed the resulting proclamation offering a total £150 in reward payments for information leading to the prosecution of the perpetrators of this latest enormity. Reverend John Ridge and all his sons signed up. Incorporated into the announcement was the threat of an application to the Lord Lieutenant to deploy the Peace Preservation Force. This was an eye-wateringly expensive measure involving the provision of a local police barracks, an annual salary of £700 for a magistrate, £150 for a chief constable, and £50 each for the sub-constables. Since half of this cost was to be born by the area under proclamation, it was considered by landed proprietors a measure of absolute last resort.

When two men were charged with the Brophy murder a fortnight later, their supporters organised a reminder to anyone who might be asked to give evidence for the prosecution at the trial. A witness in the earlier case of the killing of John Marum's animals was ambushed and shot dead on his way back from Kilkenny market in January 1821. As a final reminder, a week before the Brophy trial was due to begin, a man rumoured to be giving evidence was shot and buried in a bog. In March 1821, the two men accused of the murder of George Brophy were acquitted. Despairing at the apparent inability of the machinery of the law to deal with the succession of outrages, local magistrates applied to the Lord Lieutenant for the parishes of Eirke, Fertagh and Glashare to be placed under the protection of the Peace Preservation Act. To their dismay, the government responded by 'proclaiming' the entire barony of Galmoy, and the barony of Upper Ossory too. The proclamation of such a wide area would cost an estimated £2,450, half of which sum the residents would have to fund themselves. At least one person would gain something though. One pound per month out of this sum would go to the proprietor of the stone barn to be used as the police barracks in Eirke—John Ridge.

John Ridge's barn at Eirke: site of the police barracks under the Proclamation of 1821

The garrisoning of Eirke failed to prevent further outrages; indeed, the hot-headed reaction of the constables of the special force tended to make a bad situation worse. De Courcy Ridge became swept up in a tragedy which provided a notorious example of how the presence of the special force could inflame matters to the point of disaster. In May 1822, John's disgraced third son, whom we notice was by now hanging about in Eirke in spite of his listing in the *Treble Almanack* of that year as a commissioner for affidavits in Dublin, was among the crowd at the Fair of Bawn when trouble broke out. A dispute over money-changing led to heated words and the taking of sides amongst onlookers. Rather than trying to calm the situation, around eleven special sub-constables launched in and set about the lot of them. A runner was despatched by the sergeant to fetch the chief constable, Hugh Loyd Wray, from his dining engagement with a local gentry family nearby. Wray barged into the fair on horseback, slashing left and right with his cutlass. A stone was thrown in the over-excited Wray's direction whereupon he sheathed his sword, wheeled his horse round with one hand and drew his pistol with the other. Anticipating a shot, a man—perhaps the stone-thrower, perhaps not—ducked, and the shot went straight through the neck of the young woman behind him. She dropped to the ground, dead.

At the inquest two days later, De Courcy was among six witnesses called specifically at Wray's request. The others were Wray's dining companions at Bayswell, the sub-constable who had initially inflamed matters by turning a disagreement into a brawl, and a farmer who made the extraordinary claim that Wray could not have fired the fatal shot because the chief constable had already dismounted and handed horse, sword and pistols over to him. De Courcy was a little more evasive, joining the dinner guests in averring that Wray could not have drawn a pistol without their seeing him do so. Wray went to trial in August. Having attempted to discredit two of the prosecution witnesses, the defence wisely declined to call convicted extortionist De Courcy Ridge. He wasn't needed anyway. The evidence of the Bayswell diners swung it, and Wray was acquitted.

Those Bayswell diners were the Steele brothers, popular local landholders respected for their decent conduct towards their tenants. At the beginning of 1824 they had run into financial trouble and were ejected as landholders from the townland of Rathpatrick. The land-grabbing John Marum stepped in and snapped up the lease at the start of the six-month period of redemption, causing extreme anxiety among the sub-tenants that he would behave as cruelly to them as he had done to their neighbours in 1819. On Tuesday 16th March 1824, Marum and his son were in Rathpatrick. At dusk they set off for home at Whiteswall, passing on their way the constabulary barracks next to John Ridge's house and the churchyard at Eirke. Suddenly, in the lane leading to Whiteswall, a gang of armed men hiding in the ditch leapt out and ambushed the pair. Marum himself was knocked off his horse and stabbed to death. His son was wounded by a shot from a blunderbuss which caused his horse to bolt, carrying him to safety. Local residents rushed to the scene, and one was despatched to Eirke House to fetch the sergeant from the police barracks in John Ridge's barn. There the messenger found the special constables poring over a book of travels in India which one Patrick Kelly had thoughtfully brought along to show them that very evening.

Nerves were strained almost to breaking point amongst those connected with the despised business of tithes. Over at Gowran, where John's son Jones now acted as his father's curate, the occupants of the house were armed and ready to repel intruders. A few weeks after the murder of Marum an attempt was made to steal timber from the vicarage outbuildings. No doubt fearing an invasion of the house itself, someone fired out at the interlopers. A confidential report to the Kilkenny Sessions of 1825 remarked sardonically that when suspect houses were searched at midnight the occupants were all mysteriously absent.

Six men were brought to trial for the murder of John Marum in the following August. Most of the suspects had reason to hold grudges against the victim (it was difficult to find anyone who did not), and some had been implicated in the crimes catalogued here, as well as others. One of them, Thomas Seales, had been evicted by Marum for non-payment of rent. Seales' father was a stonemason who had worked in the past for Reverend Ridge, so that pillar of the community De Courcy Ridge was called upon as a character witness. As before, De Courcy gave a non-committal, law-yer's answer by stating that he had never heard anything said against Thomas Seales. Hardly a ringing endorsement, but the interesting point is that this time De Courcy was speaking on behalf of the supposed-attacker, not the attacked. Does this suggest that he was genuinely impartial in the struggle between oppressed and oppressors? Or that he was prepared to assist Wray, a Protestant, but not Marum, a Catholic? In any event, De Courcy probably shared in the widespread feeling at all levels of society that Marum was a bad lot who had it coming. Two days later, all six defendants were hanged. The scaffold was erected near to the site of the murder, so the last view that the condemned men would have looked upon was the hill of Eirke.

In the summer of 1826 John Ridge died in his bed in the house on that same hill at the age of 73. In his youth, he misinterpreted the stroke of luck he enjoyed when his sister stole the heart of a viscount as a sign that his family's hardworking ways could now be left in the past. His father and brother knew better. They realised that the Ash-brook connection would only provide a sort of leveraging of opportunity: instead of aspiring to improve their lot as fishermen by becoming inn-keepers, they might now graduate from inn-keepers to gentlemen. But the same degree of commitment and effort would be required to make the transition.

Once he was released from family expectations of a legal career, and with the benefit of having had his brother William go before him to do the heavy-lifting, John rapidly grasped the principles of the patronage system, and entered wholeheartedly into the requirements it placed upon him. In return for putting himself at the disposal politically of his social superiors, he enjoyed the relatively leisurely life of an eighteenth-century parson which allowed him to pursue his bucolic interests in improving agriculture and bothering game. By the time he had six sons of his own, John recognised the importance for a young man of modest fortune and the right contacts of applying himself to a career. It is therefore even more remarkable that he avoided the mistake his father Thomas had made in attempting to impose his own choice of profession on his son; instead John allowed his eldest boy, John Agar, to follow his own inclinations by taking up farming.

Whether Reverend Ridge was well-liked in his role as a clergyman is difficult to ascertain. The Ridges had never shown themselves to be particularly observant before—indeed their approach to religion appears to have been a pragmatic one. If John had displayed particular piety from boyhood, it seems unlikely that his father would have objected to his studying divinity at Oxford instead of law. But it would be unwise to claim any certainty in relation to John's conscience. In the Irish Midlands his flock would anyway have coincided closely with his social circle, whose members were all fulfilling the requirements of their own particular place within the patronage system with greater or lesser degrees of conviction. Both of Betty's brothers no doubt looked upon the struggles of the Irish labouring poor and thought their own thoughts, but their overwhelming response was probably one of relief at having escaped a similar fate.

THE HONOURABLE Caroline Flower was probably still at Pryse Loveden Pryse's seat of Gogerddan when news arrived of another death in the family. This time it was Caroline's aunt Elizabeth Flower, that unmarried lady who dutifully stood by her widowed sister-in-law Lady Ashbrook and then witnessed Betty's will upon her remarriage to Dr John Jones. Arguably, it was Elizabeth Flower who paid the highest price for her brother's determination to marry an Oxfordshire fisherman's daughter. Had William Ashbrook returned to Castle Durrow after obtaining his degree from Oxford University, his sister would have served as his hostess until he found a wife and, as the elder daughter of one of the foremost families of the Anglo-Irish aristocracy, would perhaps have married well herself. As it was, she was removed to the manor at sleepy Shellingford where she lived a life of obscurity in a household where she found herself inferior in rank to a water gypsy.

She died in March 1813 aged 72 in Charles Street off Berkeley Square and was buried with other members of the Tatton family in the church of St John's at Hillingdon in Middlesex. Her niece Caroline composed the tribute on her monument which reminds the world that Elizabeth was 'the eldest Daughter of the first Henry Lord Viscount Ashbrook of the Kingdom of Ireland and Grand daughter of Lieutenant

Crescent Terrace, Cheltenham: home of Betty's unmarried daughter Caroline

General Tatton' whose 'mild gentle and Unaffected Manners preserved uninterrupted the Friendships of her early years'.[54] It would seem only proper that Caroline, recipient of a legacy so hefty that the liquidation of family assets was required to meet it, should express due deference to her co-operative aunt. Elizabeth's final address off Berkeley Square suggests that perhaps the former Tatton home in Hillingdon had indeed formed part of the Cowley estate put up for sale by third Viscount Ashbrook in the last years of his life.

Precisely when Caroline moved to Cheltenham is unclear. The Middletons having transferred to Shrubland Park, Crowfield Hall was empty by 1820, and Caroline was certainly established in her own home in some elegance by 1823. We know this courtesy of a somewhat unlikely source. The rich Yorkshire landowner and notorious lesbian Anne Lister records in her diary a conversation with her matchmaking friend Lady Astley in August 1823 concerning Caroline's unmarried Warneford nieces. The young ladies were said to be expecting £20,000 each. The youngest, Harriet, was reported to be 24 or 25 (in fact she was 20) and dismissed as 'very large'.[55] But Lady Astley spoke more highly of the elder sister Caroline. Proposing Caroline Warneford as a companion for Lister, she explained that: 'She is determined not to marry but to live like her maiden aunt Caroline; single & in good style.'[56]

Caroline Flower's chosen home was number 3 Crescent Terrace on the north-eastern side of the finest Regency development in Cheltenham, the Royal Crescent. The row of five white-stucco houses faced south-east across gardens, on the north-west

---

54 Monument to William Tatton Esq, church of St John the Baptist, Hillingdon, Middlesex.
55 Helena Whitbread, ed., *The Secret Diaries of Miss Anne Lister 1791–1840* (London, paperback 2010), p. 298.
56 *Ibid.*

side of which was the magnificent sweep of the Royal Crescent. A fancy, wrought-iron verandah to the first floor of Caroline's house gave views of the gardens and, being central to the row, number 3 was crowned with a pediment. Whilst the house was tall and narrow, it was double-depth, so there were plenty of rooms for Caroline to fill with lovely things, and this is what she proceeded to do.

Perhaps it was a shopping trip that took her to Marshal Thompson's hotel at 28 Cavendish Square in London for the last two weeks of July 1824. The Honourable Miss Flower enjoyed the sort of financial pulling power that would have had jewellers and haberdashers queuing to attend upon her in her rooms at the hotel, but there is no reason to suppose that Caroline avoided indulging in the relatively new pastime of shopping—browsing the luxury goods on display in the bow-windows of Regency Mayfair. Oxford Street, too, already enjoyed the reputation it retains today as a shopper's paradise. A tourist reported to her children at home an evening stroll there in 1786: 'Just imagine, dear children, a street taking half an hour to cover from end to end, with double rows of brightly shining lamps, in the middle of which stands an equally long row of beautifully lacquered coaches, and on either side of these there is room for two coaches to pass one another.'[57] Pavements wide enough to stand six people deep in comfort allowed visitors to gaze upon the luxuries arrayed behind the handsome glass windows of the watchmaker's, the fan shop, the silversmith's and the china shop. Caroline lost the fleshly battle to resist these twinkling temptations. She wore a favourite diamond brooch every day, and chose from two gold watches, a repeating one and another with her initials engraved upon it. Also amongst her personal jewellery were two bracelets set with miniatures of her father, William second Viscount Ashbrook, and her grandfather, Henry first Viscount. A miniature by Engleheart of Caroline's brother William third Viscount Ashbrook, was enclosed in a gold case and therefore probably designed to be worn too. As one of the greatest English painters of portrait miniatures, at the height of his fame George Engleheart could command fees of anything up to twenty-five guineas for one of his exquisite watercolour likenesses painted onto ivory.

Just like Lady Astley, Caroline Flower was tempted to try a little match-making for her reluctant Warneford namesake. The local parson at Crowfield Hall was John Longe, whose parish included nearby Coddenham as well as Crowfield. Reverend Longe's son, also John, was due to inherit the Longe family seat of Spixworth near Norwich from a childless cousin, and this young man seems to have piqued Caroline Flower's interest as a suitable husband for her niece. Reverend Longe recorded in his diary that in June 1826 he received a letter from John informing him that he had visited Miss Flower in Cheltenham, that she was well and had received him very kindly. A straightforward enough duty-call upon a venerable family acquaintance, perhaps. But a few months later Reverend Longe reports that events had moved on: 'My son

---

57   Molly Harrison, *People and Shopping* (London, 1975), p. 87.

John received a friendly letter from Miss Flower, respecting her niece Miss Caroline Warnford, & proposes that John should go to Cheltenham next month, when Miss Flower will be at home, & expects Miss C. Warnford on a visit to her.'[58] In December, John wrote from Cheltenham that he had received every civility and encouragement from the two ladies. In June 1829, once the issue of John Longe's inheritance of Spixworth Park had been settled, Betty Ridge's first grandchild Caroline Warneford married Sir John Longe at St George's, Hanover Square. Sadly, events would soon show that Caroline would derive little happiness from her aunt's matchmaking efforts.

Sufficient evidence survives to allow us to take a tour of Caroline Flower's house at Crescent Terrace. Portraits of family and friends featured strongly among the artefacts she collected. Betty Ridge's second husband Dr John Jones, whom Caroline had known all her life, was depicted both in pastels and in silhouette-form in a black frame. An oil painting of Caroline's friend Reverend Francis Close hung on the wall, and there was another Engleheart, this time of her friend Mrs Stead. This lady qualified for two black profiles, one of which was to be found in the back drawing-room and the other in an ivory box turned by the late Mr Stead and having this gentleman's own profile on the outside. The rooms were furnished with a mixture of family heirlooms and elegant Regency pieces. Caroline's favourite bureau had belonged to her mother (evidence that Betty mastered reading and writing eventually?), and Caroline herself owned an old mahogany writing desk. This latter is described as usually standing on a small table, so perhaps it was more in the way of a writing box than a desk. An antique silver inkstand and three glass bottles with silver tops plus another ebony-inlaid inkstand and bottles completed the paraphernalia essential to a lady of copious correspondence.

On the chimney-pieces were clocks by Caroline's preferred maker, Dwerrihouse of Berkeley Square, as well as ornamental china figures. The lady of the house served tea every day from a silver teapot which perched on a silver-plated stand and was accompanied by a small, embossed silver cream jug. All sat on a little round table with a pie-crust edge. Afternoon callers (and they were numerous, including Reverends Close, Demainbray and Smithwick, Miss Lloyd, Miss Pelham, Miss Uniacke, the Misses Margaret, Marianne and Isabella Pemberton, Miss Servis, Mrs Murray, Mrs Sykes, and especially Eliza Lady Ford) might find themselves taking tea from china cups and saucers which belonged originally to Caroline's father and displayed the Ashbrook family arms. A pair of silver-plated candlesticks with glass shades provided light essential on winter days when Caroline might reach for her embroidery from her French work-box. Two cocoa-wood candlesticks with silver nozzles and mahogany stands were especially treasured, having been turned by someone she described coyly in her will as 'a particular friend'.[59]

---

58 Michael Stone, ed., *Diary of John Longe, Vicar of Coddenham, 1765–1834* (Woodbridge, 2008), p. 109.

59 National Archives, 'Will of the Honourable Caroline Flower', PROB 11/2001, 26th July 1844.

On her bookshelves was a ten-volume edition of Shakespeare's plays with notes by Samuel Johnson and George Steevens. A valuable, six-volume edition of Scott's Bible was accompanied by Alexander Cruden's heroic single-handed opus, *A Complete Concordance to the Holy Scriptures*, first published in 1737 as a sort of index to the King James Bible. Another commentary on the Bible was that by Reverend Dr Richard Mant, published in three volumes under the direction of the Society for Promoting Christian Knowledge. Visitors sufficiently impertinent to venture upstairs into Caroline's bedroom would have found a bedstead topped with a feather mattress and pillows, all covered by a patchwork bedspread made by Betty, a relic especially prized by her daughter. A sofa bed in the dressing-room provided somewhere to rest during the day. And at the windows in the next room were hung the patchwork curtains worked by Betty to accompany the bedding.

In spite of her obvious love of fine things, the clue to Caroline's main interest was there on her bookshelves. She was a passionate believer who saw it as her Christian duty to fund causes designed to benefit both the less fortunate and society as a whole. Her chief accomplice in this endeavour was the charismatic Reverend Francis Close, evangelical Anglican rector of Cheltenham and noted foe of alcohol, tobacco, horse-racing and theatrical amusements. This was an unpromising manifesto in the context of fun-loving Regency Cheltenham. Even so, Close was a popular figure who is remembered in the town to this day. He was keen to improve the quality of children's education by establishing a training college for teachers, and Caroline expressed her own enthusiasm for the subject of education by taking an interest in the Cheltenham National School and in the Cheltenham Infants' School in St James's Square. In 1832 she joined the committee of her uncle Samuel Wilson Warneford's favourite among

Charismatic preacher Francis Close, one of Caroline's closest friends

his many projects, the Warneford Lunatic Asylum in Oxford, now the Warneford Hospital. Caroline undertook to subscribe £2 2s per annum. In her will, as no doubt in life, she provided for the Cheltenham General Hospital, the Female Orphan Asylum in Winchcombe Street, and the Cobourg Lying-In Charity.

Caroline Flower, daughter of second Viscount Ashbrook of Castle Durrow, County Kilkenny, and Betty Ridge of Northmoor, would live on in this comfortably charitable way until July 1844, queen of her own little court at Crescent Terrace. As other maiden ladies who have lived lives of unblemished purity have been known to do, Caroline rather touchingly attempted to introduce a note of intrigue into her last testament. As well as that hint about a 'particular friend', she left to Mrs Murray, daughter of the Honourable Mrs Pelham, what she described as 'a very valuable pebble broach which she knows the history of'. The sad truth is that probably very few people cared about any small secrets Caroline may have had. The main beneficiary of the childless Caroline's will was Eliza Lady Ford, widow of Sir Francis Ford of Conway House in nearby Charlton Kings. The precise nature of the relationship between the two women is unclear and even were correspondence between them to emerge, the extravagant terms in which female friends customarily addressed one another at the time would probably leave us none the wiser. In addition to the customary bequests to her aristocratic relatives there is one striking legacy of £50 to her cousin, Reverend Jones Ridge, son of John Bagshot Ridge, and by now a keen and active clergyman and newly-appointed rector of Cahir in County Tipperary. Caroline had many Ridge cousins who seemed to play no part in her life, but the fact that she remembered Jones in her will surely supports the idea that the boy spent time in the Jones household with Caroline when he was growing up.

Caroline insisted upon being buried with minimal fuss: 'If I depart this life at Cheltenham aforesaid it is my express wish and desire to be interred in a vault under the Church there called Holy Trinity Church in the most plain and unostentatious manner.'[60] And there she still is, number 1427 in row XX, tomb D, and the inscription in the crypt says simply: '1844 July 1, Flower, Caroline, Hon'ble'. There is no monument to her memory.Before sneering at the lady-bountiful who salved her conscience with charitable donations whilst enthusiastically surrounding herself with furniture and precious objects produced by the finest craftsmen of the time we must remember that, in Caroline's world, she was simply fulfilling her expected role—just like her Ridge uncles in Ireland. She was the gracious lady of refinement and taste, giving liberally of her ample means for the benefit of society. Mindful of the transience of life, the eternity to come, and the inevitable crumbling to dust of all human flesh, she determined to be buried with all possible humility. Caroline knew her role in life, and she performed the part in all its aspects, as her Warneford niece would have said, 'in good style'.

---

60   *Ibid.*

7

A Regency lord

RAPID REMARRIAGE following bereavement is seen by some as a compliment to the departed spouse. The widowed party was so content with the married state, the reasoning goes, that they wish to recreate it as quickly as possible. A period of formal mourning doubtless prevented many a hasty rush to the altar on the part of the newly-bereft of past generations. Aristocrats would adopt full mourning-dress for around a year, and then the women might perhaps go into half-mourning for a further period. For men and women alike, appearing at a party or ball during the first twelve months of widowhood would be seriously frowned upon. However, even this enforced hiatus could not guarantee a felicitous subsequent union.

Following the death of his wife Deborah, Henry Jeffrey fourth Viscount Ashbrook first appeared in public socially at that local gathering at the Assembly Rooms in Staines in April 1811, thirteen months after his bereavement. Even then he was in the insulating company of his sister Caroline and his friend the Duke of Clarence, younger brother of the Prince Regent. Clarence was newly-single too, having recently separated from his long-term mistress Dorothea Jordan. Henry's first recorded appearance in London society was at a magnificent ball and supper given in May 1811 by Mrs Calvert in Mansfield Street off Portland Place. Amongst the fashionables present was one Lady Metcalfe, ambitious wife of a rich husband and mother to a daughter of marriageable age. Lady Metcalfe, the former Susannah Sophia Selina Debonnaire, was married to Sir Thomas Theophilus Metcalfe, and the family's London home was a few steps from Mrs Calvert's in Portland Place. After a military career in India, Sir Thomas became a director of the Honourable East India Company and MP for Abingdon. In the latter capacity he very probably encountered Henry Jeffrey who was deputy lieutenant for Berkshire, the county of which Abingdon was then a part. The Metcalfes had recently purchased handsome Fernhill Park, an H-plan, red-brick mansion set in a 200-acre estate on the opposite side of Windsor Great Park from Beaumont Lodge.

Fernhill Park: family home of the Metcalfes on the edge of Windsor Great Park

Sir Thomas had been created a baronet only a few years previously. 'Metcalfe is certainly a very ancient name,' says *Debrett's* carefully. 'Honourable mention is made of Captain Metcalfe who served in the field of Agincourt; in the fifteenth century Thomas Metcalfe was sheriff of York, and was attended to the assizes by 150 Metcalfes mounted on white horses.'[61] Whilst no evidence is offered of direct descent from these picturesque figures, the claim is made that Sir Thomas was a seventh-generation descendant of the chancellor of the duchy of Lancaster in the reign of Richard III. Whatever were their forebears, at the advent of the Regency the Metcalfes of Portland Place were sufficiently eminent to be invited to attend royal receptions, and Lady Metcalfe took her elder daughter, 21-year-old Emily Theophila, along to the Drawing-Room held to celebrate Queen Charlotte's birthday in January 1810.

Later that same year, when George III was finally overtaken by mental illness, the King's indisposition provided the Metcalfes with the opportunity to express their elite credentials by despatching at least one family member to call at St James's Palace every few days to enquire after the monarch's health, as was society custom. Lady Metcalfe had for some time been chaperoning Emily around society balls and concerts, and news that the widowed Lord Ashbrook had once more embarked upon the social scene would not have escaped her notice. During the week following Mrs Calvert's ball, Lady Metcalfe put aside the feelings of her domestic staff in the interests of a greater cause and gave not one, but two May balls at Portland Place—one on the Monday and one on the Thursday. Meanwhile that October it became clear just how highly

---

61   John Debrett, *Debrett's Baronetage of England,* Volume 2 (London, 1824), p. 1005.

the Prince Regent's younger brother, the Duke of Clarence, valued the friendship of Lord Ashbrook. During an inspection visit to Deal in his new capacity as Admiral of the Fleet, there were four other lords in the Duke's suite, but what particularly marks out Henry Jeffrey as something more than simply one of the Duke's cronies is the role he played at a ball and supper hosted by Clarence at the Albion Hotel in Ramsgate during the trip.

Guests arriving at the Albion just before the dancing commenced at ten o'clock one Monday evening found the entrance into the ball and supper rooms transformed into a garden illuminated with lamps suspended from shrubs. Members of the Somerset militia carrying halberds were stationed as yeomen of the guard at the entrances, and the strains of favourite airs played by the militia band drifted out from within. In deference to the Duke of Clarence in his capacity as Admiral of the Red, the ladies were dressed principally in white and red satin embroidered with gold. The gentlemen mostly wore the Duke's uniform of blue and buff, the candlelight picking out the crowns embossed on their buttons. Supper was announced at half-past one, and the guests crowded into the three rooms laid out for the refreshments. In the principal room the Duke presided at the centre table and, in the absence of a legitimate duchess, the role of co-host was performed by Henry Jeffrey, son of a Northmoor fishergirl. After supper the dancing continued until six o'clock in the morning, when presumably quarter had to be given to the staff arriving to clean up the hotel ready for the coming day's business. Off went the Duke's guests, the ladies in their specially-made gowns and the gentlemen with nothing pressing to get up for on a Tuesday morning, and all of them expecting to slumber undisturbed until midday.

Henry returned to a London humming with rumour as to the identity of the next Lady Ashbrook; the front-runner was a well-respected lady-in-waiting at Court, the Honourable Mrs Egerton. But more meetings and negotiations between Henry Jeffery and the Metcalfes must have taken place during the next few months because in June 1812 35-year-old Henry Jeffrey married Emily Theophila Metcalfe at St George's, Hanover Square. The bride had celebrated her twenty-second birthday just seven days earlier. A watercolour portrait of Emily painted around this time shows an archetypal, dark-ringletted Regency nymph swathed in vaguely Grecian drapery and perched on a bank amidst a bosky grove. She has set down her books and taken up her lyre, a reference to the love of music which she inherited from her mother. A more recent inheritance were the five young children from her husband's first marriage: Susannah, almost nine, Henry, six, Caroline, four, William, three, and Harriet, two. Acquiring such a large brood overnight would be a challenge to any 22-year-old, but it is unlikely that Emily would have involved herself in the day-to-day care of the children any more than she chose to do. She became pregnant immediately, and Henry was doubtless in high spirits in August when he attended Abingdon races with Emily's brother.

But the New Year of 1813 brought the first of several blows. In January, after six

Emily Theophila Metcalfe: musical second wife of Betty's son Henry Jeffrey

months of marriage, Emily gave birth prematurely to a still-born son at Beaumont Lodge. Thanks to the efforts of Henry's first wife Deborah in producing an heir and a spare in the form of Henry and William this was a personal tragedy not a dynastic one, but a painful event nonetheless. Within days, news arrived from Wales of the grisly death of Henry Jeffrey's sister Harriet Pryse following the mysterious fire in her bedroom, and a few weeks after that Henry's maiden-aunt Elizabeth Flower died in London. But any formal mourning undertaken by Henry following the deaths of his sister Harriet in January and his aunt Elizabeth in March did not prevent him from accompanying the Duke of Clarence to the Prince Regent's levée at Carlton House in May.

It was around this time that Emily, too, made an important royal friend. When residing at Windsor, Princess Charlotte Augusta of Wales, 17-year-old daughter of the Prince Regent and second-in-line to the throne, occupied Lower Lodge, making her a neighbour of the recently-married Ashbrooks.[62] The Princess and Lady Ashbrook shared the same masters for music and drawing. During a party at Windsor Castle, Princess Charlotte approached Lady Ashbrook and confessed that she was intrigued to meet the prodigy whose industry and perseverance their mutual instructors urged her to emulate. This cheerily self-deprecating introduction initiated a friendship that was to last for the rest of the Princess's life and brought her great comfort during the isolation of her forthcoming disagreement with her father over her marriage. It would be unfair to attribute the connection solely to Henry Jeffrey's ambitions concerning his family's status. His wife's love of music was shared by the Princess, and anyway Charlotte's own correspondence shows that, in spite of her youth, she was well aware of the difference between true friends and hangers-on. For example, of Lady Anne Smith and her daughters she remarked crisply: 'There is nothing time serving they will not do.' By contrast, in the same letter she wrote: 'The Ashbrooks [are] a most excellent, steady, quiet people… they will stand firm by whoever is ill-used.'[63]

This first full year of Henry and Emily's married life had not started well, and worse was to follow. In the autumn, a couple of months after his fifth birthday, Henry's

---

62   Lower Lodge was formerly known as Burford House, and is now absorbed into the Royal Mews.

63   A. Aspinall, ed., *Letters of the Princess Charlotte 1811–1817* (London, 1949), p. 149.

younger son William Flower died. Not only was this a devastating personal loss for Henry Jeffrey, but the death of his younger son also left a dynastic vacancy. Childhood was a perilous phase during this period, and Henry's hopes now devolved upon one small boy. The particular history of the Ashbrook inheritance was an object-lesson in the aristocratic need for insurance in the form of extra sons. Henry Jeffrey himself had inherited as the 'spare' when his brother William died young; William had inherited the title as a child when their father, Betty's husband William, died young; his father Henry inherited as a younger son, the elder brother Jeffrey having died at the age of 13. Henry Jeffrey himself had no surviving brothers, and the only one of his sisters who had children, Elizabeth Warneford, had produced two daughters and no sons. The fourth Viscount Ashbrook could perhaps be forgiven for attaching a new urgency to his expectations of his young wife.

For Emily, there was more sadness to endure before the dreadful year of 1813 was out. In November her father Sir Thomas Metcalfe attended the Prince Regent's levée, and three days later he fell ill. Three days after that, he died. 'My dear Lady Ashbrook,' wrote Princess Charlotte to her friend, 'Lord Ashbrook will I trust, have done me justice with you in saying how sincerely I felt for you and participated in your affliction, and how much I felt obliged for your having availed yourself of the only moment you could dispose of in coming to see me, as also for having sent him at such a moment when you most wanted comfort and support to give me an account of yourself.'[64]

Emily was one of the few people who acknowledged Princess Charlotte's eighteenth birthday in January 1814. Even before the Princess's dispute with the Prince Regent over his project to marry her to Prince William of Orange reached its height in the summer of that year, she had always suffered shabby treatment resulting from his jealousy of her popularity and his desire to isolate her from society. This probably contributed to a singular absence of organised national celebration on the occasion of the heir to the throne's eighteenth birthday. Charlotte spent the day alone, with only a handful of presents to mark the day out from any other. She wrote to acknowledge the gift of jewellery she had received from her steadfast friend Emily: 'My dear Lady Ashbrook, I take the first opportunity of thanking you for your very kind letter, and the dear little guitar which is really the prettiest bijou of the sort I ever saw, and I am sure I shall never fail wearing it with great pleasure as being your gift.'[65]

While the deaths of Henry's sister and aunt at the beginning of 1813 had not apparently warranted deep mourning, the death of a son in October and of Emily's father in November were another matter. It was not until July 1814 that the press spotted Lord and Lady Ashbrook at a social event. That summer the entire country was united in convulsions of joy celebrating the Duke of Wellington's victory over

---

64 Mrs Herbert Jones, *The Princess Charlotte of Wales: an Illustrated Monograph* (London, 1884), p. 57.
65 *Ibid.*, p. 68.

Napoleon in the Peninsular War. Naturally the most extravagant entertainment of all was that given in the new Duke's honour at Carlton House by the Prince Regent, and the Ashbrooks were on the guest list.

The gardens were brilliantly illuminated with lamps, a particular novelty among which was a pyramid of multi-coloured lights which rotated in constant motion. A veritable village of inter-connecting marquees ('temporary rooms'[66]) allowed the Prince to express his famously devil-may-care attitude towards taste. Golden ropes wreathed in flowers supported tents decorated in a theme of white and rose pink. Dozens of antique alabaster lamps were suspended throughout, and huge mirrors at strategic points amplified the drama of the spectacle. Musicians played from within a temple constructed of flowers, and a Corinthian temple stood at one end of the vast promenading tent, backed by a mirror and topped with a cut-glass 'W'. Within the temple stood an antique column supporting a marble bust of the man-of-the-moment, the Duke of Wellington. The Prince Regent who, in his capacity as acting head of state, privately regarded himself as the Corsican's true conqueror, strutted about in a uniform emblazoned with English, Russian, Prussian and French Orders. Supper was at 2 am, and the guests lingered on past six o'clock.

Life passed rather more peacefully for Henry Jeffery and Emily over the next couple of years. Emily continued to support her friend Princess Charlotte through her difficulties with the Prince Regent. After Charlotte finally broke off her engagement to the Prince of Orange in June 1814, relations between father and daughter reached such a pass that Charlotte was virtually imprisoned during July and August. During this upsetting period, Emily was in constant correspondence with the Princess at Cranbourne Lodge on the Windsor estate. Doubtless she would have preferred to visit Charlotte in person, but the Prince Regent had banned his daughter from receiving callers. Charlotte wrote to a friend that on the whole she didn't regret the loss of these visitors with the single exception of Lady Ashbrook. When the Prince Regent at last allowed Charlotte to visit Weymouth in late summer, the Princess wrote to the same friend: 'The Ashbrooks will go there & stay a little while on purpose, wh. is most kind of them indeed, & will be quite a comfort & pleasure.'[67]

More formal engagements served to emphasise the contrast in social visibility between Henry Jeffrey Ashbrook and his two predecessors. In January 1815 the Prince Regent's mother Queen Charlotte celebrated her seventy-first birthday at Frogmore House on the Windsor estate. Her granddaughter Princess Charlotte of Wales was present, along with all of the Queen's own daughters. Only two of her seven surviving sons were invited, all of whom she despaired of on account of their extravagant and irregular private lives; the rest would probably have found the occasion too tame anyway. After a formal dinner there was tea and coffee, and then a concert which was

---

66 *Morning Post*, 23rd July 1814, issue 13573.
67 A. Aspinall, ed., *Letters of the Princess Charlotte 1811–1817* (London, 1949), p. 147.

Princess Charlotte of Wales, godmother to Betty Ridge's granddaughter Augusta, in a portrait said to have been commissioned by Emily Ashbrook

finished by eleven o'clock. The press noted the presence of Lord Ashbrook but not of his wife, who was around four months pregnant at the time. Since the death of her premature baby two years before, perhaps her doctors were especially inclined to counsel caution during those first few uncertain months.

In June 1815, Emily's loyalty was rewarded when Princess Charlotte acted as godmother at the baptism of Henry and Emily's first surviving child, Augusta Emily. The birth of a fifth daughter was no doubt a disappointment to Henry (which does not necessarily mean that he felt any less fatherly affection towards the child personally). But Emily was only 26 years old, so there was plenty of time.

EARLY IN 1815 Princess Charlotte made up her mind to marry Prince Leopold of Saxe-Coburg, and in 1816 the Prince Regent finally acquiesced to his daughter's entreaties. The Princess was at last happy, taking up residence with her new husband at Claremont House near Esher in Surrey. Her headstrong mother Caroline of Brunswick, to whom Charlotte remained determinedly loyal, had left the country to live abroad and Charlotte was free to enjoy the calmer waters of life with a husband she adored. In January 1817 she wrote to reassure Emily that her loyalty during the dark days had not been forgotten:

> *My dear Lady Ashbrook,*
>
> *I hasten to assure you with what pleasure I received and read the letter you were so kind as to write me on my birthday. I am not a little pleased at the manner in which you remember and express yourself about the hours and days we formerly spent together. Rest assured no one can look back to them with more gratitude than I do, as I never forget my friends, or kindness shown me, and never can yours and Lord Ashbrook's, to whom I owed the few, the only, pleasurable moments I spent in those times… I should like very much to see your little girl again, as I can easily conceive I should see much improvement after so many months have elapsed. I am not surprised at your being rather vain and proud of her; she must be so entertaining and such an amusing resource to you… Would it be too far for you and Lord Ashbrook to come to us on Friday next to dine and to sleep? It would give us much pleasure if it should be quite convenient and agreeable to you both… Our dinner-hour being seven, any time you may like best to arrive at before this you will find your rooms quite ready for you. We make it a rule that everybody should do what they like best in order that they should feel as much at home as possible, which I hope you will always do in a house of mine.*[68]

68   Mrs Herbert Jones, *The Princess Charlotte of Wales: an Illustrated Monograph* (London, 1884), p. 147.

In May Henry Jeffrey was again at Claremont House celebrating the first anniversary of the royal couple's wedding. A favourite pastime of the royal pair was music, and for their vocal duets a frequent accompanist on the piano was the talented Emily Lady Ashbrook. But Emily was not mentioned in press reports, so perhaps she was again indisposed. A few weeks later, however, she was up and about once more. Escorted by Henry at the Queen's Drawing-Room, she wore a show-stopping gown comprising a satin petticoat trimmed with lace and ribbon, enhanced by lace drapery and richly embroidered with festoons of roses and trimmed with blond—an especially soft French silk lace—with a train of pink and white satin. A head-dress of feathers and diamonds completed the ensemble. A perusal of newspaper reports of the period reveals that the fashion at Court was for largely plain fabrics, and not for the last time Emily took advantage of an allusion to the family name of 'Flower' by means of floral adornment on her dress to make herself stand out.

In July Henry considered a few indulgences of his own when he attended a sale at Phillips' auction house of 'Parisian Elegancies' which included a porcelain dinner service made for Napoleon.[69] These luxury goods were, by any other name, loot from the victory over the French, and the wealthy were snapping them up as they flooded into the country. In the previous year Henry and Emily had even travelled to Paris where post-war bargains were to be had. Perhaps Henry was beautifying Beaumont Lodge for VIP guests, for at the end of the month he and Emily hosted Queen Charlotte and her daughter Princess Elizabeth at a sumptuous dinner. The summer ended for the couple with another stay at Claremont, country seat of the now-expectant Princess Charlotte and her husband. During the visit Charlotte and Emily debated the choice of physician for the Princess's delivery, and the two women decided upon Sir William Knighton, whom Emily knew personally.

Upon her return from a few weeks in Rome, Emily was dismayed to discover that Princess Charlotte had been prevailed upon instead to engage Sir Richard Croft to attend her at the birth. Emily offered to be present but, as Charlotte had already refused a similar offer from the Queen herself, she felt she could not accept. In November 1817, following the birth of a stillborn baby boy, Princess Charlotte died. And fourteen weeks later, Sir Richard Croft shot himself in the head.

The paroxysm of grief that gripped the nation upon the death of the heir to the throne testifies to Charlotte's status in the eyes of the public. The outpouring of emotion was on a par with anything afforded a superstar princess today, especially as the little son to whom she gave birth was dead too. The public imagination had fixed upon her as the eagerly-anticipated break with the dissolute Hanoverian princes of the past, and now those hopes were dashed. Subscriptions were invited to fund a public monument to the Princess to be erected near her tomb in St George's Chapel at Windsor. In order to ensure that as many people as possible could feel involved in a national

---

69   *Morning Post*, 4th July 1817, issue 14493.

tribute, a maximum donation of one guinea per person was set. Henry Jeffrey and Emily were listed as each subscribing their guinea. Emily's genuine fondness for the Princess is attested to by the fact that she guarded Charlotte's letters for the remaining sixty-seven years of her own long life, only occasionally unfolding them to read their precious contents afresh.

FOR HENRY'S FRIEND the Duke of Clarence, the death of the heir to the throne and her son had other implications. Of all of George III's ten children, only the Prince Regent had presented him with a legitimate grandchild, and now she was gone. The pressure was on the unmarried royal dukes to drop their mistresses and find wives who might provide a legitimate heir. Following a messy parting of the ways in 1811, Clarence's mistress Mrs Jordan had died in 1816, and it seems very likely that the subject of the Duke's marriage came up during his stay with Henry and Emily at Beaumont Lodge during March 1818. At last a suitable candidate had been found in the person of Princess Adelaide of Saxe-Meiningen. A few weeks after Clarence's visit to his friend at Beaumont Lodge, he met Adelaide for the first time.

They married at Kew seven days later. Adelaide wore an elegant gown of silver tissue with two broad flounces of Brussels point lace, each flounce headed with rich silver-shell trimming. Bodice and sleeves were trimmed with Brussels point lace and sil-

ver tassels. A diamond clasp fastened the robe at the waist, and in her hair the bride wore a superb wreath of diamonds. The groom was 50 and a father of ten, Adelaide was a maiden of 25, just two years older than her eldest stepson George Fitzclarence.

Meanwhile, Henry and Emily had exciting family business of their own to attend to. At the time of the Duke of Clarence's marriage, Emily was already five months pregnant and in November she came to London for the birth. On 25th November at the family's London residence at 3 Mansfield Street the baby arrived: another daughter,

The Duke of Clarence, the future 'Sailor King' William IV: closest friend of Betty Ridge's son Henry Jeffrey

Charlotte Augusta. Whatever their feelings about this, the couple rallied and embarked on a round of visits and entertainments in 1819. In June they gave a grand dinner to Princess Charlotte's widower Prince Leopold. Among the company present besides his Royal Highness were the Austrian ambassador, Prince Esterhazy, the French ambassador, the Marquis de Latour Maubourg and his wife, the Spanish ambassador, the Duke de San Carlos and his wife, the Dowager Duchess of Leeds, governess to the late Princess Charlotte, the Irish Earl and Countess of Charlemont, the Earl of Shaftesbury, the Neopolitan ambassador Count Ludolf and his wife, and the Belgian Count Caraman. One cannot help wondering whether any of these cosmopolitan socialites knew of their host's humble maternal origins.

That winter, a near-riot one evening outside the Spanish ambassador's residence demonstrated the sheer unpopularity of the Prince Regent. On their way in to the Duke de San Carlos's grand, Spanish-themed ball, Henry and Emily and most of the guests from their own dinner in June were among those who had to brave an angry mob in the street which one report numbered at between three and four thousand. The fact that 'yellings, howlings, shoutings, and language of the most abominable description' could be directed at the heir to the throne seems astonishing today.[70] One section of the crowd actually tried to break in to the ambassador's house by scrambling over the top of the marquee erected for the band of the 2nd Regiment of Life Guards to play in. Inevitably, someone plummeted straight through the roof of the tent. A combination of Bow Street Runners, parish constables and firemen failed to take control of the situation so a detachment of Life Guards was despatched to help.

The guests persevered valiantly within and, at the end of an evening of the customary extravagance and luxury, the Prince Regent had to be escorted away by a party of Dragoon Guards. According to the *Morning Post*: 'The Prince Regent was cheered by the assembled multitude on his entre, and at the time of his departure (about a quarter before four), when his Royal Highness waved his handkerchief in the most

---

70   *Morning Chronicle*, 18th December 1819, issue 15798.

elegant and condescending manner.'[71] This unwise gesture may account for the volley of 'hideous yells, hisses and groans' rather than cheers that the Post's rival the *Morning Chronicle* reported as the Prince's mounted escort battled to conduct him safely home to Carlton House. The poor Duke de San Carlos must have gazed upon the aftermath of his evening of Spanish *elegancia* and wondered whether he should have bothered.

At the end of January 1820 George III's long reign ended. Henry Jeffrey took his place among the other nobles behind the muffled drums escorting the late monarch's funeral procession as it made its way into a candlelit St George's Chapel at Windsor in February. The old king was dead, but the despised Prince Regent now reigned as George IV, and the relentless Court ceremonial ground on. In June Henry and Emily Ashbrook attended the new king's birthday Court at Buckingham House (later renamed Buckingham Palace). Emily, resplendent in a gown of satin-striped pink gossamer, was again pregnant. Surely at last Henry and Emily would be blessed with a healthy son to replace William.

At Mansfield Street on 7th November 1820, Henry Jeffrey Ashbrook's seventh daughter, Sophia Georgiana, came into the world.

AT THE NEW KING'S coronation in July 1821, while Queen Caroline attempted unsuccessfully to gain entrance to Westminster Abbey, Henry Jeffrey Ashbrook, son of a water gypsy, followed George IV up the aisle and joined the other peers clustered around the throne. After the ceremony a banquet took place in Westminster Hall. Six hours having elapsed since the commencement of the ceremonial, Henry must have set about the turtle soup, salmon, turbot, trout, venison, veal, mutton, beef, braised ham, savoury pies, daubed geese, braised capon, lobster and crayfish with some enthusiasm. Sadly for Emily, crammed among the other peers' wives in double rows of galleries set high on each side of the hall, she could only gaze down with envy upon her husband's loaded plate. It was the couple's final public appearance together.

Marital separation—as distinct from plain desertion—was a luxury only the rich could afford before the twentieth century. Betty Ridge's sister Catherine Wyatt was fortunate in being able take refuge with her parents in their new house on Noah's Ark island when her marriage broke down after 1769. Labouring-class husbands had to absent themselves from the village altogether if they wished to avoid supporting an unwanted wife. Abandoned wives and children would be obliged to throw themselves on the mercy of the parish, and consequently the overseers were likely to offer a reward for the return of the miscreant. No such difficulties faced Henry and Emily Ashbrook. Indeed, with a country seat in which to ignore one another, plus a London home and perhaps a summer residence too, upper-class matrimonial combatants could live virtually separate lives if they wished. Considerable animosity would be required to make

---

71 *Morning Post*, 17th December 1819; issue 15261.

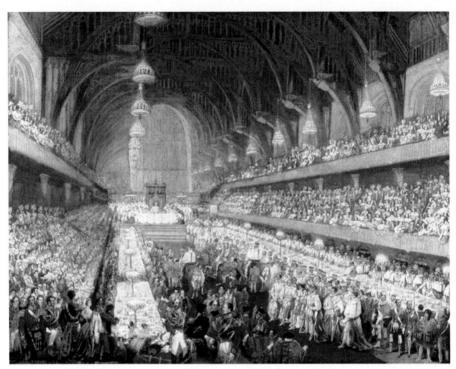

Betty's son Henry Jeffery attended George IV's magnificent coronation banquet in Westminster Hall

such an arrangement unacceptable to the parties, as it would apparently become for Henry and Emily.

In the months after the birth of Sophia, Emily had thrown herself into the dizzying round of social engagements that filled the summer of the new king's coronation—sometimes in the company of her husband, sometimes not. In the first of these, a ticketed ball at the Royal Pavilion in February designed to raise funds for the establishment of Brighton dispensary, we see the beginnings of what would become a theme for Emily as she became increasingly isolated from her husband: the association of aristocratic jollification with charitable endeavour. Perhaps she had already seen examples around her where the currency of a wife's title plummeted in value once she became estranged from her husband. The reverse, of course, was never the case. Titles followed the male line, and therefore the men retained the power. Viscountesses merely passed through—particularly if they failed to produce sons and could never therefore claim to be mother to the next viscount. Loss of influence with a titled husband meant loss of social pulling-power too. In positioning herself as a philanthropic patroness, Emily and others like her hoped to attract society grandees to functions which would enhance the guests' own patrician credentials. It was a tactic she would employ repeatedly in the coming years. Although the brief newspaper report on the charity ball stressed that the five hundred revellers comprised 'all the rank, elegance, fashion, and beauty of the place', only the lady patronesses were listed, not the guests.[72] Lord Ashbrook was not mentioned.

It seems likely that the *haut ton* saved themselves for the real thing a couple of weeks later when George IV and his sister gave a ball at the Pavilion. This time the *Morning Post* salivated over the attendant dukes, marquises, princes and princesses, counts and countesses. Lord Ashbrook was there but apparently, and perhaps significantly, not Emily. The couple did put on a united front for the reception celebrating the King's birthday in May. Both had a vested interest: Henry's daughter Susannah was presented to the King on the occasion, and so was Emily's younger sister Georgiana. Henry and Emily were also together at Prince Leopold's 'Grand Party' in May and then at the King's 'Juvenile Party' in June. The first was a matter of good form since Prince Leopold's wife Princess Charlotte had been godmother to Henry and Emily's daughter Augusta. The second, the King's 'Annual Entertainment to the juvenile branches of the Nobility, Gentry, and Persons of distinction' was an opportunity to give a social airing to Henry's daughters, Caroline, 13 and Harriet, eleven.[73]

At their home in Mansfield Street during June, Emily held two 'routs' and a ball. A rout was a kind of frantic drinks party. Reception rooms would be cleared of furniture so that society could crowd in and elbow their way round to ensure that they saw and were seen by everyone. Once this mission had been accomplished, the guests would leave and move on to the next rout. Emily's ball at the end of the month was a grander affair. From half-past eleven until gone four in the morning, three hundred guests danced quadrilles and waltzes alternately to music provided by Collinet's band. The last purely social occasion upon which Henry and Emily appeared as a couple was at Lady Warberton's ball in Albermarle Street at the beginning of the coronation month of July.

A most unpleasant incident ended what was already a strained summer for the Ashbrooks. In the early hours of a Saturday morning in September, while the family lay upstairs in their beds, two men crept silently through the grounds of the Ashbrooks' neighbour Mrs Bonnell and made their way into the gardens of Beaumont Lodge. They quietly removed a pane of glass from the parlour window using a centre-bit. Once inside, they lit the candles so recently extinguished by the household servants and proceeded systematically to rifle every drawer and cabinet in the parlour as well as the three adjoining reception rooms. Locks on several pieces of furniture were forced, or holes drilled through the fronts using the centre-bit. Amongst the articles stolen were four French ornamental clocks, a silver ink-stand, a gold box adorned with a miniature, two surtout coats, and a variety of valuable trinkets. The thieves were even so cool as to break open a tea-caddy and remove the tea. Ten days later, a sailor named Leonard and a carpenter named Smith, both of no fixed abode, were committed to Berkshire

---

72   *Morning Post*, 7th February 1821, issue 15568.
73   *Morning Post*, 16th May 1821, issue 15652; 15th June 1821, issue 15677.

In September 1821 burglars broke into Beaumont Lodge through the windows onto the gardens

gaol charged with the break-in. They had been apprehended the night before, having been found lying under a haystack opposite Egham racecourse in the company of three French clocks and a coat with Lord Ashbrook's name on it. They denied having stolen the goods, saying they had found them and that they hoped Lord Ashbrook would discover the thieves.

A LETTER FROM Emily's brother Charles Metcalfe, a British colonial administrator living in India, reveals that relations between Henry and Emily had deteriorated so badly that by the beginning of 1823 she had removed with her three daughters to her own establishment in Twickenham. Her brother wrote:

Hyderabad, 29th June 1823

My dearest Emily,

I am delighted to find by your letter of the 17th February that you are comfortably and happily settled. Really I think that your separation from your Husband is scarcely to be regretted—I now for the first time am acquainted with traits of his character which make me shudder to think that your Happiness has so long been in the power of such a being. I can never advise you to reject overtures of reconciliation; but I have little or no wish that they should ever be made, for I doubt the possibility of any comfort in a reunion...[74]

Clearly, Emily had successfully conveyed to her faraway brother that her husband was a brute of the worst stripe. A clue as to the precise form of cruelty to which Emily had been subjected emerges a few sentences later: 'I have indulged in dreams of our living together and of your occupying under your Brother's protection that station in society to which your Rank entitles you, but at present alas it is but a dream.' Evidently, in Emily's view, she was not being allowed to occupy the station in society to which her rank entitled her. And she had persuaded her brother that most right-thinking members of society agreed with her. 'I am proud to see that you are so well supported by most respectable friends,' announced Charles.

Money, we are told, is the primary cause of domestic discord. Aristocratic land-owners expected a boost to the family exchequer at least once in every generation by means of that useful mechanism of marriage. The arrival of a handsome dowry along with a wife was designed, at the very least, to ensure that the wife was not a drain on her husband's family fortune. Fathers of prospective brides who hoped to have grand-children with a higher rank in society than they themselves enjoyed were prepared to pay for the privilege, but a surfeit of daughters needing dowries was a luxury many would prefer to forgo. Emily had certainly brought a dowry with her, but she had also presented Henry with three more daughters to add to his existing tally of three legiti-mate girls and one illegitimate. All would need providing for in one way or another. The only son Emily had produced had been born dead.

The recent history of early deaths of Ashbrook heirs and the consequent reliance on younger sons has already been explored. Henry will have been aware that, added to this, the family firm had missed two opportunities for the acquisition of those handy dowries: first, in marrying Betty Ridge, William Ashbrook had wilfully put his own wishes before the needs of the family estate, and secondly, William and Betty's son, third Viscount Ashbrook, had never married at all. Henry's actions suggest that he saw in his unexpected inheritance of the title an opportunity—or perhaps a duty—to restore the prestige of the Ashbrook name. He immediately made a textbook aristo-cratic marriage to Deborah Freind: financially advantageous to the husband, socially advantageous to the wife. Suddenly swimming in Walker cash, Henry had quickly acquired a palatial base in an ideal situation on the borders of the Windsor estate from which to conduct his campaign. Naturally, he hoped that a second marriage would contribute as handsomely to his project as had his first. However, four months before the birth of Henry's sixth legitimate daughter in 1820, his first, Susannah, had reached the age of 17 and the thoughts of a dutiful father would have turned to finding her a

---

74   Lincolnshire Archives, MON/B/28/23, 'Monson Papers: Letter re Emily Lady
      Ashbrook's separation from her husband,' 29th June 1823.

husband and the first of a daunting string of dowries. This was not a tactful point at which to take out a lease on a superfluous mansion in Twickenham, but that is what Emily did.

Riverside House was a large, brick-built Georgian villa set amongst towering chestnut trees and with lawns sweeping down to a willow-fringed curve in the Thames. When Emily presented Henry with a seventh daughter to provide for rather than a son as back-up for the 14-year-old Ashbrook heir, her self-indulgence may have begun to rankle. From Henry's point-of-view, he had provided Emily with both a title and a magnificent home in which to play out the role. Emily may have felt entitled to point out in return that his own self-indulgence in acquiring Beaumont Lodge in the first place was a more direct cause of any difficulty in finding dowries for those daughters for which she was not responsible. For Henry, of course, the sheer grandeur of Beaumont Lodge was central to his mission of restoring the Ashbrook name to its proper place in society. It would be a bold move to claim an understanding of the breakdown of any marriage, far less a marriage at two hundred years' remove and in a bygone culture. But it is easy to see how, in Henry and Emily's particular circumstances, remonstrance might be met with recrimination, and deadlock might ensue.

For the remainder of the 1820s, Henry and Emily went about their business separately, conducting a delicate social *pas-de-deux* which precluded any danger of awkward encounters. Emily mopped up most of the invitations to balls; Henry seems to have been happy to concentrate on family life and cultivating his relationship with the royal family. The once-dashing soldier remained mostly at home, pottering among his coin and medal collections. The marriages his children made during these years were not the sort that depended upon his turning up at glitzy social gatherings. He remained loyal to his own circle, as evidenced by the first two matches in 1824 and 1828.

He had maintained links with his first wife Deborah's family; her grandfather, the banker Thomas Walker, was still a close associate, and would be succeeded as Henry's agent in 1836 by his son George Walker. (One can imagine in what spirit Henry's second wife might receive any rebuke over her spending habits if it were deemed to emanate from the family of his first.) Deborah had been related to the Walkers through her mother, but her father was Reverend William Maximilian Freind, who had a brother, John. Although John was born a Freind, as his maternal uncle's heir he took the name Robinson in 1793 and was created first Baronet Robinson of Rokeby Hall, County Louth, in 1819. In 1824, Henry's eldest daughter Susannah was married by the bishop of Raphoe in Ireland to Sir John's son, Reverend William Robinson at Marylebone church.

Meanwhile, Emily had developed a great taste for the Isle of Wight and spent her late summers there with her daughters. In July 1826, 'after a long and severe illness', five-year-old Sophia Georgiana died at West Cowes.[75] The little granddaughter

---

75 *Morning Post*, 21st July 1826, issue 17345.

'Afflicted mother': Emily as depicted on the memorial to her two daughters

of Betty Ridge was interred at the fashionable church of St Mildred in Whippingham near East Cowes, site of the commemoration of a clutch of princes and princesses. The following year brought no respite for Emily. In May 1827, her eldest daughter Augusta Emily, goddaughter of the tragic Princess Charlotte, died aged eleven in the resort-of-the-moment for the convalescent, Torquay. Augusta was interred in the vault at Whippingham alongside her sister. A monument to the memory of Sophia Georgiana and Augusta Emily erected by their 'afflicted mother' can be seen inside the church.

Astonishingly, in the following month, in a display of apparent opportunism and contrary to all the accepted norms of mourning etiquette, Emily mastered her state of affliction sufficiently to appear at a rout given by the Duchess of Clarence at the Admiralty. Following the death of the heir presumptive Prince Frederick, the Duke of Clarence was now George IV's presumed heir. Suddenly everybody wanted to be on good terms with the Clarences, and Emily will have known, of course, that having lost two daughters in eleven months (the most recent not yet six weeks since), Henry would not be attending a purely social event. While Henry doubtless felt sufficiently confident in his connection with Clarence not to have to join the throng at the Duchess's party, Emily perhaps realised that she could no longer afford to remain isolated from her husband's newly-powerful friends. It would therefore be unfair to accuse her of insensitivity; like her peers, she was a product of, and vulnerable to, the who-you-know system.

Henry appeared in the press only upon calling at Frogmore House in the company of his daughters Caroline and Harriet to leave a message of condolence for the old queen on the loss of her son Frederick. Then a month later, having been well enough to ride out to Frogmore with her father on the last day of July, Harriet Flower died at Beaumont Lodge at the age of 17. Henry fled to Ireland.

MAKING HIS FINAL appearance in the lives of Betty Ridge's children in this year was her second husband Dr John Jones. Since Betty's death he had lived on at Shipston on Stour for almost twenty years without re-marrying. How deeply Betty's children were affected by his death in 1827 is unknown. One small clue suggests that he certainly missed their mother. Five years after Betty's death, a wistful poem had appeared in the *Gentleman's Magazine* entitled 'On seeing a beautiful picture of the Right Honourable Lady Ashbrook'. Reproduced in full at the beginning of this book, the lines lament the demise of a beauty so striking that it could 'win an Ashbrook's and a Jones's heart'.[76] The bracketing of the name of Betty's second husband alongside that of her first strongly suggests that the poet was John Jones himself. Perhaps he sat pondering sadly upon a portrait of his wife placed within sight of his mahogany writing desk.

Much of Dr Jones's will was designed to carry out wishes expressed by Betty during her lifetime, modified by 'subsequent events which have taken place'.[77] By this he presumably referred to the death after Betty's own of her daughter Harriet Pryse in Wales and the marriages of her Oxfordshire nieces. An annuity of £25 went to Betty's elderly sister, the redoubtable Catherine Wyatt, now aged almost 90 and still living on Noah's Ark island. From the trust set up upon Betty's second marriage, her surviving unmarried daughter Caroline Flower in Cheltenham received £500. Her married daughter Elizabeth Warneford received £100, and a modest loan to Elizabeth's husband Francis was cancelled. Compounding suspicion that cash-flow problems were the cause of the trouble between Henry Jeffrey and his wife Emily is the discovery that Henry had borrowed the considerable sum of £1,000 from Dr Jones. The sum precisely matches the wildly generous annual allowance stipulated by third Viscount Ashbrook for Henry's spinster sister Caroline Flower. Was Henry obliged to undergo the humiliation of borrowing from his mother and her second husband in order to meet this expensive obligation? The loan was cancelled under the terms of the will.

A particular affection for Betty's unmarried daughter Caroline is discernible in the terms of Dr Jones's will—after all, he had known her all her life. Betty and John Jones had married in 1790 when Caroline was 16 years old, and Caroline remained by her mother's side until Betty's death in 1808. The first evidence we have of her residing anywhere other than Shipston on Stour or Shellingford is when she made the move to Crowfield Hall in Suffolk around 1811. Dr Jones and Caroline therefore lived under the same roof for perhaps twenty years. Caroline received an additional £100 from Dr Jones personally, which he requested that she accept 'as a token of my kind regard and esteem over and beyond the Legacy hereinbefore given to her'. Various pieces of needlework created by Betty were left to Caroline, who also eventually took possession of the patchwork bedding and curtains meant for Henry Jeffrey, but which he evidently

---

76 'Select Poetry for April 1813', *Gentleman's Magazine*, Volume 113, (London, 1813), p. 360.
77 University of Oxford, Jesus College, 'Will of Dr John Jones, 24th November 1827, Tredington Living papers'.

passed immediately to his sister. Perhaps they were not quite the thing for his grand Windsor mansion. But for Caroline all these items were a reminder of the quiet hours she and her mother spent bent over their embroidery frames during their thirty-four years of constant companionship.

John Jones made careful provision for his own nephew and niece, and yet he left all the treasures from his library and 'museum' to his wife's son Henry Jeffrey Ashbrook— his books, globes, pictures, and prints, his coin and mineral collections, and all the gleaming mahogany furniture in which they were housed. This might be interpreted as a sign of a special closeness between the two men, but it seems more likely to be con- firmation of the original source of all these goodies: Betty Ridge. Perhaps she bought them as presents for her new husband, perhaps some had originally belonged to her first husband and it was deemed right that they should pass at last to his son. Anyway, cash-strapped Henry appears to have overcome any feelings of sentimentality towards the items. Six weeks after probate was granted, John Jones's possessions were auctioned off at the rectory in Shipston on Stour.

HENRY JEFFREY could be reasonably certain that a warm welcome awaited him in County Kilkenny in the autumn of 1827. Following the failure of the harvest the year before, he had instituted a scheme during the summer to provide agricultural work. Two hundred men, women and children were employed to prune the extensive Ash- brook woodlands and plantations, a project designed to last through to harvest-time when work and food would become less scarce. *Finn's Leinster Journal* recorded the beneficial effects of the plan: 'Nothing could exceed the joy and alacrity of these poor people on being employed; and the comfort it has diffused amongst them generally has checked disease, and probably saved many valuable lives,' reported the paper in July.[78] 'We would strongly recommend other Landed Proprietors to imitate the example set by Lord Ashbrook.'

Happily, the scheme had immediately preceded the Irish debut of Henry's 21-year-old heir, who came to Ireland on a shooting excursion. Now in the autumn the Viscount himself was at Castle Durrow for the first time in twenty years. News emerged of orders going out to suppliers in Dublin and Kilkenny, suggesting a mag- nificent refurbishment of the castle. Rumours began to circulate that Henry's heir was planning to make the family seat his home.

Plans were indeed afoot. In the following month, Henry's son was granted the use of the name Walker as required under the terms of the Walker inheritance. A mar- riage had been agreed between Henry Flower Walker and his cousin Frances Robin- son, sister of Reverend William Robinson. Throughout the winter, Henry and his son

---

78 *Finn's Leinster Journal*, 7th July 1827.

*Betty's granddaughter
Susanna Sophia Robinson
and her daughter Caroline*

made monthly trips to London and finally, at the end of March 1828, they departed for Ireland once more. When forty cartloads containing furniture and wine from Beaumont Lodge plus an entire suite of servants rumbled across the town square in Durrow and up the avenue to the castle, local hopes were confirmed. After a break of three-quarters of a century, the family's traditional seat was to become of central interest to the Ashbrooks once more. During the visit, Henry Jeffrey reinforced his position among the great and the good of Anglo-Irish society by attending the Viceregal Ball at Dublin Castle in April, and no doubt took the opportunity to parade his heir before his peers. Perhaps he also made time to visit his daughter Susannah, now 24, at her new home near beautiful Lough Foyle. Susannah's husband William Robinson had been transferred from the unpromising-sounding parish of Scrubbey to the lucrative office of rector at Bovevagh near the little town of Dungiven in the diocese of Derry. Two months later Henry Jeffrey and his son were back in London where Henry Flower Walker married William Robinson's sister Frances.

Pragmatism of the first order is apparent once the sequence of events is complete. Fourth Viscount Ashbrook and his relative by marriage Sir John Robinson effected a spouse-swap between their offspring that rendered neutral any dowry implications. Having paved the way with a little generosity to his Irish tenants beforehand, Henry sent his heir off to raise the next generation of Ashbrooks at the family seat in Castle Durrow, leaving Henry free to stipulate in his will that Beaumont Lodge be sold after his death to release a handy chunk of cash with which to keep the Ashbrook show on the road in years to come. It was a scheme whose elegance was worthy of Thomas Ridge himself.

ONLY ONE ENTERTAINMENT was permitted to divert Henry Jeffrey from his great dynastic project in those first busy months of 1828. It was staged in March at the expense of poor Richmond Seymour of Crowood House near Ramsbury in Wiltshire. 'EXTRAORDINARY CHARGE AGAINST MR SEYMOUR OF WILTSHIRE,' bellowed a supposedly-shocked *Morning Chronicle*.[79] There followed a report on the trial of Seymour, 'a Gentleman of rank, fortune and education', and his footman, Charles Macklin, two married men who were charged with having 'attempted to commit an unnatural offence'.

The court at Salisbury was jam-packed. Among the onlookers was Lord Ashbrook as well as 'a great number of the gentry of the surrounding country', all no doubt present in their capacity as moral guardians of the masses. With rapt attention, the court listened to the various accounts of what had happened one summer's day back in 1825 when the coachman, the lady's-maid, the under nursery-maid, and two other maids happened to glance through a gap an eighth of an inch deep at the base of the door to Mr Seymour's dressing-room. Within they observed their master and the footman in a situation which the *Chronicle* felt unable to describe. The servants informed Mrs Seymour, the footman was sacked the following morning, and Seymour begged the coachman to blow his brains out. Richard Seymour, who was not present in court on account of his having absconded, claimed the whole thing was a conspiracy got up by a malicious household staff. He had, in fact, simply been leaning over Macklin's shoulder to examine a book of accounts on the bed.

After a trial lasting forty-one hours, the jury returned a verdict of guilty against both defendants. Since the crime was classed as a misdemeanour and not a capital offence, the death penalty was not available to the judge. Seymour died peacefully twenty years later at another of his family's properties near Lambourn; Charles Macklin's fate is unknown.

BY THE SECOND HALF of 1828, Henry had just one daughter, Caroline, still living with him at Beaumont Lodge. Two of his children with Deborah were dead: William and Harriet. Two were married—most importantly from a dynastic point-of-view, the Ashbrook heir Henry Flower Walker. Hopefully, news would arrive soon that the next generation was in the offing.

When Caroline married Captain Henry Every of the First Life Guards, son and heir of Sir Henry Every of Egginton Hall, Derbyshire in March 1829, Henry Jeffrey planned to ensure that he had not lost a daughter but gained a son. He built for the newly-weds on the Beaumont estate a gracious house named Ouseley Lodge, a symmetrical, two-storey, brick house with a portico over the central bay of five, and a Doric porch sheltering double entrance doors.

---

79 *Morning Chronicle*, 17th March 1828, issue 18254.

Ouseley Lodge, Old Windsor: built by fourth Viscount Ashbrook for Betty's granddaughter Caroline and her husband Captain Henry Every

There is a certain poetry in this alliance between Caroline, the granddaughter of Northmoor-born Betty Ridge, and an Every. During the seventeenth century the manor of More in Oxfordshire, later to become known as the village of Northmoor, was owned by Sir Henry Every, second Baronet. Seven generations later, Caroline would marry the son of the ninth Baronet. It is doubtful whether those present in Old Windsor church that day knew of the intriguing link. Another thing of which they were as yet unaware was the birth at Castle Durrow on that very same day of an heir to the Ashbrook title. Within a year came news of the birth of the all-important 'spare' too. (Again, the younger brother would in time be needed; William Spencer Flower succeeded his brother and become seventh Viscount Ashbrook.) As a second son himself, Henry Jeffrey must have felt an overwhelming relief when the news reached him during a stay at the Dolphin Hotel in Southampton. And within another month, his best friend would be king.

Henry Jeffrey received good news at the Dolphin Hotel in Southampton

FIVE GUINEAS REWARD.

WHEREAS a Well-Boat, the Property of Mrs. CATHARINE WYATT, of the Ark Island in the Parifh of Northmoor, in the County of Oxford, was broken open in the Night of Sunday the 20th of April, 1806, or early on Monday Morning, and robbed of a Quantity of FISH; and whereas the Door of an Out-Houfe belonging to the faid Catharine Wyatt was broken open in the Night of Wednefday the 23d of April, or early on Thurfday morning, and feveral ARTICLES taken off the Premiffes, Notice is hereby given, that EDWARD CHAPMAN, Ribbon Weaver, ftands charged by an Accomplice, who has already been apprehended, with having been guilty of the above Robberies, and that whoever will apprehend the faid Edward Chapman, fo that he may be brought to Juftice, fhall receive a Reward of FIVE GUINEAS from the faid   CATHARINE WYATT.

The faid Edward Chapman is about 5 Feet 9 inches high, of a pale Complexion, light Hair, and ftout made.

MEANWHILE, FAR AWAY from Windsor along the Thames—socially, if not geographically—an elderly lady breathed her last on Noah's Ark island in the summer of 1829. This was Catherine Wyatt, eldest sister of Betty Ridge and, at 92, the longest-lived of all of Thomas and Elizabeth Ridge's children. Having returned to her childhood home following the breakdown of her marriage some sixty years since, she stayed there for the rest of her life.

But Catherine should not be viewed as a figure of pathos. Unlike many deserted women of the period, she remained independent. The marriage of her sister Betty into the aristocracy, and her brother William's subsequent rise through the ranks of Anglo-Irish society in County Kilkenny meant that she received a decent pension to the end of her days, and the expenses for the property on Noah's Ark were paid out of Ashbrook funds. These arrangements bought Catherine the luxury of choice; unlike many eighteenth-century women, she was not forced into a second marriage on the grounds that the only alternative was destitution. She could live out her days where she chose, and she chose Noah's Ark island.

As modestly hard-working as her brother William, and as determined to retain hard-won assets as her father Thomas, Catherine even continued to operate as a weirkeeper, though doubtless employing help to deal with the arduous physical aspects of operating a paddle and rhymer weir. In 1796 she was charging 2s for each London boat at Noah's Ark. Not only that; she was also operating Pinkhill weir (next-but-one to the Ark) and charging London boats 4s. It is hardly surprising that by the 1790s things were getting on top of Catherine who was, after all, by then in her sixties. A valuation of Noah's Ark for tithe purposes made in 1798 is kept at Magdalen College. The entire messuage, including land, fishery and house, was valued at £12 12s. However, a caveat is added to clarify that this sum reflects the value 'in its present state – but [it] might with a proper tenant and repaired be worth 20 Guineas a year. The House is getting

The announcement of
Catherine Wyatt's death in
Jackson's Oxford Journal

Lately died, at the Ark, Northmoor, in her 93d year,
Mrs. Wyatt, sister of the late Lady Ashbrook.

much out of repair.'[80] This is the house that was built a mere thirty years previously. It was probably something of a relief for Catherine when the lease passed to the Nalders, a family of yeomen farmers who featured in the Northmoor parish registers between 1782 and 1868.

Other difficulties beset Catherine too. The problem of pilfering was endemic, and the targeting of elderly ladies who live alone is perennial. In the early hours of the morning on Monday 21st April 1806, a well-boat belonging to Catherine was broken open and the catch of fish being stored in the well was stolen. Three nights later the perpetrators came back, broke into an outhouse and stole several more items. One of the culprits was soon apprehended and, evidently oblivious to the principle of honour among thieves, he promptly attempted to improve his position by naming his accomplice as Edward Chapman. Catherine had had enough. She announced in the local paper that she would pay a reward of a staggering five guineas for the apprehension of Chapman, a ribbon weaver five feet nine inches tall, fair-haired and stout.[81]

A memoir written in the 1880s suggests that Catherine was sparky enough to appreciate the irony of her situation. Northmoor curate Arthur Dunlop related the story told to him some time after his appointment to the parish in 1839: 'On inquiring of the Nalders, who were an old family residing [on Noah's Ark island] and who were our College tenants, they told me they remembered [Betty's] sister, who was married, and who lived to a good old age, and who always flattered herself that if Lord Ashbrook… had seen her before her sister he would have chosen her in preference for his bride.'[82]

Perhaps it was the Nalders who took the trouble to mark Catherine's passing by placing the brief announcement in the local newspaper in July 1829 that: 'Lately died, at the Ark, Northmoor, in her 93d year, Mrs Wyatt, sister of the late Lady Ashbrook.'[83] With no family of her own and all her siblings long gone, it is difficult to determine who else, apart from her own immediate neighbours and the clergyman who conducted her burial service, would have known or cared about her death. Whether Catherine's remark about the young Lord Ashbrook was made in bitterness or with a twinkle in her eye we will never know, but her particular history suggests that a sense of humour would have been useful.

---

80 Magdalen College archive D-Y 226, 'Valuation, dated October 1798, of lands at Huntercombe in Nuffield, and at Northmoor, and at Thornborough, Bucks.'
81 *Jackson's Oxford Journal*, 17th May 1806, issue 2768.
82 Edward Walford, *Tales of Our Great Families*, (London, 1890). See Appendix C for the full account.
83 *Jackson's Oxford Journal*, 11th July 1829, issue 3976.

8

A mission accomplished

KING GEORGE had not been dead three days before everybody discovered that he was no loss, and King William a great gain,' recorded the waspish courtier Charles Greville in his diary in July 1830. 'His life has been hitherto passed in obscurity and neglect, in miserable poverty, surrounded by a numerous progeny of bastards, without consideration or friends, and he was ridiculous from his grotesque ways and little meddling curiosity.'[84] The former Duke of Clarence had apparently distinguished himself in the role of Lord High Admiral by making absurd speeches and behaving in such a way as to encourage suspicion of incipient Hanoverian insanity. Presumably therefore, Greville, who bowed to no-one in his contempt for the venality of those seeking to curry favour with the truly influential, would have approved of the loyalty of the new king's friend, fourth Viscount Ashbrook.

Henry Jeffrey had made it his mission to restore the prestige of the Ashbrook family, and had positioned himself close to the royal Court to do so. However, if Greville's assessment of attitudes towards William IV is accurate, Henry's manifestly close involvement in Prince William's life over the years suggests that the friendship was one based on genuine affection rather than hopes of preferment. Any mutual sympathy can only have been reinforced during the years when the two men were experiencing similar pressure to produce male heirs that never arrived. Henry's wife Emily had already given birth to a still-born boy and two daughters by the time William and Adelaide's first daughter died having lived for only a few hours. In the year after the birth of Henry and Emily's daughter Charlotte Augusta, Adelaide suffered a miscarriage, and in the following year another baby princess, Elizabeth of Clarence, died aged four months. In 1820 Emily presented Henry with his seventh daughter, and in 1822 Adelaide gave birth to stillborn twin boys. Henry was at least fortunate in that he had four children who survived into adulthood. And William was at least fortunate in

---

84   Henry Reeve, ed., 'July 16th, 1830', *The Greville Memoirs*, Volume 2 (London, 1874).

his choice of a wife. Adelaide was genuinely fond of his ten illegitimate children, and modified in her husband his tendency towards the behaviour of the bluff sailor—excessive drinking, swearing and general oafishness.

The day after George IV's funeral—an inappropriately jolly occasion by Greville's estimation—King William and Queen Adelaide concluded a tour of their new home at Windsor Castle by making straight for that of Lord Ashbrook at Beaumont Lodge. One imagines that, as well as lunch, hearty helpings of back-slapping and merry disbelief were enjoyed behind closed doors at the almost incredible position in which the friends found themselves. William had been transformed from a prince of very little consequence into a king, and Henry Jeffrey had brought his family back from virtual obscurity to the pinnacle of society. Three weeks later, when the monarch and his consort arrived at Windsor Castle one evening in August, Henry Jeffrey organised a special welcome. Six brass cannon taken from a French privateer during the Revolutionary War and presented by Lord Ashbrook to the Corporation were fired in Bachelors' Acre. Engraved on their sides was the inscription 'Liberté, Egalité'. Second only to the King's revered sister Princess Augusta on the guest list at the celebratory dinner in the castle on that momentous evening was Henry Jeffrey, Lord Ashbrook.

During the next few months, Henry presented at Court both his son Henry Flower Walker and his sister Harriet's nephew George Agar, who would in the following year be raised to Baron Dover. George Agar was the son of second Viscount Clifden, to whom Henry Jeffrey's cousin James Jones Ridge, son of John Bagshot Ridge, was at that time domestic chaplain (see Family Chart 2). Indeed, Jones had named his own son George Agar Ellis Ridge in honour of his patron's son. It seems reasonable to suppose that Henry and George Agar's mutual connection with the Ridge family came up in conversation at Court that day during the customary interminable waiting around. Jones Ridge's position in the Agar household was by no means a menial one; many younger sons of the gentry would be pleased to enjoy a connection with such a powerful patron. Indeed, it is perfectly possible that Henry and his son Henry Flower Walker encountered Jones socially at the Clifden seat of Gowran Castle. Readers of the works of Jane Austen are familiar with the notion that clergymen attached to aristocratic households would be expected to help entertain their patrons' guests when required.

William IV's accession appears to have prompted Henry Jeffrey to petition for confirmation of his right to exercise an inherited Ashbrook privilege. In August 1831 he set forth his case before the Lords Committees for Privileges claiming his right as his brother's heir to vote at the Election of Peers of Ireland to sit in the Parliament of the United Kingdom. Pryse Loveden Pryse MP having been called from the Commons to appear as a witness supporting his former brother-in-law's case, Viscount Ashbrook's petition was granted. Evidently Henry Jeffrey suspected no involvement on Pryse's part in the death eighteen years previously of his sister Harriet; loyalty to old friends usually repaid him.

Betty Ridge's son Henry Jeffrey attended upon the new king at his coronation in 1831

On 8th September Henry and Emily played their allotted roles at the coronation of William IV and Queen Adelaide, and on the 12th Emily was presented to the Queen. Three days later she departed for Cowes.

Meanwhile, the new king's informality and rejection of courtly stuffiness was alarming some and pleasing others. 'The King's good-nature, simplicity, and affability to all about him are certainly very striking, and in his elevation he does not forget any of his old friends and companions,' conceded the diarist Greville.[85] 'Altogether he seems a kind-hearted, well-meaning, not stupid, burlesque, bustling old fellow, and if he doesn't go mad may make a very decent King.' One old friend frequently in the King's company was, of course, Lord Ashbrook. An announcement came from St James's Palace in May 1832 that the king had appointed him one of his Lords of the Bedchamber. Eight men of noble families performed this somewhat medieval-sounding function. In reality, it meant that each in turn attended upon the king for a week at a time. Duties included assisting the king when he was dressing, waiting on him when he took meals in private, supervising access to the king in his bedchamber, and providing general companionship. Such a role gave the holder unrivalled one-to-one access to the monarch, and even as the sovereign's power decreased, his influence could be still be valuable. And as a salaried member of the royal household, a Gentleman of the Bedchamber was paid a useful £1,000 per annum.

Henry Jeffrey's schedule over the next few years reveals the commitment required of the courtier. During the twelve months prior to his appointment, Henry was recorded by the press as being in the company of the King on seven occasions. During the twelve months after his appointment that number rose to twenty-two, many of which involved Henry acting as Lord in Waiting at the King's levées. At the pro-

---

85   *Ibid.*

Henry Jeffrey became Lord of the Bedchamber to his friend King William IV

roguing of Parliament in August, Henry Jeffrey sat opposite the King in the State coach as it was pulled by eight cream horses from St James's Palace to the Palace of Westminster. And at home at Beaumont Lodge, impromptu visits from the King became so frequent that a roll of red carpet was tucked discreetly in a corner of the hall, ready for hasty deployment at short notice.

Henry Jeffrey Ashbrook was accustomed to dining at Windsor Castle but, since most of us are not, a description of the proceedings one evening in August 1832 gives an idea of the splendour of these occasions. One hundred and ten guests assembled for a dinner at the Castle just before seven o'clock. Precisely at seven, as the Queen's Band in the gal-

The King was such a frequent visitor at the home of Betty's son Henry Jefferey that a roll of red carpet was kept permanently at the ready, tucked discreetly away in the hall

lery struck up *God Save the King*, the royal party entered St George's Hall. The King and Queen took their seats amidst the dazzle of the gold dinner service, the massive gold candelabras, and the glittering of the ladies' diamonds. After feasting on a baron of beef the company toasted the health of their hosts and then retired to the Waterloo Gallery where yet more guests waited. All partook of tea and coffee, after which they adjourned to the two grand drawing-rooms for the rest of the evening.

Presumably even Betty Ridge's wildest dreams as she grew up on an island in the river Thames at Northmoor did not feature a son whose daily grind would involve waiting upon a king. On 20th March 1833, sixty-seven years to the day after she married William Ashbrook in the little church at Northmoor, her youngest son Henry Jeffrey accompanied his friends King William IV and Queen Adelaide during an afternoon of Court formalities at St James's Palace. He presented his son-in-law Henry Every who had recently been appointed a deputy lieutenant for Derbyshire. Caroline and Henry by this time had a two-year-old son Henry Flower Every. This third great-grandson of Betty Ridge later became tenth Baronet Every of Egginton Hall, Derbyshire. It was all a long way from Noah's Ark inn.

ARCHERY AS GENTEEL sport was all the rage. It was open to men and women, with the ladies wearing costumes designed specifically to cope with the required movements. An archery party was on the programme during the first visit of Betty Ridge's daughter Elizabeth Warneford and her husband Francis to their own daughter's marital home at Spixworth Hall near Norwich. Caroline Warneford and John Longe had married in June 1829, but it was not until 1831 that Caroline's parents made the difficult journey across-country from Wiltshire. John Longe had gone to considerable trouble, organising games and a fireworks display in honour of his in-laws, with the celebrations culminating in a dinner for one hundred and thirty guests.

According to the imaginative Mary Gibson, a Warneford descendant writing in the 1960s, Caroline had always been a difficult girl who exhibited only two contrasting characteristics: listlessness and hysteria. For example, there had been the embarrassment concerning her music teacher. When her elderly music master fell ill and was replaced by 28-year-old Signor Ricardo (virtually every music teacher in the country at the time claimed to be of Italian extraction), Caroline developed an urgent interest in her piano-playing. She quickly fancied herself in love, and the pair decided to elope by means of the night mail to London.

On the morning of the proposed adventure, Caroline's mother Elizabeth Warneford realised what was afoot and managed to retrieve her errant daughter from the turnpike just in time. Elizabeth insisted that the matter be kept from the girl's father Francis, whereupon Caroline threw herself in the lake, rendering the poor man all the

Spixworth Hall in Norfolk: home, briefly, of Betty's unhappy granddaughter Caroline Longe

more baffled. When, encouraged by Elizabeth's sister Caroline Flower in Cheltenham, young John Longe of Spixworth expressed an interest in taking the tiresome girl off his hands, Francis reacted with delighted incomprehension. The ceremony took place, of course, at St George's, Hanover Square.

The alliance sealed that day turned out to be one between a depressive, hard-to-please girl and a young man suffering from some form of nervous complaint which caused him chronic pain across his face. We rely on John's father, Reverend Longe of Coddenham, to chronicle the breakdown of the marriage and his diaries reveal that, contrary to Gibson's rather unsympathetic view, not all the fault should be laid at Caroline's door: 'We find Colonel Warneford & family most agreeable and friendly people. I am very sorry to observe that John does not treat them with the civility & attention which he should do, nor is he so kind to Caroline as I wish to see him.'[86]

Reverend Longe proved a perceptive observer, and eighteen months later the couple separated. Caroline wrote to her father-in-law complaining of continued ill treatment by her husband. She announced that she could go on no longer and intended to consult a lawyer in Norwich. Reverend Longe urged Caroline to refrain from taking such a drastic step just yet. He proposed a family meeting, but his peace-making efforts were to no avail. By 1834 Caroline was back at Warneford Place, her father no doubt less than surprised by the turn of events.

---

86 Michael Stone, ed., *Diary of John Longe, Vicar of Coddenham, 1765–1834* (Woodbridge, 2008), p. 132.

Charlotte Augusta Flower: Betty's granddaughter around the time of her 'coming-out' in 1834

'BEAUMONT LODGE,' announced a somewhat startled *Morning Post* in October 1834, 'the delightful chateau of Viscount and Viscountess Ashbrook, will be the scene of a brilliant Féte this evening to the rank and fashion of Windsor, including all the Officers of the Household Brigade quartered there.'[87] It was the first time Henry Jeffrey and Emily had appeared in the society columns as a couple since Lady Warberton's ball in the coronation summer of 1821. But an examination of the dates involved and their implications soon disabuses the romantically-inclined. This was no public manifestation of a personal reconciliation between Henry Jeffrey and Emily. It was an affirmation of the status of their only remaining daughter as the eligible offspring of an influential Court figure; it was Charlotte Augusta's 'coming-out'.

A watercolour of Charlotte during this period depicts her as an adorable sea-nymph in billowing pink muslin, with huge blue eyes and tumbling chestnut curls. Seashells, coral and pearls symbolise a love of the coast developed as a result of spend-

---

87   *Morning Post*, 20th October 1834, issue 19927.

The ballroom at Beaumont Lodge today

ing childhood summers on the Isle of Wight with Emily. At ten o'clock on a Monday evening in October, the haut ton of the neighbourhood arrived at the brilliantly-lit mansion and the dancing to Weippert's band commenced with a waltz. The jollity, which of course included supper, carried on until the customary English country dance signalled a conclusion at five in the morning.

In fact the ball took place over a month before Charlotte turned 16, but there was a reason for this too. As a confidant of William IV, Henry Jeffrey will have been aware that the King was about to dissolve Lord Melbourne's Whig ministry and, though unlikely, it was possible that any new administration might insist upon his own dismissal as Gentleman of the Bedchamber. (The *Morning Herald* expected Lord Ashbrook to retain his position under Wellington's Tory administration on account of his 'Conservative opinions'.[88]) Far better to introduce Charlotte Augusta to society as the daughter of a senior courtier than that of yesterday's man.

An apparent reconciliation suited Emily too. Her friendship with Princess Charlotte, who had been expected to succeed her father George IV, would have placed her in a very favourable position at Court. But Princess Charlotte had died before her father, and George IV's actual successor was Henry Jeffrey's closest ally, William IV. The turn-around in spousal fortunes was ironic and inconvenient for Emily. She had been obliged to look on from a distance while her estranged husband moved in the very highest circles thanks in part to his own determination to restore the prestige of his family name, but also in part to the vagaries of Fate in making the unlikely Clarence king. Meanwhile, she had spent her time flitting between parties, the theatre and her beloved Isle of Wight, as well as travelling extensively on the Continent. During her absence from the marital home, however, she never appeared at Court.

An incident during her exile from Court perhaps seemed to Emily symbolic of her somewhat liminal existence at the time between the proud yacht of the aristocracy and

88   *Hampshire Advertiser & Salisbury Guardian Royal Yacht Club Gazette, Southampton Town and County Herald, Isle of Wight Journal, Winchester Chronicle, and General Reporter*, 22nd November 1834, issue 592.

the humble rowing-boat of the social has-been. In the course of one of her frequent sailing holidays in 1828, Emily was returning to Southampton from an outing on the water in the company of her friend Mrs Cochrane. Emily successfully transferred from the yacht into the rowing boat intended to convey the two ladies ashore, but Mrs Cochrane executed the classic manoeuvre of attempting to retain a foothold on both vessels, and thus succeeding only in pushing them further apart. Upon seeing her friend dangling half in and half out of the water and clutching desperately to the side of the larger boat, Emily leapt to her feet in the rowing boat to effect a rescue, and was promptly precipitated head-first into the water. The *Morning Post* related the details of the ladies' 'extraordinary fortitude' with barely-concealed glee.[89]

Having for several years been noticed in the society columns for little more than falling out of a boat, Emily had shored up her anomalous social position by taking up a charity. In 1828 the Repository at Southampton under the patronage of the then-Duchess of Clarence created a fund with which to purchase in bulk the materials necessary and advance them at cost to respectable gentlewomen who had fallen on hard times so that they might craft items for sale. The lady patronesses, who included Lady Ashbrook, would then play 'shop' by serving customers at a sale, and encourage all their friends to come and make unnecessary purchases in the cause. Once the Duchess of Clarence became queen, the charity was known as the Royal Charitable Repository, Southampton, and the annual sale was held to coincide with Adelaide's birthday.

Even if Emily did contribute to her own fate, it is hard not to feel some sympathy towards her. She had endured the deaths of two of her three daughters alone. Furthermore her brother Charles's satisfaction expressed in his letter from Hyderabad of 1823 at the notion that most people sided with Emily in her dispute with her husband inevitably proved to be misplaced once Henry Jeffrey's friendship with the Duke of Clarence turned into a friendship with the reigning monarch. Now all Emily's hopes centred on her remaining daughter, and she was prepared to do whatever it took to achieve the best outcome for Charlotte Augusta. Another display of apparent conjugal togetherness by the Ashbrooks came in January 1835 with a family trip to Brighton. By now it was clear that no further heirs to the throne were going to arrive to stand between Princess Victoria of Kent and the crown. Although Henry Jeffrey had survived the dissolution and retained his post as Gentleman of the Bedchamber, there would soon be a woman at the head of the royal Court, and it was essential to the plan that Emily should be acceptable there as chaperone to her daughter Charlotte. For this, the show of unity with her husband must be reinforced.

For the remaining two-and-a-half years of the King's life, Henry Jeffrey's royal duties utterly absorbed him. As William IV faded during the spring of 1837, the two men spent more time together than ever. At the end of May Henry and Emily appeared at Court to celebrate the King's final birthday, though Henry must have done so with

89   *Morning Post*, 31st July 1828, issue 17980.

a heavy heart for his friend was now too ill to leave his rooms. William IV had never regained his strength following a severe asthma attack in April. It was clear which way the wind was blowing for the 'Sailor King', and throughout the first three weeks of June London flooded with aristocratic arrivals in anticipation of the Sovereign's death.

ON FRIDAY 7th JULY 1837, the eve of the King's funeral, his velvet-draped coffin lay in state in the Waterloo Chamber at Windsor Castle. At ten o'clock in the morning, Viscount Ashbrook, younger son of Betty Ridge, commenced a vigil at the head of the casket. There he remained, in the vast gallery where he had supported William on so many glittering royal occasions, until eight o'clock on Saturday evening. Then he took his place in the funeral procession to St George's chapel to bid a final farewell to his friend. Smart society may have considered William IV something of a buffoon, but his informality and simple tastes had endeared him to his subjects. Whilst perhaps lacking charisma, he was no fool; he had the good sense to recognise the necessity for democratic modernisation (probably against his own instincts), creating new peers for the express purpose of helping the Reform Bill through the House of Lords. And he was sharp enough to spot the manoeuvrings of the Duchess of Kent as she attempted to position herself as Regent-in-waiting to his heir, Princess Victoria. His relative frugality and pragmatism in the face of social change reduced the temperature of anti-monarchist sentiment which had been fuelled by the excesses of his brother the Prince Regent. He paved the way for the welcome bestowed upon his young successor.

On the day of his friend's death Henry Jeffrey vacated his post as Gentleman of the Bedchamber and, having presented his son Henry Flower Walker to the new Queen at her first levée at St James's Palace in July, he took his leave of Court life for good. It was Emily's turn for a place in the sun.

THE SPIRIT OF Betty's granddaughter Harriet Warneford was said for many years after her death to haunt the grounds of her beloved Warneford Place near Seven-hampton in Wiltshire in the form of a hare. Harriet's father Francis, fuelled by hatred of his cousins but having no male heir of his own, contrived to leave the estate to his favourite daughter, obliging her to make a late marriage of necessity in order to acquire the means to maintain the place.

According to Mary Gibson, a Warneford descendant writing in the 1960s, Harriet was a true country-woman. A portrait of her as a girl shows her remarkable wavy, red-gold hair which might a few decades later have been described as pre-Raphaelite. Following the death of her father Francis in 1835, Harriet took over the running of the estate, and Gibson paints a picture of Harriet struggling to keep it afloat in the face of adverse economic conditions. By now Harriet's sister Caroline Longe had returned home from her unsuccessful matrimonial excursion to Norfolk, and the sisters lived on at Warneford Place with their mother Elizabeth, Betty Ridge's first child. Harriet's financial worries were doubtless compounded by a sense of responsibility towards her elderly mother and fragile sister, and desperation propelled her towards a marriage with her father's friend, the wealthy lawyer and politician Sir Charles Wetherell.

Charles was the brother of Robert Wetherell, ecclesiastical colleague of Dr Jones at Shellingford. Like Henry Jeffrey Ashbrook, Charles was a close associate of one of George III's sons. In Charles's case his friend was Ernest Augustus, the Duke of Cumberland, who on William IV's death became King of Hanover and heir presumptive to Queen Victoria. Wetherell was a man who contrived always to swim against the tide of opinion to his own detriment. Following the Spa Fields riots of 1816 when a mass meeting in Islington in support of electoral reform descended into disorder, Wetherell's successful defence of the first defendant brought to court led to the charges of riot against all the others being dropped. In spite of Wetherell himself being a staunch reactionary, his denunciation of the methods of the Tory government convinced the court, but 'did nothing to advance his career'.[90]

Wetherell revealed himself in parliament to be vehemently opposed to almost every form of progress, including democratic reform and Roman Catholic emancipa-

---

90   Elizabeth Baigent, 'Wetherell, Sir Charles (1770–1846)', *Oxford Dictionary of National Biography* (Oxford, 2004).

Betty's granddaughter Harriet Warneford and her reactionary husband Sir Charles Wetherell

tion. Indeed, a passionate speech in opposition to Catholic emancipation resulted in his dismissal by Wellington from the post of Attorney General in 1829. The occasion was recorded in his diary by the sugar-free Charles Greville. He described how Wetherell unbuttoned his braces when speaking, and then gesticulated so wildly that his breeches drooped down and his waistcoat rode up. Mr Speaker remarked that the only lucid interval Wetherell had was that between his waistcoat and his breeches, and Greville concluded: 'He is half mad, eccentric, ingenious, with great and varied information and a coarse, vulgar mind, delighting in ribaldry and abuse, besides being an enthusiast [a fanatic].'[91]

Ignoring warnings of likely unrest in view of his well-known opposition to democratic reform, Wetherell travelled to Bristol in October 1831 in his capacity as recorder to open the assizes. He was greeted by the Bristolians with jeers and projectiles, and the sometime champion of the Spa Fields reform protestors was forced to make an undignified escape in disguise via the rear of the Mansion House. There followed the worst reform riot in the country, lasting three days and involving great loss of life. Buildings burnt down included the Bishop's Palace, three gaols, two toll-houses, and most of Queen's Square including the Customs House, the Excise Office, and the Mansion House through which Sir Charles had made his ignominious getaway.

This was the man, then, to whom Harriet Warneford turned for protection and assistance. Sixty-eight-year-old Sir Charles and 35-year-old Harriet were married in November 1838 at St George's, Hanover Square. Intriguingly, given Harriet's financial

---

91   Henry Reeve (ed.), 'March 21st, 1829, at night', *The Greville Memoirs*, Volume 2 (London, 1874).

circumstances, several newspapers reported a rumour that Sir Charles had acquired a dowry of £60,000 along with his bride. However, the reports must be regarded with some suspicion since they also endow Sir Charles with an imaginary extra wife; his marriage to Harriet is described as his third, whereas in fact he had been married only once before. From the start, according to Gibson, Sir Charles's understandable insistence as holder of the purse-strings upon interposing his own bailiff to manage the Warneford estate rankled with Harriet. Another cause of marital discord was Harriet's refusal to leave her beloved Warneford Place for her husband's residence in Berkeley Square. She declined to attend when her husband paid a call on his friend the King of Hanover in the company of her aunt Emily Ashbrook, her cousin Charlotte and her aunt Caroline Flower in August 1843. However, a show of family unity became compulsory in June 1846 when an important invitation arrived.

THE ACCESSION OF A QUEEN played nicely into Henry and Emily's hands. The Court became perforce a more feminised environment just at the point when Henry and Emily's daughter Charlotte Augusta reached marriageable age. The efforts Henry and Emily had made to present their own marriage as being back on track was intended to counteract any doubts over Emily's status and render acceptable her presence at Court as Charlotte's chaperone. Emily appears to have felt confident that she could afford to resist any urge towards a low-key, re-entry onto the Court scene. After all, what was the point of appearing at Court unless one made a splash? For the occasion of Queen Victoria's Drawing-Room at St James's Palace in April 1838, Emily selected an exuberant ensemble. The bodice and sleeves of the customary white satin dress were decorated with lace and sprinkled with diamonds, and Emily's train was richly embroidered with cerise flowers and trimmed with lace and cerise ribbon. Above her diamond tiara towered fashionable feathers, and two strips of lace known as lappets hung down from the top of her head. The gown of the Honourable Miss Flower echoed the pink-and-white theme of her mother's, as well as its figurative allusions to the family name. Charlotte Augusta's white crepe dress was trimmed with pink flowers, and her rich pink silk train was trimmed with tulle and satin ribbon. In her hair she wore pink topaz ornaments as well as the obligatory feathers and lappets.

From this point on, Emily devoted herself and her daughter to a frenzy of engagements. Apart from regular appearances at Court, there were balls including Mrs Mansfield's, Dowager Lady Cooper's, Almack's, the Caledonian in Willis's Rooms, Lady Harriet Clive's, Mrs Weir Hogg's, Viscountess Maynard's, and Lady Sondes'. Emily also paraded her daughter at parties, entertainments, after-dinner assemblies and garden parties including Countess Stroganoff's, Lady Chatterton's, Miss Burdett-Coutts', Mr and Mrs Waymouth's, the Marchioness of Hertford's, the Duchess of Devonshire's, Countess de Salis's, the Dowager Duchess of Bedford's, and the Marquis and

Marchioness of Douglas's at Connaught Place. Mother and daughter traversed the length and breadth of the land to stay at country houses where eligible bachelors might be found, from Tedworth Park in Wiltshire (the Assheton-Smiths) to Hamilton Palace in Lanarkshire (the Duke and Duchess of Hamilton).

If Charlotte was as exquisite as her portraits suggest, it must have been somewhat dispiriting when, in spite of such an exhausting campaign, one by one the aristocratic bachelors Emily pursued chose other brides than Charlotte. The dedicated duo had been based either in hotels in London or at Emily's house in Twickenham, but following their attendance at the marriage of Lord Claud Hamilton MP to Miss Elizabeth Proby in August 1844, Emily seems to have deemed it politic to go with her daughter back to Beaumont Lodge. Had the body-swerve of yet another eligible young man persuaded Emily that doubts still lingered over the regularity or otherwise of her position in society?

Her appearance alongside her husband Henry Jeffrey among the fifteen hundred or so guests at Queen Victoria's *Bal Costume* in June 1845 may have been designed to reaffirm her credentials. Poor Henry Jeffrey, who had led a blameless life since his retirement from Court attending the races and rearranging his coin collection, must surely have been less than enthusiastic at the prospect of dressing up at the age of 68 in Pompadour silks in compliance with the Louis XV theme decreed by a mischievous young Queen. (Three years previously, she had inflicted a chivalric motif upon her guests, obliging her variously-shaped and frequently elderly courtiers to prance about dressed up as medieval knights.) At least Henry's ladies did him proud. Emily opted for her favourite cerise, this time in brocaded silk embroidered with flowers and ornamented with diamonds, pearls and rubies; Charlotte wore matching cerise glacé silk and a petticoat with deep flounces of guipure lace trimmed with cerise roses.

In the months after this display of dubious royal taste, Emily launched afresh into the social round, chaperoning Charlotte at Lady Feversham's ball in Belgrave Square, at Lady Yard Buller's, and at Baroness Brunnow's at Ashburnham House (twice). At Lambeth Palace in July Charlotte Augusta endured the humiliation of serving as a 26-year-old bridesmaid at the marriage of her friend Clementina Baillie Hamilton to Edward Denison, Lord Bishop of Salisbury. A few days later she and Emily enjoyed glorious weather at the Duchess of Bedford's third garden party of the season at Bedford Lodge, and there followed visits to the Duke and Duchess of Buckingham at Stowe, to the Assheton-Smiths at Tedworth Park, and to Mr and Lady Elizabeth Dickens at Coolhurst in Sussex.

Then at last, on Monday 13th April 1846, the *Morning Post* announced that 'Viscountess Ashbrook and the Hon Miss Flower are on a visit to his Grace the Duke of Marlborough at Blenheim'.[92] Jostling mothers of marriageable daughters throughout society must have paused to hold their breath at this news.

---

92 *Morning Post*, 13th April 1846, issue 22576.

Blenheim Palace, Oxfordshire: family seat of the Dukes of Marlborough

AFTER A MARRIAGE of almost twenty-five years, George Spencer-Churchill, sixth Duke of Marlborough, had lost his wife in October 1844. Still handsome at 51—almost twice Charlotte's age—he had a colourful if unoriginal past. Before his first marriage to Lady Susan Stewart, he had fathered an illegitimate child with a scandal-prone Spencer cousin. The child, a daughter named Susan, was born in 1818, five months before Charlotte. But this was irrelevant where the title 'duchess' was at stake.

The Duke was one of the highest-ranking aristocrats in the country, and enjoyed the subsidiary titles of Marquis of Blandford, Earl of Sunderland, Earl of Marlborough, Baron Spencer of Wormleighton and Baron Churchill of Sandridge. However, whilst long on titles he was short on cash. His father the fifth Duke was a renowned profligate who had spent most of the family fortune on the gardens and library at Whiteknights near Reading, plus extravagant parties therein. The sixth Duke, therefore, had commenced a programme of selling off assets to raise cash, one of which might be said to be the title of Duchess of Marlborough. The death of George's poor wife would be regarded by ambitious society mothers merely as giving rise to an exciting opportunity. In the face of such competition, therefore, how did the invitation to Blenheim come about? We have traced the links between the Ashbrooks and the Churchills over the years, but they were no greater—and probably far fewer—than those between the Churchills and many other aristocratic families. It may be that, initially, Emily's energetic approach combined with a peripatetic existence simply led her to be in the right place at the right time.

As widowers have so often done over the years, the Duke consoled himself follow-ing his wife's death with a new toy; he commissioned the construction of the 205-ton schooner *Wyvern* which was launched at Gosport in the spring of 1845. No doubt to the frustration of networking dowagers, the Duke had never been a regular attender at Court functions such as the June ball. But he did enter into his new hobby with enthu-siasm, being elected in the same year a member of the Royal Yacht Squadron. Henry Jeffrey Ashbrook had been a founder member of the original club at Cowes in 1815, and Emily developed a passion for the place. George Spencer-Churchill's membership brought him into that aristocratic sub-set, of which Emily was a steadfast member, which took advantage of the cooling sea breezes on the Isle of Wight in the late sum-mer. It seems a strong possibility, therefore, that the annual aristocratic jamboree on the Isle of Wight in 1845 was the occasion upon which Charlotte Augusta Flower caught his Grace's eye. Emily's habit in the years in when she was not travelling on the Continent was to go to the Isle of Wight in August, sometimes later. That September, the Duke challenged Mr Hope's *Zephyretta* to a race over the Eddystone course with £1,000 at stake. Soon after setting out, the sleek racing yachts encountered weather which their anxious owners considered too dangerous for their beloved craft. To the merriment of the local press, the gallant seafarers ran for home. 'Many a fruit schooner would have weathered the breeze,' one local paper scoffed, 'and would certainly have contended longer for the thousand pounds.'[93]

Society mothers nurturing hopes for their daughters cared not a jot what the locals thought: George Spencer-Churchill was a duke. Neither would the man himself have cared, and for the same reason. His social position was utterly secure; his financial one was not. Thanks to Henry Jeffrey's canny arrangements for his other children and, it has to be said, the loss of three unmarried daughters, Lord Ashbrook was in a posi-tion to provide an attractive dowry to accompany Charlotte—a major attraction from the Duke's point of view. In his particular circumstances, this would easily make up for any slight taint hanging over her mother. The obvious charms depicted in Charlotte's wedding portrait can only have been enhanced by a dowry of £15,000 (five thousand of which was to go directly into the pocket of the Duke for his personal use), plus a third share of £20,000 raised by Lord Ashbrook upon his estates in Ireland.

Any financial negotiations would have been well out of the way by the time of Emily and Charlotte's visit to Blenheim Palace in April. At the end of the month, and to the chagrin of matrons everywhere, the news was out. Simpered the *Morning Post*: 'We are enabled to announce that his Grace the Duke of Marlborough is about to lead to the hymeneal altar the Honourable Charlotte Augusta Flower, daughter of Viscount and Viscountess Ashbrook.'[94]

---

93 Montague Guest and William B. Boulton, *The Royal Yacht Squadron* (London, 1902), p. 189.
94 *Morning Post*, 29th April 1846, issue 22590.

Betty Ridge's exquisite granddaugter Charlotte Augusta, pictured on her wedding day

A FEW MINUTES before midday on Wednesday 10th June 1846 the exquisite young bride arrived at Lambeth Palace, London residence of the Archbishop of Canterbury, in the company of her mother. Upon the news of her arrival, a gaggle of marquises, earls and countesses moved out of the Archbishop's drawing room and rustled their way into the chapel in their finery. Emily Ashbrook's moment of triumph was upon her. She may not have been destined to give birth to a viscount, but from that day she would be mother to a duchess. The Honourable Charlotte Augusta Flower, resplendent in a white, polished-silk gown encrusted on the bodice with jewels and trimmed with

George Spencer Churchill, sixth Duke of Marlborough

deep flounces of Brussels lace, was escorted up the aisle by her uncle, Lord Monson. Her father, too ill to attend, was at home in Old Windsor. Her beautiful face was obscured by a veil secured with a wreath of orange blossom, and in her hands she carried a fragrant bouquet of more orange blossom and jasmine. Six brides-maids attended upon Charlotte in white muslin dresses, the deep necklines of which were made modest by pink fichus. Matching pink bonnets completed their ensembles.

Conducting the ceremony was William Howley, Archbishop of Canterbury. Nine years previously he had been among that early-morning delegation sent to Kensington Palace to inform Princess Victoria that she was Queen of Great Britain and Ireland. The bride arrived at the altar, the groom stepped forward to take up his position on her right hand and the marriage was solemnised. Simultaneously, a nineteen-gun salute rang out over Portsmouth harbour where the Duke of Marlborough's yacht *Wyvern* lay, decked out in flags for the occasion. The Archbishop followed the newly-weds back to his library for the legal registration of the marriage. The guests then retired to Vis-countess Ashbrook's residence in Chesham Place for a sumptuous wedding breakfast. The arrival of further guests brought the number up to sixty, all of whom were stunned by the spectacle of the magnificent wedding cake: 'one of the most successful achieve-ments of the confectionery art ever seen.'[95] The light-pink cake was smothered in orna-mental sugar work and topped by raised sugar basket. Clustered round the basket, five horns of plenty discharged orange blossom and maiden-blush roses. Perched on fancy scrolls at the summit was a vase of orange flowers, convolvulus, and roses. Equidis-tant around the sides of the cake were the arms of the Marlborough and Ashbrook families emblazoned on shields, surrounded by fancy designs; posies of orange flowers and lily of the valley tied in white satin rosettes filled any gaps. One cannot help but seize gratefully upon the reporter's assurance that all this exuberance was 'tastefully

---

95 *Jackson's Oxford Journal*, 13th June 1846, issue 4859.

arranged'. As for the Duke, even the heroic efforts of Gunter, Mayfair's most fashionable confectioner, were insufficient to detain him. Before the feast had begun, he had spirited his bride away from London to her new life as Duchess of Marlborough and chatelaine of Blenheim Palace in Oxfordshire.

LYING IN HIS BED at Beaumont Lodge on the day of his youngest daughter's marriage, Henry Jeffrey could reflect with satisfaction on the forty-four years since his dash back from Egypt to his sick brother's bedside in England. At the time, the family's future was in some doubt. Both the second and third viscounts, Henry's father and his brother William, had failed to attract dowries into the Ashbrook exchequer. In the case of Henry's brother William, the reason for his failure to marry is unknown and it cannot therefore be assumed that his lack of a bride was a wilful dereliction. His visit to a spa town as a young man of 19 and his subsequent early death at 34 conspire to suggest that he may have endured ill-health for most of his life. Henry Jeffrey's father, on the other hand, had cast aside family considerations and stubbornly followed his heart in marrying a penniless fishergirl. He had then buried the family in an obscure Berkshire hamlet, albeit probably out of consideration for his wife, and neglected his responsibilities in Ireland to such a degree that the name of Ashbrook was despised among those who considered themselves Irish patriots.

When Henry Jeffery found himself unexpectedly succeeding to the Ashbrook title at the age of 26, he seized upon the opportunity to restore the family fortunes and prestige. He swiftly made an advantageous and, as it turned out, happy marriage with the wealthy heiress Deborah Freind, and with his finances thus buoyed, he purchased a magnificent mansion adjacent to the royal estate at Windsor. From this strategically-placed base, he commenced a campaign that took him right to the very top of society. Of course, nobody could have predicted that the Duke of Clarence would succeed to the throne, and Henry's proximity to the monarch arose partly by sheer luck. But it was also a result of that same streak of loyalty he displayed by providing for his powerless Minorcan mistress Josepha Fernandez and their daughter for the rest of their lives.

Being a friend of the king did not in itself guarantee riches, and Henry had spent heavily on purchasing Beaumont Lodge. His good luck was balanced by what would have been regarded in his circle at the time as the misfortune of being presented with a surfeit of daughters. His solution was masterful: he married his son and daughter to the daughter and son of relatives of his first wife, thus neutralising any dowry implications. He then despatched his heir to reside at the family seat of Castle Durrow, solving at a stroke the twin problems of mounting resentment among the family's Irish tenantry against Ashbrook absenteeism, and of providing for his heir without further outlay a suitably grand establishment within which to raise the next generation. Future

Ashbrooks now had no need to hover so close to the centre of the action because Henry Jeffrey had restored the profile of the family to its rightful place.

This was the culmination of a scheme of positively Ridge-like ingenuity, reminiscent of Thomas Ridge's plan to contain the problem of his wayward son John's first wife Elizabeth Trinder by marrying her to his deceased daughter's widower Thomas Holford—a man to whom he had already passed the valuable asset of his victualler's licence. Henry Jeffrey was far more Ridge than Flower. It must be acknowledged that his father's marriage to Betty Ridge dealt the family fortunes a blow, but it is surely undeniable that the characteristic dynamism, loyalty, determination and instinct for careful planning which enabled Henry Jeffrey to restore the family's position came to him through his mother. Betty brought with her, and passed to her younger son, the very qualities which would prove the means of counteracting any damage her marriage may have done. She also brought with her a brother William who, deploying these same Ridge family traits, devoted his life to preserving the Ashbrook interests in Ireland from which Henry and his heirs benefitted. Henry must have considered his job done by the time his son was established with a family at Castle Durrow and the prospect of future funds from the sale of Beaumont Lodge. But there would be one more call upon his loyalty. His estranged wife Emily was understandably ambitious for her remaining daughter, but the irregularity of her position as a separated wife was a potential obstacle. She and Henry set aside their personal differences and presented a picture of unity that helped towards their achievement for Charlotte Augusta the most glittering marriage in the entire history of the Ashbrook family.

EVENTS IN THE months following the marriage seemed almost to conspire to bring to a conclusion the astonishing family episode which began with an Ashbrook viscount marrying a fisherman's daughter. First, a resolution of sorts for unhappy Harriet Wetherell was provided by the final animal-related death in this history. Having dutifully attended the marriage of his estranged wife's niece at Lambeth Palace in June, Harriet's husband the bigoted Sir Charles Wetherell journeyed into Kent in August to inspect a property he intended to purchase. Irritated by one of his carriage horses falling out of step, Sir Charles seized the reins from the driver and made his displeasure known to the offending beast. The horse returned the compliment and tipped him out of the carriage, causing a head wound that killed him a few days later. Harriet, newly-rich as a result of her husband's death, promptly changed her name back to Warneford by Royal licence.

Twelve days after the death of Sir Charles, Harriet's sister Caroline Longe died. In *Warneford: being the life and times of Harriet Elizabeth Wetherell Warneford*, family descendant Mary Gibson, who enjoys portraying a Caroline barely in possession of

Betty Ridge's granddaughter Harriet Warneford: described at her mother's death as one of the richest heiresses in the kingdom

her reason, has her dying in the somewhat cheerless surroundings of 'a back room of a "Home for Nervous Cases" at Accacia House, 22 Allsop Terrace, Marylebone'.[96] The 1841 census does indeed put Caroline in Marylebone, but in the sub-district of Cavendish Square. At 28 Cavendish Square stood Marshal Thompson's hotel, sometime London base of Caroline's namesake aunt, the woman who had taken such an interest in her. The thought of Caroline living out her final days in a suite in a familiar London hotel is somewhat more palatable than Gibson's 'Home for Nervous Cases', but the possibility that Gibson was referring directly to family papers remains.

Seven months after the death of Caroline Longe, her mother Elizabeth Warneford, first child of William Flower and Betty Ridge, died at Warneford Place in the spring of 1847. She was the longest-lived of all the Shellingford siblings, countering the fiction that her birth eight months after her parents' marriage was a result of prematurity. Few babies born early in the eighteenth-century attained the venerable age of 81. According to the press, her death meant that all the Warneford estates in Wiltshire and Ireland passed to her daughter Harriet Wetherell Warneford, making her, it was said, one of the richest heiresses in the kingdom.[97]

---

96   Mary Gibson, *Warneford: Being the life and times of Harriet Elizabeth Wetherell Warneford* (Private publication, 1966) p. 85.
97   *Morning Post*, 6th April, 1847, issue 22881.

Betty Ridge's son Henry Jefferey died at home just yards from the waters of the river Thames

ON 4th MAY 1847 Henry Jeffrey managed some broth for lunch in his room. Soon afterwards he was seized with a fit, and within ten minutes he died. Outside, the waters of the river Thames flowed on by, as they had done a few hours earlier past his mother's birthplace on Noah's Ark island at Northmoor.

Just after nine o'clock on the morning of Wednesday 12th May 1847 passers-by in Burfield Road in Old Windsor would have seen a procession of eight carriages emerging from the gates of the Beaumont estate. First came the hearse, drawn by six horses and carrying the remains of Henry Jeffery Flower, fourth Viscount Ashbrook, youngest son of an Oxfordshire water gypsy named Betty Ridge. Next came six mourning coaches, each drawn by four horses sporting nodding black plumes and velvet mantles. Inside were the family members, including the new, fifth Viscount Ashbrook.

Henry Jeffrey's personal carriage came last, empty, following the fifteen-mile procession to the village of Hurley where Henry had asked to be buried alongside his first wife, Deborah. In every parish along the way a single church bell tolled as the cortège passed by.

Epilogue
A deserted island

A FOOTPATH off the lane through the village of Northmoor in Oxfordshire leads down towards the river and then along the bank to Noah's Ark island. Even after the drainage and flood-defence work of the Victorian period this remains marshy country, so on a dripping autumn day I hitched a lift with the shepherd who grazes his sheep in these fields. We bumped and splashed our way down to the river's edge in his truck. My driver and his father-in-law, the current tenant of Noah's Ark island, taught me something important. During the course of my research I had been told variously-embroidered and distorted versions of the Ashbrook story. But the aspect related to me by these inheritors of the Ridge lease was the only one which proved absolutely accurate. Memories are long in the world of landholding, and farming works only where boundaries are well-known and respected. There is no room for spinning yarns or passing on hearsay. I shall continue to listen to local tales from any source, but I shall always pay especial attention to farmers where the land itself is concerned.

All is now quiet on the island, save for the occasional dog-walker following the Thames path. The plethora of small weirs along this stretch of the river were consolidated in the 1890s into one large weir with an accompanying lock roughly halfway between here and Rainbow bridge, a footbridge on the site of the old Hart's weir. Where once life on Noah's Ark would have been lived against a constant background noise of tumbling water, now the great river moves almost silently by.

The island is bigger than I expected. Poking about in the straggling growth obscuring the junction between the main watercourse and the stream on the landward side of the island, the farmer revealed the remains of a sluice and perhaps a boat-house. In a dry summer, he explained, the plan of a sizeable, square house, including its walls, doorways and hearths, emerges from the usually sodden ground in the form of stone and brick foundations. Sometimes traces of large, rectangular depressions can be detected in the turf too, the shepherd added—the remains of holding tanks, perhaps, for someone in the fishing trade. It would have been a straightforward enough matter to arrange a channel for a flow of fresh river water in at one side of the island and out at the other. Having expected from my trip to the island nothing more than a self-indulgent interlude of imaginary communion with the spirits of a long-departed family, in fact I received from these pragmatic men an object lesson in how the piece of land I had seen represented only on parchment actually functioned.

The palisade of greenery is interrupted on the north-eastern flank of the boat-shaped island where the shore slopes down to the river. Just perceptible to the patient viewer on the river surface is the diagonal line of Thomas Ridge's fish weir reaching across to the Appleton bank—the faintest dimpling in the general flow, a slight, glittering change on the moving water. But everything that once made the island a tiny, self-contained kingdom is gone: the bustle in the house, the dairy and the brew-house, the chickens, the pig and the house-cow. The orchard that once blossomed here and was known as 'Grassham' is nowhere to be seen. And of course, the family that charmed a viscount: Thomas and Elizabeth Ridge and their laughing, squabbling children, brothers and sisters of the pretty little girl whose son would become the best friend of the king of England. We have traced the history of Betty and her brothers, but what about her sisters. Where did they go?

Eldest daughter Catherine, we know, went nowhere, and out of choice. She remained on the island of her birth until the day she died, working the weirs even though she had no need to do so financially. Her parents Thomas and Elizabeth disappear from the record after that final clue when Betty included them in her will written in 1790. Perhaps they were with her in Shellingford, or living in smart Bampton. Perhaps they accompanied their son William to Ireland, in which case the image of old Thomas Ridge, one-time fisherman, putting up his feet beside the fire at Castle Durrow and sipping on a glass of port from the Ashbrook cellars becomes almost irresistible. But perhaps Betty's parents simply stayed on Noah's Ark, with their daughter Catherine to look after them in old age.

Two years after Thomas and Elizabeth's next daughter Anne died in 1782, her widower Thomas Holford had married John Ridge's first wife Elizabeth Trinder. But Holford was dead within the year, and the subsequent histories of his children suggest that they were probably sent back to Holford relatives in Bampton. Perhaps their stepmother of eleven months accompanied them, perhaps not. She was certainly not abandoned to her own fate; family papers show that she remained on the Ashbrook payroll as late as 1804. Eighteen months after the death of Betty's son third Viscount Ashbrook, the family solicitor met with Lord Ashbrook's sister and executrix Caroline to discuss 'a Debt due by the late Lord Ashbrook to Mrs Holford of £140'.[98] The debt, plus interest, was duly paid via the agent of Betty's husband Dr John Jones, suggest-

---

98   ORO, F/122/20/F/6, 'The Honorable Miss Flower Executrix of the late Lord Ashbrook, Bill from Philip Deare, 1803–1806'.

ing that Betty was at the very least aware of the lady's whereabouts almost thirty years after the ill-fated marriage to John Ridge. The eldest Holford child, Maria, married a Bampton man called John Adams in 1799, and in 1827 she received £50 in the will of Dr Jones, presumably at Betty's behest. This and other bequests in Dr Jones's will show that Viscountess Ashbrook's exalted social status did not estrange her from her sisters' children; indeed, she followed the established pattern by arranging for widowed relatives and fatherless children to be provided for after her death.

Betty's younger sister Sarah married Joseph Winter, a fisherman and son of the ferryman at Swinford near Eynsham. In 1777 the Swinford ferry was replaced by a bridge and this may be why the family removed to that old Ridge stronghold of Buckland. Joseph Winter was renting Old Nan's and Rushey Weirs in 1796. At the age of 28, Sarah's son Joseph Winter the younger was in trouble. Apparently reduced from a fisherman to the status of a labourer, he came before a jury in early 1800 accused of thrashing a certain Richard Wright to within an inch of his life. To be fair to Joseph, he countered the accusation with a similar charge against Wright and, since the fight occurred on 26th December, it seems possible that festive drinking may have played its part and that the two men may have been equally culpable.

In 1817 a Joseph Winter drowned at Rushey Weir. Tempting though it is to imagine a vengeful Richard Wright creeping up behind his enemy one dark night and shoving him, drunk, into the rushing waters of his own weir, the fact that Joseph the younger lived to have another son in 1819 suggests that the corpse examined by the coroner on 27th September 1817 was that of Sarah's 76-year-old husband. However, Joseph the younger had definitely died by 1825 because his widow Elizabeth received a bequest of £50 in the will of Dr Jones, wherein her deceased husband was referred to as a fisherman once more. Perhaps he took over Rushey Weir after his father's death. Joseph the younger and Elizabeth's surviving children, probably Ann, Thomas and Joseph, were left £160 to be divided between them.

It is difficult to argue that Betty Ridge's marriage to the second Viscount Ashbrook made very much difference to the lives of her sisters. Thomas Ridge was already an ambitious man before William Ashbrook came along in the summer of 1763. The marriage of his first daughter Catherine into a family of bargemasters seems to have been an acknowledgement that the fishing trade was in decline, and that industrialisation would create a transport boom. His second daughter Anne also married away from the fishing trade. Her husband Thomas Holford was a cordwainer in Bampton who took on Thomas Ridge's hard-won victualler's licence, a family asset which might otherwise have passed to Betty's elder brother William. It is telling that, following Betty's marriage to Viscount Ashbrook, Thomas Ridge permitted his youngest daughter Sarah to marry a fisherman. It seems that, once the family's connection with the aristocracy was formalised, Thomas felt that the pressure to guide his daughters away from a future with a husband in the fishing business was off.

It is true that, courtesy of Viscount Ashbrook, Catherine Wyatt could return from a failed marriage to a substantial new house on Noah's Ark, and all three sisters benefitted from the pensions their brother William Ridge obtained for them as high sheriff of County Kilkenny. But none of this appears to have made a lasting difference to the fates of the sisters' descendants, and this could not be better illustrated than by the return of the family of Betty's sister Sarah Winter to the weirs and locks of Buckland itself.

CHANGING ECONOMIC circumstances which drastically reduced the importance of the river meant that the island in the Thames where the Ridge family made their home could not hold on to the glory days either, once the influence of the Ashbrooks passed. Three years after the death of Betty's indomitable sister Catherine Wyatt it was described in the following terms: 'Little variety of scenery occurs until the arrival at… Noah's Ark, where the banks become more wooded, and the river is divided into three separate streams; between the two broadest is an ait [island], with a pretty rustic cottage'.[99] Already, the once-substantial brick house was just a 'pretty rustic cottage'. As an ageing woman living alone, Catherine had difficulty keeping the place in good repair, and probably inhabited only a fraction of it anyway. But the extent of the original building and its outhouses can be gauged by the fact that whatever did remain by the 1840s still provided homes for no less than six families: the leaseholder John Nalder and his wife, farmer William Keen and his family, and four other families of agricultural labourers. In all, Noah's Ark had a population of thirty-one people according to that year's census—but no fishermen. (There was even a resident Trinder, though only as a servant in the Keen household.)

The orientation of the village was shifting away from the river. The fishing trade was dead, and the goods generated by the factories of the industrial revolution were transported in large barges along purpose-built canals. Ten years later there were sixteen residents left on Noah's Ark, with three dwellings unoccupied. Nalder began to harvest the stones and bricks from the neglected property for his building projects on the other side of the moor in the centre of the village. He is said to be responsible for the half-timbered row known as Red Lion Cottages, and since these are the only red-brick buildings of the appropriate age in Northmoor, they were very likely built from materials salvaged from Noah's Ark.

There was sufficient plunder to last for sixty years. At the turn of the twentieth century, Fred Thacker documented every nook and cranny of his beloved Thames, and reported of Noah's Ark that:

---

99   W. G. Fearnside, *Tombleson's Thames* (London, 1832), p. 29.

Red Lion Cottages (left): as the only brick-built dwellings of the appropriate age in the village of Northmoor, they were probably built using materials salvaged from the Ridge home on Noah's Ark

Noah's Ark island: its distinctive boat-shape can be seen clearly from the air. The foundations of the family home become very obvious during dry weather such as the summer of 1976, pictured

> *Four elms tower towards heaven at its lower end; and close by a large thorn leans over the stunted brick wall of the old weirkeeper's cottage. "Leans," I say; and indeed so it did when I first landed to view it in August 1910. But as I returned a week later a cart was busy removing the brickwork; and only the shallow hollow remained beneath the bush.*[100]

---

100 F. Thacker, *The Thames Highway, Volume 2: Locks and weirs* (Newton Abbott, 1968, first published 1920), p. 87.

Appendix A
Ridge family solidarity

FISHING THE THAMES was still a viable way of earning a living at a time when transport difficulties meant that this important part of the diet had to be caught locally. Provided a tenant acquired the right to harvest a section of the waters, he could hunt all that the river had to offer including perch, dace, and pike. A legal dispute of 1713 gives us a glimpse of the mutually-supportive nature of the Ridges when grandfather Thomas and his sons Thomas and John (fathers to the runaway couple in chapter 1) maintained a united family front before the justices of the peace in the matter of the theft of John's fishing gear.[101] Detachment from the community at large evidently did not mean that the people of the river altogether avoided disharmony amongst themselves.

Charles Pemberton, variously described as a labourer and a bargeman, was accused of taking a 'trunk' (a box for fish[102]) belonging to Elizabeth's father John out of the river at Chimney in March 1712. John's brother Thomas supported him by making a deposition on oath that Pemberton came with John's trunk in his boat to Thomas's house on the Oxfordshire bank, that he recognised his brother's trunk and seized it back. An incensed Pemberton, clearly a man with a limited future in the world of crime, appears rather to have lost his head at this point. According to Thomas, Pemberton blurted out that he had also taken two 'Jacks' (pike) out of John's keep-net as well, and that if he had his chance again, he would have finished the job properly and torn the net to pieces.Four documents survive pertaining to the case, and John Ridge's signature is accompanied variously by that of both his brother Thomas and their father.[103] The case and its documentation reveal so much about the Ridge menfolk: their confidence in themselves and in one another, their loyalty to and focus upon mutual family interests, and the importance of literacy to those entrepreneurial types not closely dependent throughout life upon one landowner for work, housing and wages.

---

101 ORO, QSD RI 1713 E2/E3/E9/E10, 'Information of theft in Chimney, 9th March 1712'. Intriguingly, in 1623 grandfather Thomas's master John Curtis had a dispute with the 'Pemerton' family of fishermen and boatmen; could the ill-feeling have persisted between the Pembertons and Curtis's affiliates, the Ridges, hence the apparently motiveless mischief-making revealed in the legal case of 1713? See Mary Prior, *Fisher Row: fishermen, bargeman & canal boatmen in Oxford 1500–1900* (New York, 1982), p. 102.

102 *Chambers Dictionary*, 11th edition (London, 2008).

103 On the initial deposition John signs with a mark, but thereafter a perfectly confident signature appears for him as well as his father and brother, suggesting that an actual signature was regarded as optional and held no particularly totemic power. All three give their name as 'Ridge', not 'Rudge'.

IN JUNE 1739 Robert Brain, described as a 'husbandman', was bound over to appear at the next General Quarter Sessions in Oxford.[104] His alleged crime was the 'Assaulting and wounding of Thomas Rudge and Assaulting and Braking of John Hewet'. While there was a member of the other Northmoor Rudge family called Thomas, the fact that this one was in the company of a John Hewett and there were no Hewetts in Northmoor up to this date strongly suggests that he is our Thomas Ridge.

Thomas's wife Elizabeth had a younger brother, William, who would eventually marry Katherine Hewett, and Katherine had a brother called John. Thomas would have been about 27 years old in 1739 and John Hewett 19[105]; however proficient Robert Brain may have considered himself in the pugilistic arts, it seems highly likely that anyone taking on two strong young men simultaneously may have been enjoying a measure of optimism that could only be alcohol-fuelled. If an alehouse was indeed involved, Thomas and John could simply have been fellow drinkers who got into a brawl. On the other hand, the case raises the possibility that Thomas was already in charge of an alehouse, and enlisted a family friend to eject an unruly customer. Either way, the incident is of interest in that it also hints at continuing contact between Thomas and Elizabeth Ridge and their Buckland connections at this point.

A Rudge family already living in Northmoor when Thomas and Elizabeth arrived is recorded as far back in the village as are the Ridges in Buckland. Indeed, it may be that Thomas's grandfather Thomas Rudge de Buckland was brother to Richard Rudge who died in Northmoor in 1678. It was 'Thomas, son of Richard Rudge, labourer of Northmoor' who was apprenticed to John Curtis in 1666.[106] If so, the labourer Richard Rudge may have been father both to Richard who had a family with Eleanor in Northmoor, and Thomas who had a family with Mary in Buckland.

Both families are recorded over the generations using both spellings, 'Ridge' and 'Rudge'—as well as a few others. Illiterate country people doubtless stared blankly at a minister asking them to spell their name for the register entry, and he would simply have to do the best he could phonetically. It would be understandable for an Oxford-educated clergymen from far-off parts of Britain to assume that these new Ridges coming before him to mark important life events belonged to the Rudge clan that he had seen listed in the parish registers for generations.[107] It is remarkable, though, that once again Thomas uses a name to make a point. Wherever he signs his own signature

---

104 ORO, QSD, RI 1740 Ep2.
105 ORO, Parish burial registers, St Denys, Northmoor, 15th July 1799, records the burial of 'John Hewitt', aged 70. Katherine Hewett's brother John was baptised in Buckland in 1720, but the age of 70 may simply be a guess. The John Hewett buried in Buckland in 1742 is probably John and Katherine's father because when their mother dies in 1748 she is described as a widow.
106 Mary Prior, *Fisher Row: fishermen, bargeman & canal boatmen in Oxford 1500–1900* (New York, 1982), p. 102.
107 From 1555 the vicarage of the church of St Denys, Northmoor, was in the gift of St John's College, University of Oxford.

from this point onwards, 'Ridge' begins to predominate over 'Rudge'—sometimes even where an official has already written 'Rudge' on the same document.[108] The change does not occur overnight, but it is fair to say that, as Thomas rose up the social scale in the village, what better way was there to distance his family from their doubtless respectable but rather less dynamic Rudge cousins? Perhaps family solidarity went only so far. And by the time Thomas's sons were dealing with their own affairs, they were exclusively 'Ridge'.

---

108 It is this signature on the various documents referred to in this account which distinguishes our Thomas Ridge from the Thomas Rudge born in Northmoor in 1701. However, it must be noted that Thomas Rudge's brother Joseph also held a victualler's licence.

Appendix B
The Flower family

UNDER ELIZABETH I, Francis Flower was an attendant upon the Queen's favourite, Lord Chancellor Sir Christopher Hatton, but Francis's son George opted for the military life. The outbreak of the Nine Years War, or 'Tyrone's Rebellion', provided George with the opportunity to shine and sowed the seeds of the Flower family's three-hundred-year involvement in Ireland. At the height of the rebellion in April 1600, George led an expedition into County Cork which marched for a week through rebel country, utterly laying it waste. Captain Flower reported briskly that: 'We burned all those parts and had the killing of many of their churles and poor people, leaving not one grain of corn within ten miles of our way wherever we marched and took five hundred cows which I caused to be drowned and killed.'[109] Returning from this jamboree of destruction, Flower and his men fell into a rebel ambush from which, after much chasing about, they managed to extricate themselves. As ever, estimates of the casualties on each side vary considerably, but Flower claimed that his forces had disposed of 137 rebel fighters, while he listed just one lieutenant and nine soldiers of his own killed. Other eyewitnesses put the number lost on Flower's side as high as one hundred and more but readers will be relieved to learn from the author of *The Peerage of Ireland*, written in the eighteenth century, that, whatever the number was, it did not include 'any person of note'.[110]

One method used to crush the rebellion was the granting of the possessions of troublesome Irish landowners to English and Scottish settlers, a policy dubbed the 'Plantations'. The policy was wildly successful at uniting the hitherto bitterly divided 'Old Irish' and 'Old English' (Anglo-Norman) lords into one opposing movement, and this led inevitably to further trouble breaking out in 1641. The wars dragged on, and in 1648 George Flower's son Sir William was among a group of officers suspected of defection to the rebel side, and consequently arrested. Happily for Sir William, the restoration of King Charles II in 1660 led to his release at last, and thereafter he began to serve the king in various capacities and to amass land grants in return. By 1664 he was renting the old castle at Durrow from the Duke of Ormonde, who had had the county boundaries changed by act of Parliament. Apparently the Duke's object was 'to repress the outrages committed by the Fitzpatricks against his tenantry, who when tried in the Queen's county were always acquitted, but when brought to Kilkenny never escaped

---

109 'Captain Flower, Journey into Rosscarberry, 1st April 1600', Daniel McCarthy, *The Life and Letter Book of Florence McCarthy Reagh, Tanist of Carberry* (Dublin, 1867) p. 242.
110 J. Lodge and M. Archdall, 'Flower, Viscount Ashbrook', *The Peerage of Ireland* (Dublin, 1789) p. 283.

with impunity'.[111] Durrow found itself transplanted from Queen's County to Kilkenny. The political pendulum swung again for Sir William's heir Thomas. In 1689, six years after his marriage to Mary, fourth daughter of Sir John Temple, Attorney-General of Ireland, Thomas was served by King James II's parliament with an attainder sequestering his estates and his personal fortune of £700. A thousand barrels of wheat provided from Thomas's own granaries to the benefit of William of Orange's invading army did the trick, for the victorious William promptly restored his lands and fortune upon becoming king. Thomas managed to acquire the Durrow estate by means of a mortgage before his early death in c.1700, and his son William spent his youth under the guardianship of his uncles Temple and Palmerston. Finally in 1708 William obtained a release of the estate from the Duke of Ormond to himself and his heirs forever at an annual rent of £68 13s 4d plus 'three fat beeves' or £4 8s 6d in lieu.[112]

Now at last the family had total control of the estate at Durrow, so William, still in his early thirties, began building a family seat suitable to his aspirations and the times. Since King William's victory at the Battle of the Boyne, a new Protestant aristocracy was in the ascendancy, and the need for fortified strongholds receded. What better way to express your effortless superiority and cultural supremacy than by building an elegant country mansion in a style harking back to a Classical age, with no reference to such tiresome vulgarities as military threat, and no danger of confusion with the farmhouses of an earlier age? William married Edith Caulfeild, granddaughter of the first Viscount Charlemont and a member of a family originally from Oxfordshire which had been granted land in Ireland in return for service to King James I. The couple had two sons, Jeffrey and Henry, and two daughters, the first of whom died young and whose name has not come down to us, and then Rebecca. William was chosen to represent County Kilkenny in parliament in 1715, and Portarlington in 1727.

A collection of letters survives which gives an insight into family life first during a period prior to William's marriage from c.1702 to 1710, and later from 1729 to 1738.[113] The correspondence is conducted between William and his maternal aunt Jane, née Temple, Countess of Portland. Aunt Jane's husband Hans William Bentinck, first Earl of Portland was born in the Netherlands and had followed William of Orange to England in 1688 in order to serve the new king. Aunt Jane seems to have rallied round to do her best for her sister Mary's fatherless boy, and their letters show that young William spent time at the Hague and in Utrecht. Teasingly, Jane suggests that her nephew will be wasting an opportunity at Wateringbury Place near Maidstone if he does not pay court to his host Sir Thomas Style's sister. She pretends to sulk when she suspects

---

111 William Tighe, *Statistical observations relative to the county of Kilkenny* (Dublin, 1802), p. 3.
112 J. Lodge and M. Archdall, 'Flower, Viscount Ashbrook', *The Peerage of Ireland* (Dublin, 1789), p. 286.
113 Lincolnshire Archives, 'Goulding Papers 4A/2', 23 letters from Lady Portland to William Flower, later first Baron Castle Durrow, c.1705–1738.

that he is too taken by a beauty of Dundalk to reply to her own letters, and then betrays the reason for her jauntiness: she has her little granddaughter Sophia staying with her, and she mischievously expresses the hope that William will never fall down the stairs while carrying the child as he apparently once did when carrying the infant's mother as a babe-in-arms. Once William had children of his own Aunt Jane fussed over them too, and her letter of condolence sent from Whitehall on 8th December 1730 (upon being widowed, she had become governess to the daughters of George II) is touchingly endorsed by William: 'Lady Portland, Whitehall, December 8th on Death of my dear son Jeff.' A letter of July 1731, a year when William was serving as sheriff of County Kilkenny, reveals that his surviving son and heir Henry is not strong either. Aunt Jane expresses her relief at hearing good news of Henry, and opines that his 'fainting fit' must have been due to fatigue. In 1733 she is among the first to congratulate him on the news of his being raised to the peerage as Baron Castle Durrow. William was also called to serve in George II's privy council, but by 1735 the delicacy of the constitution of the Flower male is again on Aunt Jane's list of concerns, and she hopes that temperance and exercise have cured William's own dizziness. If not, he had best try Ward's remedy. (In the year of Aunt Jane's letter, this preparation was enjoying a predictable surge in its popularity following attempts by Ward's critics to inform the public of its dangers.)[114] In 1738 the health of William's heir Henry seems to be giving cause for concern once more, for the young man is apparently to stay longer at Caen, a place 'in reputation for their care of youth'. In fact, William lived on to the respectable age of 61, having seen both of his children make good marriages.

THERE IS A TOUCHING brevity to the wills of the widows of aristocratic men in the eighteenth century. Not for them the careful disposition of vast landed estates and the anxious, repetitive clauses designed to retain the estate's integrity whatever the future might hold; the will of Henry, first Viscount Ashbrook, plods on doggedly for eleven pages, that of his widow Elizabeth runs only to four. She spent her widowhood essentially as a pensioner of her husband's family estate, albeit a pensioner with free use of his 'House, Demesne and all [his] carriages and Coach Horses during her natural life'.[115] But none of this was hers to pass on, and in a way those of us with an interest in the daily lives of our predecessors are the richer for it; these wills give a glimpse of the warmth of the relationship between a lady and her long-serving and trusted maid, the consideration given to widows in or close to the family, and they show us the fabulous

---

114 Philip K. Wilson, 'Exposing the Secret Disease', Chapter 4 in L. E. Merians, ed., *The Secret Malady: Venereal Disease in Eighteenth-Century Britain and France* (Kentucky, 1996), p. 78. It must be clarified without delay that Joshua Ward's 'Pill & Drop' was used to treat various disorders, not just venereal disease.

115 National Archives PROB 11/802, 'Will of The Right Honorable Henry Lord Viscount Ashbrook of Kingdom of Ireland', 6th June 1753.

nature of some of these privileged ladies' personal possessions. After the customary preliminaries, Elizabeth dives straight in:

> ... *I Give and bequeath to my two Brothers the Reverend Doctor Tatton and Colonel Neville Tatton Fifty pounds apiece for mourning or to purchase Rings as tokens of my affection and Esteem for them*
>
> *Also I Give to my Olde Servant Mary Lynham three hundred pounds to be paid to her within Six Months after my Decease*
>
> *Also I Give and bequeath to my Daughter Elizabeth Flower my Watch with a Blue Enameld Case with the Steel Chain and Trinkets belonging to it And also my Two Bracelets One of her Father my late Lord Ashbrook and the other of her Brother the present Lord*
>
> *Also I Give to my Daughter Mary Flower my Finger Rings of all Sorts and also my Dressing Table and everything belonging to it*
>
> *And I do Recommend it to my Son William Lord Viscount Ashbrook to permit my said two Daughters or either of them at his discretion to Wear and have the use of my Brilliant Diamond Earrings my Seven Brilliant Roses for the Stays my Brilliant Sprig for the Hair and my Brilliant Diamond Egret until the marriage of my said Son or Daughters either of them*
>
> *Also I Give and bequeath to my said Son my Epagne and Square Silver Tea Table and also the Old Family Silver Watch which belonged to Sir John[?] Temple [maternal grandfather of her husband 1st Viscount Ashbrook]*
>
> *Also I Give and Bequeath all and every other my Household Goods and Furniture and all other my Earrings and Trinkets to my said Two Daughters Equally to be Divided between them by my Executors hereafter named*
>
> *My Wearing Apparel and Wearing Linen (Excepting as my Daughters shall choose to keep for themselves) I Give and bequeath to my said Servant Mary Lynham*
>
> *And I desire my Executors to Give to my said Daughters such of my Books as they shall think most Suitable and proper for them and the remaining part of them to my said Son*
>
> *... And I do hereby charge and make chargeable all and every the said Lands Tenements Hereditaments and Real Estate in the hands of the first person or persons aforesaid who shall come into and be in possession of the same by virtue of this my last Will Twelve Compleat Kalendar Months at least with the payment of the sum of Five hundred Pounds to the Honourable Jane Ponsonby (Widow of the Honourable Folliott Ponsonby) as a token of my Friendship and Regard for her.*[116]

---

116 National Archives PROB 11/843, 'Will of The Right Honorable Elizabeth Lady Viscountess Ashbrook Dowager', 17th February 1759.

Appendix C
Published accounts of the romance

A CENTURY AFTER the event, and at a time when sentimentality had become acceptable—possibly even compulsory—Edward Walford describes 'The Romance of the House of Ashbrook' in his *Tales of our Great Families*, published in 1890:

THE ROMANCE OF THE HOUSE OF ASHBROOK

The Flowers, who enjoy the honours of the Irish peerage as Viscounts and Barons Ashbrook, and who, in the present century, have become allied by marriage with one of the a proudest and noblest ducal houses in the land, namely, that of Marlborough, are not, I have reason to believe, at all ashamed of a slight dash of plebeian blood which, about a century ago, became by accident intermixed with their sang azul. Whether they are of Norman or of Saxon origin I will not undertake to say for certain, though I incline to the belief that there were 'flowers' of many kinds in England before the Norman Conquest; and the heralds tell us no more than that they were formerly seated near Oakham, in Rutlandshire, which county they represented in Parliament as far back as the reign of Richard II, when one of the Flowers was not only M.P. for Rutland, but also the first Commoner in the land, being chosen to fill the Speaker's chair.

It appears that in the reign of Elizabeth one of these Rutlandshire Flowers went over to Ireland as a soldier of fortune, and distinguished himself in the wars against the natives, as also did his son, who became Governor of Dublin during the Irish Rebellion, in the reign of Charles I. His son and his grandson became the owners of Castle Durrow, in the county of Kilkenny, and the latter holding a seat in the Irish Parliament, won a peer's coronet under George I.

This nobleman and his son were each born, married, and died, and 'slept with their fathers,' after the usual fashion: but about his grandson William, the third Baron and second Viscount Ashbrook, I have a little tale to tell which will interest such of my readers as are fond of romantic incident, and who have not forgotten the story of Mr. Cecil and his humble-born bride, who found herself one day Countess of Exeter and Mistress of Burleigh House, near Stamford Town.

This young nobleman, when scarcely out of his teens, or, at all events, when very young, and residing as a student at Oxford, was struck with the beauty of a peasant-girl named Betty or Elizabeth Ridge, whose father was in the habit of punting a ferry-boat across the Thames, or rather I should say the Isis, at Northmoor, in the vicinity of Cumnor, near Oxford the village made so famous by Sir Walter Scott in his 'Kenilworth' as the home of Amy Robsart. The love-sick youth took every opportunity of cultivating the society of his beloved water-nymph, but carefully concealed from his parents the impression which she had made upon his susceptible heart.

He was at that time an undergraduate of some college in the University, it is said of Magdalen College; but he was too young to think of matrimony, nor was the object of his affection either old enough or sufficiently educated to become his wife. She had been reared among the peasant class, and was wholly uninformed in matters of the world, though she could read and write pretty well, as is proved by her signature 'Betty Rudge' in the Register Book of Marriages at Northmoor; but the young collegian fancied that, in spite of these disadvantages, he could perceive an aptitude of mind and soundness of intellect united with great amiableness of temper in addition to her personal perfections. Under these circumstances he conceived the romantic idea of submitting her to the superintendence of some respectable lady capable of rendering her, through the influence of education, an associate suitable to his wishes and to his rank.

The lovely ferry-girl was accordingly placed under the tuition of a lady, a few miles off, at whose house Ensign Flower occasionally visited her, and where he marked from time to time, with all the enthusiasm of a romantic lover, her progress in various polite accomplishments. Elizabeth Rudge remained in this situation for about three years, when the efflux of time, as well as some domestic occurrences, conspired in enabling Capt. Flower to reap the reward of his constancy and honourable conduct by a matrimonial union; and so the knot was tied, the blessing was given, and the blushing daughter of the ferryman became ultimately the Viscountess Ashbrook and Lady of the Castle of Durrow, on whose walls her early charms are still commemorated in an authentic portrait. By the Viscount she had several sons and daughters, among the former two who each succeeded to the Viscountcy in turn; and the daughter of one of these sons, the peasant-girl's grandchild, was married to George, fifth Duke of Marlborough, the lord of princely Blenheim.

The peasant-girl, ennobled in the manner related above, showed herself in after life well worthy of the promotion which she had gained, and died early in the present century at a good old age, honoured and loved by all her husband's family.

A friend of mine, who was for some years curate of the parish of Northmoor, has kindly sent me the following memoranda as a supplement to the story as told by myself:

'The living, as you know, belongs to St. John's College Oxford, and when, as one of the Junior Fellows, I was appointed to it in 1839, I can well remember looking through the registers, and being much struck with the strangeness of a marriage, where the bridegroom signed himself "Ashbrook" and the bride signed herself (not indeed by her mark, but in her own hand) "Betty (not Elizabeth) Rudge." On inquiring of the Nalders, who were an old family residing there and who were our College tenants, they told me they remembered her sister [Catherine], who was married, and who lived to a good old age, and who always flattered herself that if Lord Ashbrook, or, as he then was, Mr. Flower, had seen her before her sister he would have chosen her in preference for his bride. From what I could learn by tradition, Mr. Flower was a gentleman-commoner of Magdalen College, and coming over there to fish occasionally, was brought into contact with the ferryman's daughter, and this ended in their marriage. He afterwards erected in the parish, at the riverside, a large quadrangular building, one portion of which existed in my time, and was let in cottages, the rest having been pulled down. I never heard anything to the contrary of Betty Rudge being a good and devoted wife, and it is very possible that the education mentioned by you might have been bestowed upon her to make her more suitable for the mistress of a gentleman's household. She was also, doubtless, the ancestress of the Duchess of Marlborough. I remember in my younger and more imaginative days, it always struck me as a romantic history, and as I used to wander along the banks of the Isis at Northmoor, on the summer evenings when I was in my parish, I used to picture to myself her waiting so anxiously to ferry Mr. Flower over on his way back to College, and thought it might form the basis of an interesting story for one of the Magazines; but I never got further, and am glad that you have placed the story on record permanently. I think she must be credited not only with superior personal attractions, but also with a high tone of moral principle, to have induced her inamorato to make her his wife. I do not know whether she lived long, or what was the place of her death or her burial.'

I may add that I am told that in the parish of Shellingford, near Farringford[117], Berkshire, there is a tablet to Lady Ashbrook's daughter or granddaughter, connecting her with the Marlborough family. There is a portrait of her to be seen at Castle Durrow, as stated above.[118]

---

117 Faringdon. Betty is commemorated on a tablet and also on her husband's monument at St Faith's, Shellingford and her daughter Caroline is mentioned on William, fourth Viscount's monument opposite; her granddaughter Charlotte Augusta has a monument at St Bartholomew's church, Yarnton.

118 Walford, Edward, *Tales of Our Great Families* (London, 1890).

In spite of its handful of inaccuracies—William's parents, being dead, were in no position to offer an opinion on his choice of wife, his college was Christ Church, not Magdalen, he was never an ensign or a captain, and the evidence of a signature by Betty herself is highly ambiguous—the account is valuable for its inclusion of the 'memoranda' of Walford's clerical friend, whom the parish registers show was Arthur Philip Dunlop, perpetual curate in Northmoor from 1839 to 1842. As for Betty's education in the household of a suitable lady, unfortunately Dunlop can confirm only that such an arrangement was 'very possible'. Since Walford himself gives no hint of where he has this particular titbit from, we can only speculate.

A HIGHLY-EMBROIDERED version of the story, apparently based upon Walford's account, appeared in the Ladies' Column of the *Auckland Star* in 1907. It may prove hard-going for those with weak stomachs, but newspaper editors of the time knew perfectly well that ladies could not possibly be expected to digest their history without the accompaniment of copious quantities of saccharine. Whilst not to modern tastes, this version does illustrate how the story had evolved from being an uncomfortable but undeniable fact in 1789 via Walford's apologia in 1890 and from there into a fairytale romance emphasising the spotless motives of both parties:

THE STRANGE LOVE STORY
OF THE ISIS FERRY

'In the very nick of time, Festing, my boy![119] Here she comes, and by Jove! if it is not actually a "she"! No grim Charon to ferry us over the Styx this time; but, unless my eyes play me false, a maiden with the form of a sylph, and I dare swear, when we see it, a face as bewitching as her figure. The two young men, fishing-rods in hand and with the day's spoil in baskets slung over their shoulder, stood on the bank of the Isis, silhouetted against the golden glory of the setting sun, while the punt, with its solitary passenger and its fair ferry-maid, nosed its way across the river towards them. A few moments later the passenger was stepping on shore, and a sweet, flushed face was looking up at the young men on the bank, only to turn away in coy confusion at the ardour of the glances that met hers.

BEAUTY IN THE BOAT

'Didn't I tell you, Festing?' whispered the taller and handsomer of the two

---

119 A John Festing did indeed shadow William's steps from Eton to Christ Church, but the alumni records show that he arrived at Eton the year after William left, and did not matriculate at Oxford until 1773, eleven years after William.

youths to his companion. 'I knew that figure had a face to match its beauty. Gad! if I don't believe it's Amy Robsart come to life again to steal our hearts away. Madam,' he continued, with a sweep of his gold-laced hat and a courtly obeisance, 'may two unworthy wights have the honour of your company to the opposite shore?'

'If you please, sir,' the maid answered, with a demure curtsey and downcast eyes, 'that is what I am here for.'

'And indeed, madam, your presence is an honour for which we were little prepared, but which we highly esteem,' answered the young gallant, as he followed his companion into the boat. 'But you must allow me the privilege of being ferryman'; and, taking the pole from her hands, he pushed off from the shore. Never in the history of the Northmoor ferry had the distance been so long or seemed so short from bank to bank; and never surely has ferryman proved so incompetent or required so much instruction. When at last the opposite bank was reached, 'I vow, my dear lady,' he said, 'I am so fatigued by my exertions that I must rest awhile before resuming my journey to Oxford. Before I go, may I inquire the name of the fair maiden who has brought so much sunshine into the close of a rather dreary day?'

'My name, sir, is Betty Ridge,' was the demure answer. 'Some call me "Elizabeth," but I love "Betty" best; and my father, who is the ferryman, has had to go into Oxford, so I have had to take his place.'

'Indeed, Mistress Betty, I must make the acquaintance of your father to congratulate him on having such a lovely daughter. Don't you know, child, how beautiful you are?'

'Oh, fie, sir!' the maid answered, as the crimson flooded her cheeks; 'you would not say that if you could see my sister; she is beautiful, if you like.' But already the sun has sunk below the horizon, and, as darkness was falling swiftly over the land, there was little time left for the paying of mere compliments; and with farewells and with promises to return again soon to make Mistress Betty's better acquaintance, the young men resumed their tramp towards Oxford.

THE BEGINNING OF THE ROMANCE

Such was the opening scene in one of the prettiest romances in the history of our peerage; though as yet the ferryman's fair daughter little dreamt of all that was to follow that chance meeting on the Isis, over which the setting sun threw its glamour. Betty knew nothing of the handsome gallant whose admiring glances and flattery had made her cheeks flush and her heart go pit-a-pat; but she knew that between her and him there was a great social gulf. He was obviously a gentleman; she was a peasant's daughter, and she was too sensible a girl to attach much importance to the pretty speeches of a man so much above her. And the young gallant himself, we may be sure, was equally unsuspecting of the trap Cupid had laid for his undoing.

There follows an account of the accomplishments of William's ancestors sufficiently glowing as to throw into sharp relief the sheer insignificance of the Northmoor peasantry. And, of course, the scion of such a valorous line is not going to give up the campaign easily. The following day, William and his gold-laced cap are back:

LOVE LAUGHS AT LINEAGE

But long descent and blue blood notoriously count as naught in the eyes of Cupid, who had matched against them the charms of the lowly-born Betty Ridge, whose 'milk and roses,' blue eyes, and wealth of rippling hair were more potent spells than all the blood of the Howards. Nor was it long before the spell began to work, for the very next day young Flower, fishing-rod in hand, found himself again at the ferry; and once more Cupid seemed propitious, for Betty, looking more radiantly beautiful than ever, was standing, framed by the rose-covered porch of the cottage, as if awaiting his coming. But if she felt any pleasure at the sight of the tall, handsome fisherman, whose eyes and tongue had already begun to play such havoc with her peace of mind, she gave little evidence of it.

'Good morning to you, Mistress Betty,' was his greeting. 'I vow you look sweeter than ever in the freshness of the morning.'

'You should not say such things,' Betty flashed out, flushing hotly, 'and I don't think you would if my father were here. It is not wise for a gentleman to pay such compliments to a poor girl like me.'

'But, Betty, if I mean them,' protested the young man, 'as I vow I do?'

'Then, sir,' Betty said, 'you would not be so ready to speak them on such slight acquaintance.'

And her father coming up at that moment, she walked indoors, and not another glimpse of Betty did Mr Flower see that day or for many a day after.

'I LOVE YOU BETTY'

If Betty, instead of being a simple rustic maid, had been an accomplished coquette, she could not have done more to fan the flame of her lover's passion. Her maidenly modesty inspired his respect, which must always be a factor of true love; her coldness hardened his resolve to win her favour. Day after day he made his way to the ferry without catching even a glimpse of the fair young face that haunted him day and night, until at last his opportunity came—as it always does to the patient wooer. And this time, he succeeded in convincing her that his worship was sincere.

'I love you, Betty,' he said, in a voice trembling with the sincerity of is passion; 'and your coldness drives me to distraction. I vow you are far dearer to me than all the world. I cannot bear the thought of life without you. Cannot you give me just a little love in return?' Betty drooped her beautiful head, but made no answer.

'I have little to offer you at present,' he continued, 'but some day I can make you a great lady, as you are now and always will be queen of my heart.'

It is as if by declining the chance of winning the laurels of his ancestors, William's actions are no longer an embarrassing dereliction of aristocratic duty; now he is performing a selfless sacrifice in the most honourable of causes as only a truly well-bred gentleman could do.

'Ah,' Betty said at last, as she looked timidly up into her lover's face; 'that is it! You are a gentleman and I am but a poor little nobody. How can I know that if you make me your wife you will not despise me instead of loving me?'

'I swear it, Betty, I swear it! Cannot you trust me when I say that as my wife you will be dearer to me than ever? Say that you love me and that you trust me!'

WOOED AND WON

What maiden could resist such pleading? Certainly not Betty; for from the first her heart had gone out to her handsome young lover, and try as she might and did, she could never recover it. And then at last she confessed that she did love him, 'just a little'; and thus it was that troth was plighted between the Viscount's son and the peasant-maid on the banks of the Isis, a century and a half ago. It was only after Mr Flower had won his bride that he revealed to her his rank and the position she would some day fill as his wife and lady of the Castle of Durrow.

More follows in this same vein, and the reader may be grateful to be spared its horrors. Alternatively, the stout-hearted may resort to the reference given below.[120]

---

120 [http://paperspast.natlib.govt.nz] (retrieved 18th May 2012). No doubt the story was syndicated from London around the British Empire.

Appendix D
Who married Elizabeth Trinder?

ACCORDING TO the parish registers of the church of St Denys, North-moor, on 1st October 1775 'John Rudge' married Elizabeth Trinder. Under-graduates were absolutely not allowed to be married at this date, so could this John be someone other than William and Betty Ridge's little brother?

Several puzzles surround this register entry. Both John and Elizabeth sign with a mark rather than a signature—not unusual for a working-class bride, but for a groom who has already studied at Oxford University for four years…? It is the only one of the Ridge siblings' marriages where we know that a member of the family is not present as a witness, though that does not necessarily signify that they were not present at all, simply that they, too, preferred not to attach their signatures to the occasion. Instead two regular witnesses of Northmoor marriages did the job: yeoman farmer William Kent and former licensed victualler Henry Smith who was for many years the parish clerk.

The marriage was performed by banns, so it was not a secret from the couple's families. More likely, both the mark for a signature and the absence of any other iden-tifiable Ridge family member in the register suggests a degree of obfuscation in view of the fact that documentary proof of such a marriage would jeopardise the groom's academic prospects at Oxford. A mark as opposed to a signature would serve both to throw an unwitting clergyman off the scent, and also to provide that same clergyman with what is today called 'deniability' if he was later questioned over his role in a cer-emony that breached university regulations.[121]

As we have seen, there was another Rudge family in the village in the eighteenth century but, according to the parish baptismal register, the contemporaneous genera-tion of that family in fact consisted of two Elizabeths, an Ann, an Augustine and a Mary. An uncle of this generation was indeed named John. But that John, 'son of Augustine, labourer, and Anne', died in 1742, thirty-three years before the marriage in question. Although an absence of a baptismal record does not necessarily rule out the existence of an unbaptised John, there is no evidence that the Rudges were neglectful of the sacrament on any other occasion, and any second John Rudge also managed somehow to avoid dying and thus appearing in the register of burials.

Could the John Rudge marrying in 1775 be from outside the village, someone who has come to the village to marry a Northmoor girl? This seems unlikely because the wording of the register entry is quite specific: 'John Rudge & Elizabeth Trinder *both of this Parish*'. An outsider would in that case have had to lie successfully to the

---

121 The officiating curate was John Cobb, a Fellow of St John's college since 1764.

clergyman that he was from within the parish simply in order to avoid the necessity of obtaining a licence. Why bother? Licences were straightforward enough to obtain, and it seems unlikely that a bride's family would allow her to make a potentially invalid marriage.

A refusal to accept that John Ridge could have signed the marriage register with a cross back in 1775 must be accompanied by an explanation as to why it is *more* likely that an unbaptised or alien John married a girl who lived nearby to our Ridges in 1775, why he and his wife then failed to appear ever again in any capacity in the parish registers, why a similarly-unbaptised Elizabeth Ridge appeared out of the blue in Shellingford, a village where not one member of a Ridge or Rudge family features in the parish registers between the late 1500s and 1899—and moreover appeared during that brief period when a Ridge reigned as the lady of Shellingford manor—and how she came to remarry to that same Lady Ashbrook's widowed brother-in-law Thomas Holford in a village a couple of hours away in the same year that the lady's own brother also remarried.

The use of the word 'spinster' in the register entry for Elizabeth Trinder's second marriage is interesting. Before the introduction of divorce as we now know it, the word 'divorcée' was unknown. A single woman was either unmarried or she was a widow. A description frequently used for a bride at this time was 'a maiden'. However, the word carried clear implications of sexual innocence, and no clergyman was going to risk recording a bulging bride as a maiden when he might be recording the baptism of her child just weeks later. The term 'spinster' was a useful catch-all where a woman was undeniably single but was perhaps older than the traditional blushing bride, or where the whole parish was familiar with her lively romantic career. This may explain why it was deemed appropriate in the case of Elizabeth Ridge of Shellingford.

On the balance of probability, therefore, the John Ridge who signed with a cross when he married in Northmoor in 1775 was Betty's brother, and Elizabeth Trinder who became Elizabeth Ridge on the same day was the Elizabeth Ridge who returned from Shellingford to marry Betty's widowed brother-in-law Thomas Holford in 1784.

Appendix E
Poetry Corner

FROM *FINN's Leinster Journal*, 1st November 1783, upon the occasion of Betty's visit to Castle Durrow with her children William, aged 16, and Elizabeth, now 17 and 'out' in society:

On the Arrival of LADY ASHBROOK,
LORD ASHBROOK, and MISS FLOWER,
at CASTLE DURROW.
AN ODE. By Mr. LYNCH.

RECITATIVE.
DURROVIAN Nymphs, in whose joy-streaming Eyes
Th'o'er flowing Tears of Gratitude arise,
Whose Words but faintly express th'extatic Heat,
Wherewith your all-enraptur'd Bosoms beat;
What tho' no high-caul'd Towers your Tresses grace,
With Pendant Ribbands strung or Dresden Lace,
But (void of Fashion's tantalizing aid)
In humble, home-spun, self-wrought Stuffs array'd;
What tho' such courtly Steps to you b'unknown,
As Pirrouette, Pas grand, or Riggadoon;
And tho', with salient Airs, you ne'er essay'd
Quick Conter-tems, or Tip-toe Promenade;
Yet never blush in the Irish Jig to advance,
And lead the glee-inspiring jocund Dance:
Let all with vocal Melody conspire,
Responsive to the Soul-enliv'ning Lyre.

AIR I. Tune, Britannia Rule the Waves.
Hark she appears! let all unite
In Mirth and Dance and Roundelay;
She comes! she comes! prepare each Rite,
To hail our Patroness this Day;
Rejoice glad Durrow, Durrovians now rejoice,
And to her Praises tune each Voice.

RECITATIVE.

In far sublimer Strains, by ev'ry Tongue,
Let Psalmodies of Gratitude be sung,
To her who doth such Charity unfold,
That Objects unreliev'd she can't behold;
Who now (while meagre Famine's Harpey-Train
O'erspreads our Isle with Penury and Pain)
Bids drooping Mis'ry smile, cheers up the Poor,
And ope to all her hospitable Door.

AIR II. To the preceding Tune.

Vain Flatt'ry hence, with Zeal sincere
We pour the tributary Lay;
And she must sure with Pleasure hear,
The duteous grateful Vows we pay.
Rejoice glad Durrow, Durrovians now rejoice,
And to her Praises tune each Voice.

RECITATIVE.

Who with parental fost'ring Care refin'd
And form'd young William and Eliza's Mind,
With em'lous Zeal to catch each Kindred Flame,
And climb the arduous Precipice of Fame.

AIR III. To the preceding Tune.

No more we envy Sharon's Vale*
Her Rose renown'd in sacred Strains,
But those two blooming FLOWERS hail,
Who glad and ornament our Plains.
Rejoice glad Durrow, Durrovians now rejoice,
And to their Praises tune each Voice.

RECITATIVE.

Trumpets and Drums resound, still louder rise,
With Incense of Thanksgiving fill the Skies,
To him, in whose Deportment, Mein [sic], and Face,
The Force of Irish Ancestry we trace;
Who, of all boyish Affectation clear,
And with magnanimous Contempt of Fear,
Early, with patriot Emulation warms,

To bear the loud tumultuous Din of Arms;
And by his own Example to inspire
His gallant Volunteers with heroic Fire;
While he (delightful Task) from File to File,
Approves their Zeal, with an applausive Smile,
To check Oppression's overbearing Tide,
Impos'd by Britain's Selfishness and Pride.

AIR IV. Tune, How imperfect is Expression.
Lo! Ashbrook's noble Line, auspicious,
Still reviving in our Peer,
Who'll yet to Durrow's Vows propitious,
Her to Shellingford prefer:†
Who, in Bloom of Youth Appearing,
And with every Virtue blest,
Ev'ry Heart to him endearing,
Reigns in each Durrovian's Breast.

RECITATIVE.
But ah! while Freedom deigns our Isle t'adorn,
And plenteous Peace pours forth her copious Horn,
While Slav'ry (bound in adamantine Chains)
No longer wastes our long-devoted Plains,
And while we may exchange, without Controul;
Our rich commodities from Pole to Pole,
Shall Manufacture unreliev'd remain?
Or hence transport her Wealth-augmenting Train?
And shall fair Science ('fore his Lordship here)
Unpitied drop the Heart-distressing Tear?
No, no, my Lord, be thine (whose Bosom glows
With ardent Zeal to heal your Durrow's woes)
The glorious Toil, the pleasing Talk be thine,
To bid both Arts and Manufacture shine:
Be thine (nor shall our gen'rous Guardian now
Neglect those Wreaths which here await his Brow)
Maecenas-like, to make poor Genius thrive,
And bid expiring Sciences revive;
Philosophy's illuming Rays t'advance,
And check all superstitious Ignorance:
Then shall our native Wits record thy Fame,

And to Futurity transmit their PATRON'S Name.

AIR V. To the preceding Tune.
O! the Prospect now how pleasing,
Still protected by a FLOWER,
And we in Opulence encreasing,
Shall our Ashbrook e'er adore;
Whom, his noble Sires transcending,
(Praises still to Durrow dear)
Arts and Sciences defending,
We, for ever, must revere.

* For Sharon's Rose consult the Bible.
† Shellingford, his Lordship's Seat in England.

FROM *FINN's Leinster Journal*, 15th December 1790, in memory of Juliana Lidwill Ridge, who died in 1789:

EPITAPH, for the late mrs. Ridge,
wife of William Ridge, esq; of Castle-Durrow.
Beneath this marble tells the mortal past
Of her who once delighted every heart;
How good she was, and what her virtues were,
Her guardian angel can alone declare,
All moan her death, her virtues long were tried,
They knew not how they loved her till she died,
The friend that now this little tribute pays,
Too exquisitely feels to speak her praise.
Yet, would'st thou know the pious life she spent,
How many from her hands received content,
How many breasts that poverty had chill'd,
Her charity with peace, with rapture, fill'd,
The voice of penury shall greet thy ears,
And tell thee, some with words, but most with tears.

Bibliography

A. Aspinall, ed., *Letters of the Princess Charlotte 1811–1817* (Home and Van Thal, London, 1949)

Anonymous, *A Slight Sketch of the Life of the Late Whitlock Nicholl MD* (Private publication, London, 1841)

T. F. T. Baker, J. S. Cockburn, R. B. Pugh, eds., Diane K. Bolton, H. P. F. King, Gillian Wyld, D. C. Yaxley, *A History of the County of Middlesex: Volume 4: Harmondsworth, Hayes, Norwood with Southall, Hillingdon with Uxbridge, Ickenham, Northolt, Perivale, Ruislip, Edgware, Harrow with Pinner* (Boydell Press, Woodbridge, 1971)

Jonah Barrington, *Historic Memoirs of Ireland,* Volume 1 (Richard Bentley for H. Colburn, London, 1833)

John Bennet, *Poems on Several Occasions* (Private publication, London, 1774)

Sir Bernard Burke, *Landed Gentry of Ireland* (Burke's Peerage, London, 1912)

John Bernard Burke, *A Visitation of the Seats and Arms of the Noblemen and Gentlemen of Great Britain,* Volume 1 (Hurst and Blackett, London, 1852)

George Dames Burtchaell & Thomas Ulick, eds., *A Register of the Students, Graduates, Professors, and Provosts of Trinity College in the University of Dublin* (Williams and Norgate, Dublin, 1924)

John H. Chapman, ed., *The Register Book of Marriages belonging to the Parish of St George, Hanover Square in the County of Middlesex,* Volume 2, *1788–1809* (London, 1888)

W. Laird Clowes, *The Royal Navy: a history from the earliest times to the present* (S. Low, Marston, London, 1901)

G. E. Cokayne; with Vicary Gibbs, H. A. Doubleday, Geoffrey H. White, Duncan Warrand and Lord Howard de Walden, eds., *The Complete Peerage of England, Scotland, Ireland, Great Britain and the United Kingdom, Extant, Extinct or Dormant,* new edition, Volume 3 (1910–1959; reprint in 6 volumes, Alan Sutton, Gloucester, 2000)

William Combe, *An History of the River Thames* (W. Bulmer for John and Josiah Boydell, London, 1794)

Sir Charles Coote, *General View of the Agriculture and Manufactures of the Queen's County* (Dublin Society, Dublin, 1801)

John Debrett, *Debrett's Peerage of the United Kingdom of Great Britain and Ireland,* Volume 2 (G. Woodfall, London, 1824)

John C. Erck, *Ecclesiastical Register* (Board of First Fruits, Dublin 1820)

Henry Farrar, *Irish Marriages, being an Index to the Marriages in Walker's Hibernian*

Magazine, 1771–1812 (London, 1890)

W. G. Fearnside, *Tombleson's Thames* (W. Tombleson, London, 1832)

Mary Gibson, *Warneford: Being the life and times of Harriet Elizabeth Wetherell Warneford* (Private publication, 1966)

Montague Guest and William B. Boulton, *The Royal Yacht Squadron* (John Murray, London, 1902)

Mr and Mrs S. C. Hall, *The Book of the Thames from its Rise to its Fall* (Published by Arthur Hall, Virtue, London, 1859)

Molly Harrison, *People and Shopping* (Ernest Benn Ltd, London, 1975)

A., E. and M. Innes, *Annual Peerage of the British Empire* (Saunders and Otley, London, 1829)

Mrs Herbert Jones, *The Princess Charlotte of Wales: an Illustrated Monograph* (Bernard Quaritch, London, 1884)

E. Keane, P. Beryl Phair and T. U. Sadleir, *King's Inns Admission Papers 1607–1867* (Dublin Stationery Office, Dublin, 1982)

James Kelly, *'That Damn'd Thing Called Honour': Duelling in Ireland 1570–1860* (Cork University Press, Cork, 1995)

Edward Kimber, The Peerage of Ireland: *A Complete View Corrected to January 20th 1768*, (H. Woodfall, J. Fuller, G. Woodfall, R. Baldwin, W. Johnston [and 9 others], London, 1768)

James B. Leslie, *Ossory clergy and parishes* (Fermanagh Times, Enniskillen, 1933)

Lady Llanover (ed.), *The Autobiography and Correspondence of Mary Granville*, Volume 3 (Richard Bentley, London 1861)

J. Lodge and M. Archdall, *The Peerage of Ireland* (J. Moore, Dublin, 1789)

Daniel & Samuel Lysons, *Magna Britannia, being a concise topographical account of the several counties of Great Britain*, Volume 1 (T. Cadell and W. Davies, London, 1806)

Daniel McCarthy, *The Life and Letter Book of Florence McCarthy Reagh, Tanist of Carberry* (W. Clowes & Sons, Dublin, 1867)

R. B. McDowell, *The Church of Ireland 1869–1969* (Routledge & Kegan Paul, London, 1975)

Pádraig Ó Macháin, *Six Years in Galmoy: Rural Unrest in County Kilkenny 1819–1824* (Poddle Press, Dublin, 1992)

Lewin G. Maine, *A Berkshire Village, its History and Antiquities* (J. Parker, Oxford and London, 1866)

Graham Midgley, *University Life in Eighteenth-Century Oxford* (Yale University Press, New Haven & London, 1996)

James Mullalla, *A View of Irish Affairs Since the Revolution of 1688* (T. Henshall, Dublin, 1795)

John Preston Neale, *Views of the Seats of Noblemen and Gentlemen in England, Wales,*

Scotland and Ireland (Sherwood, Neely and Jones, London, 1822)

John Nott, trans., *Selected Odes from the Persian Poet Hafez* (Cadell, London, 1787)

Edward O'Brien, *An Historical and Social Diary of Durrow 1708–1992* (Millfield Press, Durrow, 1992)

Patrick O'Kelly, *Killarney: a Descriptive Poem* (P. Hoey [printer], Dublin, 1791)

William Page and P. H. Ditchfield, eds., *A History of the County of Berkshire:* Volume 4 (Boydell Press, Woodbridge, 1924)

John Payne, *Universal Geography,* Volume 1 (Zachariah Jackson [printer], Dublin, 1794)

Francis Plowden, *An Historical Review of the State of Ireland* (William F. McLaughlin, Philadelphia, 1805)

Roy Porter, *English Society in the 18th Century* (Penguin, London, revised edition 1991)

Mary Prior, *Fisher Row: fishermen, bargeman & canal boatmen in Oxford 1500–1900* (Clarendon Press, New York, 1982)

Thomas Prior, *A List of the Absentees of Ireland and an estimate of the yearly value of their Estates and Incomes spent Abroad* (George Faulkner, Dublin, 1769)

Henry Reeve, ed., *The Greville Memoirs,* Volume 2 (Longmans, Green, London, 1874)

W. Senior, *Rivers of Great Britain: the Thames, from source to sea* (Cassell, London, 1891)

Michael Stone, ed., *Diary of John Longe, Vicar of Coddenham, 1765–1834* (Boydell Press, Woodbridge, 2008)

Walter G. Strickland, *A Dictionary of Irish Artists* (Maunsel, Dublin, 1913)

F. Thacker, *The Thames Highway, Volume 2: Locks and weirs* (David and Charles, Newton Abbott, 1968, first published 1920)

R. G. Thorne, ed., *The History of Parliament: the House of Commons* 1790–1820 (Secker & Warburg, London, 1986)

Emma Elizabeth Thoyts, *History of the Royal Berkshire Militia (J. Hawkes* [printer], Reading, 1897)

William Tighe, *Statistical Observations Relative to the County of Kilkenny* (Dublin Society, Dublin, 1802)

Amanda Vickery, *The Gentleman's Daughter: women's lives in Georgian England* (Yale University Press, New Haven & London, 1999)

Edward Walford, *Tales of Our Great Families* (Chatto & Windus, London, 1890)

Maureen Waller, *The English Marriage* (John Murray, London, 2010)

Francis E. Warneford, *The Warnefords: an English family through eight centuries* (Private publication, 1991)

Helena Whitbread, ed., *The Secret Diaries of Miss Anne Lister 1791–1840* (Virago paperback, London, 2010)

James Wills, *A History of Ireland in the Lives of Irishmen,* Volume 5 (A. Fullarton, Dublin 1897)

Cooper Willyams, *A Voyage up the Mediterranean in His Majesty's Ship the Swiftsure* (first published London, 1802, Cambridge University Press, New York, 2010)

Adrian Wilson, 'The ceremony of birthing' in ed. Valerie Fildes, *Women as Mothers in Pre-Industrial England* (Routledge, London, 1990)

C. H. Wilson, *A compleat collection of the resolutions of the Volunteers, Grand Juries &c of Ireland* (Joseph Hill [printer], Dublin, 1782)

Philip K.Wilson, 'Exposing the Secret Disease', Chapter 4 in L. E. Merians, ed., *The Secret Malady: Venereal Disease in Eighteenth-Century Britain and France* (The University Press of Kentucky, Kentucky, 1996)

William Wilson, *The Post-Chaise Companion: or Travellers' Directory through Ireland* (Printed for the author, Dublin, 1818)

Reference

A List of the Officers of the Army and of the Corps of Royal Marines 1821 (War Office, London, 1821)

Rugby School Register, Volume 1 1675–1849 (Rugby School, Rugby, 1881)

Treble Almanack and Dublin Directory (Dublin, 1822)

First Report of Commissioners for Inquiring into the Condition of the Poorer Classes in Ireland, House of Commons Papers, Appendix D, Volume 31 (HMSO, London, 1836)

Return of Sums Voted and Applied in Aid of Public Works in Ireland (House of Commons, London, 1839)

Return of Dignities, Benifices, and Parishes in Ireland, prepared by Remembrancer of First Fruits (House of Commons, London, 1831)

Office-Holders in Modern Britain, Volume 11 (revised), Court Officers, 1660–1837 (Institute of Historical Research, London, 2006)

Oxford Dictionary of National Biography (Oxford University Press, Oxford, 2004) Elizabeth Baigent, 'Wetherell, Sir Charles (1770–1846)'; Kenneth Milne, 'Agar, Charles, first earl of Normanton (1736–1809)'

Presentments of the Grand Jury, County Kilkenny, 1832 (Grand Jury of County Kilkenny, Kilkenny, 1832)

Presentments of the Grand Jury, County Kilkenny, 1834 (Grand Jury of County Kilkenny, Kilkenny, 1834)

Dodsley's Annual Register, 1828, Volume 70, Edmund Burke (London, 1829)

Journal of the House of Lords, Volume 63, 1830–1831

Periodicals

'The Pryse family of Gogerddan and the decline of the great estate, 1800–1960', Richard Colyer, *Welsh History Review*, Volume 9, no. 4, December 1979

Bonaventure Kelleher & Ken Jones, 'Captain John Lloyd: a research note', *Brycheiniog*, Volume 35, 2003

T. U. Sadleir, 'The Register of Kilkenny School (1685–1800)', *Journal of the Royal Society of Antiquaries of Ireland*, Sixth Series, Volume 14, no. 2 (31st December 1924)

'Pensions on the Civil Establishment of Ireland', *Walker's Hibernian Magazine 1786* (Dublin, 1786)

Press

Belfast Newsletter (Belfast, Ireland), 30th September 1834, issue 10152

Bristol Mercury (Bristol, England), 24th March 1894

Bury and Norwich Post (Bury St Edmunds, England), issue 1040, 2nd June 1802

Christian Examiner and Church of Ireland Magazine, Volume 8, January–June 1829 (Dublin, 1829)

Court Journal (London, England), 31st January 1835, issue 301; 25th April 1835, issue 313

Daily News (London, England), 6th April 1860, issue 4337

European Magazine and London Review (London, England), Volume 41, January–June 1802

Era (London, England), 16th August 1846, issue 412; 23rd August 1846, issue 413

Finn's Leinster Journal (Kilkenny, Ireland), 4th June 1774; 26th December 1772; 6th March 1771; 18th January 1775; 23rd January 1779; 13th January 1785; 28th September 1782; 26th April 1783; 3rd August 1782; 1st November 1783; 31st December 1783; 16th January 1816; 4th April 1789; 21st–25th September 1793; 5th November 1796; 14th February 1789; 22nd October 1791; 12th September 1792; 21st December 1793; 22nd October 1803; 4th March 1820; 20th January 1821; 15th December 1790; 20th September 1794; 4th October 1794; 2nd March 1791; 28th June 1786; 1st July 1786; 11th November 1797; 15th and 19th June 1793; 11th February 1792; 10th June 1795; 29th August 1796; 7th July 1827

Freeman's Journal (Dublin, Ireland), 13th January 1785; Tuesday 21st December 1830; 5th February 1838; 14th August 1839

Gentleman's Magazine (London, England), Volume 64, Part 1; Volume 55, 1741–1794; Volume 91, 1802; Volume 12, JulyDecember 1839; Volume 83, Part 1, 1813; Volume 113, 1813; Volume 11, January–June 1839

Hampshire Advertiser: Royal Yacht Club Gazette, Southampton Town & County Herald,

Isle of Wight Journal, Winchester Chronicle, & General Reporter (Southampton, England), 27th March 1830, issue 349; 21st August 1830, issue 370; 22nd November 1834, issue 592

Hampshire Telegraph and Sussex Chronicle etc (Portsmouth, England), 25th August 1828, issue 1507; 4th April 1831, issue 1643

Hull Packet (Hull, England), 23rd February 1813; 21st December 1838, issue 2819

Ipswich Journal (Ipswich, England), 20th July 1844, issue 5492; 11th July 1818, issue 4233

Jackson's Oxford Journal (Oxford, England), 13th June 1846, issue 4859; Saturday 29 March 1766; 29th September 1832, issue 4144; 13th May 1847, issue 22913; issue 2862, 5th March 1808; 1st August 1812, issue 3092; 13th October 1821, issue 3572; 17th May 1806, issue 2768; 11th July 1829, issue 3976; 10th May 1862, issue 5689; 8th September 1883, issue 6808

London Gazette (London, England), issue number 12628, 12th March 1785; issue 13796, 14th July 1795; issue 13098, 19th May 1789; issue 13507, 2nd March 1793; issue 13739, 10th January 1795; issue 16239, 21st March 1809; issue 15024, 2nd June 1798; issue 15706, 29th May 1804; issue 16070, 22nd September 1807; issue 16311, 31st October 1809; 13th September 1831, issue 18848; 25th May 1832, issue 18939; 28th April 1848, issue 20850

Morning Chronicle (London, England), 19th January 1810; issue 13255, 1st November 1811; 20th January 1815, issue 14263; 26th September 1817, issue 15102; 31st December 1817, issue 15184; 13th July 1818, issue 15350; 18th December 1819, issue 15798; 28th June 1827, issue 1802; 17th March 1828, issue 18254; 20th June 1832, issue 14881; 21st March 1833, issue 19833; 28th May 1834, issue 20204

Morning Post (London, England), issue 22627, 11th June 1846; issue 10222, 2nd June 1801; issue 10291, 12 October 1801; 22nd April 1811, issue 12551; 22nd August 1811, issue 12658; 16th, 24th and 31st July 1824; issue 12569, 13th May 1811; issue 12180, 9th February 1810; 14th January 1813, issue 13098; 12th November 1813, issue 13357; 25th July 1814, issue 13574; 23rd July 1814, issue 13573; 28th June 1817, issue 14488; 4th July 1817, issue 14493; 27th March 1818, issue 14722; 24th June 1819, issue 15110; 9th September 1819, issue 15176; 17th December 1819, issue 15261; 16th June 1820, issue 15366; 7th February 1821, issue 15568; 23rd February 1821, issue 15582; 4th May 1821, issue 15642; 16th May 1821, issue 15652; 15th June 1821, issue 15677; 26th June 1821, issue 15687; 5th July 1821, issue 15695; 2nd October 1821, issue 15771; 22nd May 1824, issue 16668; 16th July 1824, issue 16715; 24th July 1824, issue 16722; 31st July 1824, issue 16728; 21st July 1826, issue 17345; 9th May 1827, issue 17597; 9th August 1830, issue 18614; 15th September 1831, issue 18959; 30th June 1832, issue 19207; 23rd August 1832, issue 19253; 13th September 1833, issue

19584; 14th September 1833, issue 19585; 18th September, issue 19588; 19th December 1833, issue 19667; 20th December 1833, issue 19668; 21st December 1833, issue 19669; 23rd December 1833, issue 19670; 20th October 1834, issue 19927; 22nd October 1834, issue 19929; 25th October 1834, issue 19932; 31st July 1828, issue 17980; 17th April 1835, issue 20081; 2nd 1837, issue 20775; 28th November 1838, issue 21186; 27th April 1838, issue 21013; 27th May 1845, issue 23203; 17th July 1845, issue 22346; 13th April 1846, issue 22576; 2nd May 1845, issue 23182; 29th April 1846, issue 22590; 6th April, 1847, issue 22881; 6th May 1847, issue 22907; 13th May 1847, issue 22913

Racing Calendar (London, England), Volume 22, 1794

Royal Cornwall Gazette, Falmouth Packet & Plymouth Journal (Truro, England), 27th November 1813, issue 544

Sporting Magazine (London, England), Volume 9, 1797

Standard (London, England), 11th June 1846, issue 6813; 31st July 1827, issue 62; 17th July 1830, issue 990; 9th June 1845, issue 6509; 11th July 1845, issue 6537; 12th June 1846, issue 6814

Sydney Morning Herald (Sydney, Australia), 20th November 1837

Teetotaller (London, England), 21st November 1840, Volume 1, no. 22

The Times (London, England), 19th July 1787, issue 798; 23rd July 1795, issue 3361; 23rd June 1790, issue 1715; issue 6322, 2nd May 1805; issue 6430, 6 September 1805; 21st May 1813, issue 8917; 3rd May 1817, issue 10138; 13th September 1831, issue 14642

Documents

BRO = Berkshire Record Office
ORO = Oxfordshire Family History Centre
LFHC = London Family History Centre

National Archives, PROB 11/2057, 'Will of The Right Honourable Henry Jeffrey or Jeffry Lord Viscount Ashbrook', 12th June 1847

BRO, Parish registers, church of St Mary the Virgin, Buckland

BRO, Parish registers, church of St Faith, Shellingford

BRO, Parish registers, church of St Lawrence, Besselsleigh

ORO, Parish registers, church of St Denys, Northmoor

ORO, Parish registers, church of St Mary the Virgin, Bampton

ORO, OPI-60394, Oxford Freemen Index 1663–1997

University of Oxford, Magdalen, DY-33 'Lease from Mabell Wheeler and others to Thomas Ridge for 12 years', 10th March 1740

ORO, QSD, V/1-4 'Licensed Victuallers, Northmoor 1754–1772'

National Archives, PROB 11/759/400, 'Will of Jane Bedford, widow, Northmoor, Oxfordshire', 13th February 1757

Lincolnshire Archives, 4A/2, 'Goulding Papers: 23 letters from Lady Portland to William Flower, later first Baron Castle Durrow, c.1705–1738'

Lincolnshire Archives, MON/B/28/23, 'Monson Papers: Letter re Emily Lady Ashbrook's separation from her husband,' 29th June 1823

National Archives, PROB 11/802, 'Will of The Right Honorable Henry Lord Viscount Ashbrook of Kingdom of Ireland', 6th June 1753

National Archives, PROB 11/843, 'Will of The Right Honourable Elizabeth Lady Viscountess Dowager Ashbrook', 17th February 1759

ORO, PAR248/13/1D/23, 'Lease for 14 years, William Marchant, Gent *(et al)*', 21st September 1787

University of Oxford, Magdalen, MP/2/Oxon./1, 'Map, with detailed reference key, of estates at Northmoor by John Gutteridge, dated 1768'

ORO, Oxon. Archd. c.556 Marriage Bonds & Allegations, 'Ashbrooke & Rudge', 1766

University of Oxford, Bodleian Library, 'Shellingford Manor' by J. C. Buckler.

National Archives, PROB 11/1069, 'Will of The Right Honorable William Lord Viscount Ashbrook of Kingdom of Ireland', 21st October 1780

National Archives, PROB 11/1369, 'Will of The Right Honorable William Lord Viscount Ashbrook of Kingdom of Ireland', 25th February 1802

Monument to William, second Viscount Ashbrook (1744–1780), St Faith's church, Shellingford, Berkshire

National Archives, PROB 11/985/172, 'Will of William Ridge, now captain in the 17th Regiment of Foot, Bishop's Waltham', 3rd February 1773

University of Oxford, Magdalen, D-Y 226, 'Valuation, dated October 1798, of lands at Huntercombe in Nuffield, and at Northmoor, and at Thornborough, Bucks'

ORO, RI 1770 Ep 26 'Recognizance Robert Wyatt Lechlade/Henley', 6th November 1769

National Archives, PROB 11/1155/157, 'Will of William Hanson, Castle Durrow, Kilkenny', 5th July 1787

Hampshire Record Office, 21M57/B23/9 'Lord Clifden recommending Mr Ridge, January 1793', Ecclesiastical papers of Charles Agar, 1st Earl of Normanton (1736–1809)

Warwickshire Record Office, EAC560, 'Catalogue of musical instruments, music, books, household effects of Rev Dr John Jones', 2nd–3rd January 1828

National Archives, PROB 11/1478, 'Will of the Right Honorable Elizabeth Dowager Viscountess Ashbrook', 5th May 1808

University of Oxford, Jesus, 'Thomas Evans to Rev John Jones', 22nd May 1795

Monument to William, third Viscount Ashbrook (1767–1802), St Faith's church, Shellingford, Berkshire

ORO, F/122/20/F1, 'Draft statement of account shewing the Deficiency to be raised from Real Estates in Ireland in order to satisfy the Trusts of the late Lord Ashbrook's Will', March 1811

ORO, F/122/20/F2, 'Rent roll of the estates of Dowager Lady Ashbrook', March 1809

ORO, F/122/20/F3, 'Bill of Costs relating to Enfranchisement of the Estate at Cowley… from the Year 1798 to 1809'

ORO, F/122/20/F4, 'Particular of Lord Ashbrook's Estates', 1797

ORO, F/122/20/F5, 'Recapitulation of the Account of the sale of the Estate of the late William Lord Viscount Ashbrook situate in the County of Brecon', 24th October 1803

ORO, F/122/20/F/6, 'The Honorable Miss Flower Executrix of the late Lord Ashbrook, Bill from Philip Deare, 1803–1806'

ORO, F/122/20/F7, 'Account of Money paid and due to the Younger Children of the late Lord Ashbrook', 2nd March 1795

ORO, F/122/20/F8, 'Account of the Younger Children of the late Lord Ashbrook with Philip Dear', 3rd May 1795

ORO, F122/20/F/9, 'General abstract of the account of the younger children of William Lord Ashbrook', 4th October 1788

ORO, F/122/20/F10, 'Inventory of Lord Ashbrook's plate, received by Philip Deare on 24th September 1796'

ORO, F/122/20/C/1a, 'Extract of letter from C. Deare to the Honorable Miss

Flower,' 17th March 1810

RCB Library, Vestry minute books, church of St Fintan, Durrow, 1781–1796

National Archives of Ireland, IAR/1833/F/159, 'Robert Ridge, 1833', Index of Irish Wills 1484–1858, Volume 4/237/33

Hampshire Record Office, 21M57/C24/1, 'Letter from Rev J. Ridge to Agar, 10th April 1790', Ecclesiastical papers of Charles Agar, 1st Earl of Normanton (1736–1809)

Hampshire Record Office, 21M57/C29/37, 'Letter from Lord Clifden, Ramsgate, to Archbishop of Cashel about the living of Gowran [etc]', Ecclesiastical papers of Charles Agar, 1st Earl of Normanton (1736–1809)

Durham University Archive, Ponsonby Papers GRE/E516 Castleview, 'Brother of Elizabeth wife of second Viscount Ashbrook', 13th April 1806

National Archives of Ireland, 'Irish Prison Registers 1790–1924'

National Archives of Ireland, 'Tithe Applotment Books 1823–1837'

National Archives, PROB 11/2001, 'Will of the Honorable Caroline Flower', 26th July 1844

University of Oxford, Jesus, 'Will of Dr John Jones, Tredington Living papers', 24th November 1827

Northumberland Archives, ZCE/F/4/1/3/2, 'Watercolour painting of Miss Flower [the Honourable Charlotte Augusta Flower], later the Sixth Duchess of Marlborough, by Harriet Carr'

ORO, BOR4/36/29D/1, 'Assignment of mortgage, John Knapp, gent, William Winter of Swinford, ferryman'

ORO, RI 1800 Ep4, 'Bampton assault, Joseph Winter'

ORO, QSD A1817 M1, 'County of Oxford to Wm Macey Coroner'

LFHC, Registry of Deeds, Memorial Number 1785/530281241 'Ridge to Lidwell'; 1795/483/273313813 'Rev Oliver Flood & wife (Mary Fitzpatrick) to Ridge'; 1795/499/316316651 'Mark C. Lidwell to Ridge'; 1797/511/319/331990 'Anne Lidwell to Ridge'; 1814/672/556/465098 'Rev John B. Ridge, Judith Ridge o'wise Bathorn & DeCourcy Ridge to Chambers'; 1815/686319/471853 'DeCourcy Ridge to Ringwood'; 1818/522497257 'Bell to Ridge'; 1825/802256541391 'Ridge to Woodroffe'; 1825/802257541392 'Ridge to Hill'; 1825/802279545014 'Ridge to Woodroffe'; 1826/81334547769 'Ridge to Purcell'; 1826/815177549112 'Ridge to Woodroffe'; 1827/821532553067 'Ridge to Farrell, in trust'; 1827/827189556324 'Ridge to Powell, in trust'; 1827/820418552353 'Ridge to Woodruffe'; 1827/821/256/552791 'Ridge to Box'; 1828/835242561177 'Ridge to Grace'; 1828/563458 'Ridge to Woodroffe'

For further copies of this book, please visit:

FeedARead.com

Lightning Source UK Ltd.
Milton Keynes UK
UKOW03f1157070414

229525UK00002B/58/P